GREAT BIBLE STORIES

AND MASTER PAINTINGS

A COMPLETE

NARRATION OF

THE OLD AND NEW

TESTAMENTS

by Owen S. Rachleff

ILLUSTRATED WITH

ONE HUNDRED AND FOUR

WORKS OF ART

FROM GIOTTO TO COROT

GREAT
BIBLE STORIES
AND
MASTER
PAINTINGS

ABRADALE PRESS · Publishers · *New York*

Library of Congress Catalog Card Number: 68—29485
Published in the United States of America, by
ABRADALE PRESS, INC., NEW YORK

PREFACE

AN EVENING OF BIBLE READING might be compared to a night at the opera for many of us. We arrive at the theater knowing that it is considered a rich and rewarding experience to hear Mozart or Verdi. We watch patiently as an intricate action unfolds on stage and listen, in puzzlement, to a foreign language sung by a variety of characters. Of course, there is always the great music. But our appreciation even of the music may be impaired by an overall lack of comprehension. Thus, a meaningless, perhaps painful evening results. How different things might have been, had we read, beforehand, a concise version of the plot and a description of the music.

This book of Bible stories has been written as such a preparation for Bible reading. It attempts to provide, for young and old alike, a basic narrative of the Biblical text, so that the reader may be moved to explore the original with a clear understanding of the events and themes related by the ancient scribes. Like a retelling of a complicated operatic plot, the present text aims for simplification without condescension. Essentials are given in some detail, but involved sub-plots, and characters not germane to the major action—such as the minor kings of Israel and Judah—are abridged or entirely omitted. Quotations of stirring Biblical poetry and prose, however, appear frequently in order to provide some familiarity to carry the reader along when he delves into the Scriptures, and to acquaint him with the meter and tone of Biblical writing. Similarly, the author here has striven to suggest, in modern terms, something of the concise, poetic language of the Bible, so that the reader may be prepared for the sudden shifts in emphasis and the laconic descriptions of earthshaking events that often appear in the original narratives.

A sense of history and continuity from one Book to the next, and across the Apocrypha to the New Testament, has been carefully sought, in the same way that one would try to give unity to the separate acts of a difficult opera or play. The reader will therefore find explanations of historical events where they are absolutely required. But theological digressions, interpretations, and moralistic evaluations in depth are not pursued. They are left to the reader, and may serve to underscore the plots, as the music of an opera permeates the action on stage.

Besides attempting a clear and inviting retelling of the Bible's stories, the current book also offers certain special educational features that, it is hoped, will appeal to parents and teachers. For instance, each story has a carefully keyed chapter-and-verse reference in order to induce further study in the original. There is also a pronouncing glossary of Biblical names and places. The major tales of the Apocrypha, missing in so many other books, appear here with the same documentation and treatment as other sections. And—perhaps as the most distinctive feature of all—over one hundred full-page color plates of the world's greatest Biblical paintings serve as illustrative material, as a kind of visual counterpart to the majesty of the Bible's content and language. Many of these masterpieces have been seen infrequently, absent not only from Bible stories, but from art books as well. Along with the more familiar works, they cover the greatest periods of traditional art, from Giotto to Corot, and are drawn from the finest collections in the world.

O. S. R.

CONTENTS

THE OLD TESTAMENT

Stories from the Book of Genesis

The Story from
the Book of Ruth

Stories from the First Book
of Samuel (also known
as the First Book of Kings)

Stories from the Second
Book of Samuel (also known as
the Second Book of Kings)

THE APOCRYPHA

NOTE: Many stories overlap in the various books of the Bible. This is especially true of stories in Exodus, Leviticus, Numbers, and Deuteronomy; the Books of Samuel and of the Kings, Chronicles, Isaiah, and Jeremiah; and the Four Gospels of the New Testament. In most cases the primary chapter and verse source of each story is indicated in parentheses in the Contents pages.

The First and Second Books of Samuel and the First and Second Books of Kings, so called in most Protestant Bibles, are generally known as the First, Second, Third, and Fourth Books of Kings respectively in Catholic Bibles.

A word about the illustrations: in most cases the entire painting is reproduced; but often, for dramatic emphasis, only the major and most relevant portion is shown.

THE OLD TESTAMENT

THE BOOK OF GENESIS

The Story of the Creation of the World; of Man's First Sin and Punishment; of Cain, Who Murdered His Brother Abel; of Noah and the Flood; of the Tower of Babel.

Stories of Abraham, the First Leader of the Hebrews; of Isaac, His Son; of Jacob and Esau, the Twins; of Joseph and His Brothers; and the Coming into Egypt of the Jews.

IN A TIME before time, in dark and empty space that stretched endlessly away, there existed only God, the Creator.

There was neither night nor day. No planets spun throughout the universe. Even as much light as glimmers on a distant star could not be seen. This is how it was in the beginning.

Then God arose and ended the infinite darkness by commanding, "Let there be light." And when the light broke against the blackness, God, even God, was pleased. Thus began the first day of creation.

On the second day, God created Heaven, the vast dome of the universe, which hovered over the silent waters and the heavy clouds.

On the third day, God brought forth land from among the waves of the waters—and mountains, forests, valleys, and the earth brought forth grass, and herbs, and trees bearing fruit. And God saw that it was good.

It was a strange and awesome world. God had fashioned it as easily as a potter molds his clay. And yet, the most wonderful creations were to follow.

For, on the fourth day, God took a handful of the light He had made and formed it into the flaming sun, so that time would be divided into night and day. And, to give comfort during the blackness of night, God, with a smaller handful of light, made the moon and placed it in the heavens. And he made the stars and the planets besides. And God saw that it was good.

When the fifth day dawned, the earth was made, but there was no life upon it. So God filled the seas with fish and the skies with birds. And he said to them, "Be fruitful and multiply, and fill the waters in the seas, and let the fowl multiply in the earth."

The Creation of the World

Plate 1. THE CREATION OF ADAM, by Michelangelo (Italian,
1475–1564), Sistine Chapel, the Vatican, Rome.

Now the sixth day began, and God was astir with marvelous works. He would create the animals of the world—lions and tigers, horses and cows, elephants and camels—to live among the trees and to roam the forests and deserts and vales. And so it was done that morning.

But, on the afternoon of the sixth day, God conceived His greatest plan. He would fashion, from the very earth, a creature in His own image who was able to think, who was free and wise, and who would be able to rule all other creatures and make the earth his home as God had made heaven His dominion. And thus, gathering the dust from the earth, the Almighty fashioned Man and blew the breath of life into his fragile being, and said: "Be fruitful and multiply, and replenish the earth and subdue it."

Six marvelous periods of time had come and passed since the world began. God had labored greatly over this creation; and, when the seventh day dawned and the work was complete, the Lord Himself rested in His heaven, and the man, whose name was Adam, rested on earth.

Adam and Eve

THE GARDEN OF EDEN was the first home of man. It was more like heaven than any place we know on earth today. Here Adam was placed by God to live an untroubled life. At his fingertips lay all the food he needed. The springs ran fresh and clear. The days were cool and the nights were comfortable.

God brought all the animals He had created to this earthly paradise. It was Adam's task to give them names. Adam did as the Lord said and gave names to all cattle, and to the fowl of the air, and to every beast of the field.

Such activity kept Adam very busy. But when it was done and he was idle, a feeling of sadness and emptiness came over him—for he was alone.

God recognized this mood, and therefore decided to create another human being to be a companion to Adam in his paradise. This was to be woman. And since God wanted woman to be part of man, He fashioned her from a rib, which He removed painlessly from Adam while he slept. The first woman was named Eve, or "mother of the earth," and when Adam saw her, he exclaimed: "This is now bone of my bones, and flesh of my flesh; she shall be called Woman, because she was taken out of Man."

Like innocent children, naked and serene, they walked hand in hand throughout the Garden of Eden, enjoying the beauty of the flowers and vines and the perfect protection of God.

And in the Garden of Eden flowed four streams of a great river, and there was also in that garden the Tree of Life which was intended to sustain man forever. Another tree stood close by.

One day, Adam pointed to that tree, and said to Eve, in a serious voice:

"God has given us everything we need and told us to do as we please, except for one thing. We may not eat the fruit of the Tree of Knowledge of Good and Evil, which stands in the middle of the garden. If we do eat that fruit, we shall die, and lose our paradise and our comfort forever."

Eve understood, and said that she would obey the commandment.

ALL THE ANIMALS had feelings and ambitions in those days. One of the most intelligent was the serpent, who then had legs and walked, like a lizard. The serpent was cunning, and wanted to bring on the downfall of man.

So he lurked in the thicket near the forbidden tree, knowing that Eve often wandered in that direction when Adam was asleep beneath the noonday sun. When she came his way, he raised his head, pretending friendship.

"Why is it," he asked, "that you and Adam are not allowed to eat the delicious fruit of this Tree of Knowledge?"

"Because it is forbidden to us by the Lord, and we shall die if we do," she answered.

The serpent smiled.

"You will not die," he replied. "All that will happen is that you will become as wise as God. This will be a great pleasure to you—your eyes shall be opened and you will be as gods, knowing good and evil."

Eve was not used to this kind of sly trickery, for she had known only trust and contentment. Therefore, the serpent's questions and insinuations began to trouble her mind. She thought that Adam might have misunderstood the Lord about eating these fruits. Besides, whatever was forbidden seemed so tempting to Eve at the moment as to be almost irresistible.

Did she dare? After all, Eve was free to choose to obey or disobey. Like Adam, she had been made in the image of God.

How long it took her to make her fateful decision—and what conflicts ran through her mind—we can only guess. But, in the end, she plucked the forbidden fruit, ate half of it, and immediately persuaded

The First Sin— and God's Punishment

OPPOSITE: Plate 2. THE FALL OF MAN (ADAM AND EVE),
by Titian (Italian, about 1487–1576), The Prado Museum, Madrid.

BELOW: Plate 3. THE GARDEN OF EDEN, by Lucas Cranach, the Elder
(German, 1472–1553), Kunsthistorisches Museum, Vienna.

Adam to eat the other half. As soon as the man and woman had tasted the fruit, their eyes were opened. They were confused. Previously, they had felt no shame over their naked bodies. Now, they were embarrassed, and hid from each other in the foliage. Indeed, Eve would not show herself until she had covered her body with leaves and insisted that Adam do the same. Ridiculously clothed, confused and frightened, they attempted to hide from God, who came at twilight into the midst of the Garden. They heard him and feared He knew what they had done.

But, though He knew, God wanted man to admit his own guilt freely, and so He asked Adam:

"Why do you hide?"

And Adam, in his confusion, answered that he was ashamed.

"Why are you ashamed?" God demanded. "Have you eaten the forbidden fruit?"

"The woman made me do it," cried Adam desperately. Already he had become petty, and wanted to pass on the blame for his own mistake.

Eve was no better.

"The serpent made *me* do it," she said.

But God was greatly angered. He called to Adam and said: "Because you have listened to your wife and have eaten of the tree which I forbade you to eat, therefore cursed is the ground for your sake; in sorrow shall you eat of it all the days of your life. Thorns and thistles shall it bring forth to Thee; and thou shall eat the herb of the field; in the sweat of your face shall you eat bread, till you return into the ground; for out of it you were taken: for dust you are, and unto dust shall you return!

Adam and all his descendants were no longer to live in the Garden of Eden. And woman, though she would always wish to be a mother and have children, would do so forever in pain. But, worst of all, eternal life was no longer their earthly lot. They would become old and die, like the leaves in winter, and return to the dust from which they had come.

The serpent was punished to the full extent. No longer would he walk proudly on his legs, but forever crawl on his belly as the lowest creature on earth. Man would hate him and he would hate man, and they would always attack each other on sight.

The Lord made coats of skins for Adam and Eve and so clothed them from that day on.

It was a terrible day for man and beast. And, as the sun began to set, God decreed His final punishment. Man and woman were to be expelled from the Garden of Eden, lest they eat fruit from the Tree of Life and so outwit their punishments. And, if they tried to return, they would be halted by angels who were placed at the gate of Eden, and armed with a flaming sword that turned this way and that way so that no one could ever enter Eden again.

Cain
and
Abel

EASTWARD FROM EDEN, the land was hard and wild. Here, Adam and Eve came when they were expelled from paradise. Their easy life was over. No longer could they walk with God in the gardens. No longer could they gaze on His majestic being. His voice, however, remained in their hearts, and, for this reason, they did not lose faith. With work, the earth produced good food, and, soon, a son was born to the world's first family. Adam was proud and Eve gratefully said, "I have gotten a man from the Lord."

The baby was named Cain, and he was soon followed by a brother named Abel. The boys grew up in their parents' care, never knowing anything of the Garden of Eden, except what they heard from Adam. They were, nevertheless, healthy and strong, and, eventually, they began to help their father with the work of the fields. Cain became a farmer tilling the soil; Abel was a shepherd, and tended the sheep in the pastures.

At certain times, the whole family gathered together to worship God. They did this by building altars of stone upon which they burned the things that they raised, believing that the rising smoke would ascend to God and that He would be pleased with the sacrifices they offered unto Him.

Cain and Abel had separate altars upon which they made their sacrifices. Cain, because he was a farmer, usually placed corn and oats on his altar. Abel, the shepherd, offered up a lamb from the flock.

One day, the smoke from the meat and fat on Abel's altar rose upward toward Heaven, but the thinner smoke from Cain's offering of grain blew back in his face, causing him to choke and cough, for God did not respect Cain's offering, because Cain was insincere in his homage. He grew so sullen that the Almighty spoke to him and warned him of the evils of anger and envy.

"If you do well," said the Lord to Cain, "you shall be accepted. But if you do not do well, then sin is waiting at your door to ensnare you."

At first, Cain may have tried to heed this warning. But, like his father before, he could not always obey God's voice—and so he lurked about the fields, building up hatred in his soul against his innocent brother.

His hatred grew unbearable; one day while has was in the fields with Abel, he suddenly grabbed up a stone and struck him on the head.

Abel fell. Even Cain, the murderer, was alarmed. Why didn't Abel move or revive? Terror gripped his heart, and he fled like a deer to hide from his crime.

But again he heard the angry voice of God.

"Where is your brother Abel?" asked the Lord.

"I don't know," the murderer answered. "Am I my brother's keeper?"

"I know where your brother is," thundered God. "His blood is crying to Me from the earth where you killed him; and from such a crime you cannot hide. From this time forth you shall be accursed and wander as a fugitive on earth."

And then God placed a mark on Cain's brow so that no one would murder him during his wanderings.

Overwhelmed with fear, Cain was forced to leave his home, a marked and hated man. But God again was merciful, as He had been with Adam. Instead of death, Cain was to know only endless wandering and hardship. For it was God's hope that somehow he would repent—even he, a murderer.

After these terrible events, other children were born to Adam and Eve, and the world's population began to grow. But what kind of people would these children be? In so short a time, it seemed that only wickedness could flourish on the earth. Was a good man anywhere to be found?

Noah and the Great Flood

THE WORLD became crowded, and men lived to be very old. Methusaleh, for instance, died when he was 969 years old, for, in God's eyes, he was a good man deserving of reward. This was true of Enoch, his father, who died at 365 and went straight to Heaven. Perhaps this was the only decent family on the earth at that time, because God became so angered with the rest of the world that He determined to destroy it. To destroy everyone, that is, except Methusaleh's grandson Noah—who loved God and, "found grace in the eyes of the Lord."

All around, people broke the law and were dishonest, and said that God no longer existed. This deeply angered the Lord. "My spirit shall not always strive with man," He said, except for Noah and his family, I will flood the earth as it used to be before Creation."

Noah, who tilled the soil with his sons, often heard the voice of God in his heart; and, one day, when he was alone at his vineyards, God came to him again, and presented an amazing plan.

"The world will be ended by a flood," said the Lord. "But I love man in spite of his sins, and, therefore, I shall save your family and one pair of every bird and beast in existence, so that the world may start afresh."

Noah was overcome.

"How shall we survive such a flood, Lord?" he asked.

"In a wooden boat," said God, "in an ark three hundred times as long as your forearm, large enough to house your sons, their wives, your own good wife, and the many, many animals that I shall select. You shall make this ark three stories high, with many rooms and one window; it shall be fashioned of the strongest wood, and sealed against leaks with tar—and, on the side, you shall hinge a great door to be an entrance for the animals. This is how I shall save you."

Upon hearing these instructions, Noah and his sons immediately set to work to erect the frame of the boat with the strong timbers of trees that God had provided especially for this purpose. The ark was finally finished exactly as God had specified to Noah. And then according to God's command, Noah and his sons, Sham, Ham, and Japheth also prepared food and necessities for their families and for the countless animals that were to be taken aboard the ark and kept there during the long days of the flood.

ONE DAY, Noah saw the skies grow very dark and fill with clouds, and he knew the time had come for the flood. Carefully, he prepared the last details of construction, making sure that there would be no leaks in his ship and providing for all the necessary comforts that his family would need. Then, after sounding a horn, he stood back to allow the great procession of animals to pass before him, two by two, up the ramp and into the ark.

What a great spectacle! Led by lions and elephants and long-necked giraffes, with monkeys and spiders, and speckled beetles and orange birds, followed by lizards and frogs and turtles, by tiny mice and great brown horses with flowing manes, by chickens, ducks, scarlet flamingos. . . .

And still they came, cows, and sheep (seven each of these, because they would provide food for Noah and his sons). Indeed, all the species of the world entered the ark—all save the fish, who would be quite safe in the water.

And then, when every creature was settled inside, all quite calm and obedient, Noah led his wife and his sons and his daughters-in-law

The
Animals
Enter
the
Ark

through the great hinged door, just in time, as the black clouds darkened the skies and great big drops of water began falling on the smooth white decks of the ship. One after another, faster and louder, the raindrops came, until, suddenly, there was a great clap of thunder. God then lowered the door of the ark and commanded the Heavens to open their floodgates without mercy!

As the Bible says: "In the same day were all the fountains of the great deep broken up and the windows of heaven were opened. . . . And the waters prevailed and were increased greatly upon the earth; and the ark went upon the face of the waters."

Forty days and forty nights, the heavens poured down great torrents of rain, so that nothing could be seen or heard, and the rivers swelled and spilled over and carried away vast cities and farmlands in their wake. Mightier than a waterfall, constant and roaring, the great rains came. And rich men, beggars, and great beasts of the fields, all fled to the mountains and caves, but in vain, for the waters, the endless waters, followed them upward and onward until the entire world was one vast sea. Nothing could be seen upon this sea except the lone ark, from which Noah and his family watched fearfully and with tears in their eyes, as the world was swallowed up beneath them in the waves.

AFTER DAYS AND DAYS, the great rains ended. Yet, for many months, the waters remained at full tide on the earth, and the ark merely floated from one wave to another.

Then, at last, a beam of sunlight pierced the eternal gloom, and Noah felt the ark strike against the top of a mountain. He rushed to the window and looked out through the clouds. Here and there, he could see the pinnacles of mountains emerging just slightly above the waters. It was time for an experiment.

He brought a raven to the window and released it, hoping that it would return with some evidence that dry land was emerging. But the raven could fly for many days without stopping. When it didn't return, Noah realized that he had chosen the wrong kind of bird.

So he turned to the small white dove. He knew that this bird could not fly long and would have to return if the land was still under water. After many hours, the dove flew back to the ark, having found no better resting place.

A few days later, Noah tried again, and released another dove from the window. It returned a short time later, bearing in its beak a leaf of an olive tree, which it had found nearby at a place where the waters were receding.

Hope filled Noah's heart. Seven days later, he freed the dove again and this time she did not return, for she had found a nesting place where the earth was dry. Now Noah knew that the time of waiting had

The

Flood

Recedes

33

ended. Hand in hand with his family, he stepped onto the deck of his ark. Before him lay the bright green hills and meadows sparkling with droplets of water. Joyously and thankfully, Noah led his family and the birds and the beasts onto the land again.

When all of them had settled on a grassy plain, Noah built an altar of stone and offered up a sacrifice to God for His mercy. The sun beamed more brightly than ever before, but Noah felt a great sadness in his heart for all those who had perished. Surely, he prayed, God would not destroy the world again. And as this prayer fell from his lips, he suddenly beheld in the sky a beautiful rainbow of many colors. And God's voice was heard:

"This rainbow is a sign of My promise that I will never again destroy the earth and that all the seasons will come and go as before. But, because I know man to be weak and forgetful, once more I will tell you, as I told Adam; the earth is yours to rule in goodness and justice. It will feed you and comfort you. But you must take care of the earth, and of one another, as well. Above all, I hate murder and bloodshed, for it is the same thing as denying God, in whose image man was made. Remember this, and I will keep My promise."

And thus, the flood was ended, and Noah and his sons began to till the soil. Soon children were born to Noah's daughters-in-law, and life seemed pure and happy.

But as God had warned, man is weak and sinful. One day Noah drank too much wine, and he fell down in a deep sleep on the floor. His son named Ham found him this way. He thought it quite a joke, so much so that he ran out and called his brothers Shem and Japheth to come in and see how foolish their father looked on the floor. But his brothers had greater respect and would not take part in such a mockery.

When Noah awoke, he was angry to see his laughing son. With heavy heart he ordered Ham and his family out of the house, for he was afraid that Ham would influence other people to become disrepectful and to laugh at their parents.

And so it was that Ham took his possessions and his wife and children and left that part of the world, forever to bear the scorn of his brothers—for he had mocked a righteous man.

The Tower of Babel

MANY YEARS PASSED, and the sons of Noah had many descendants. Most of them settled in the area that we know today as the Middle East. There, it is said, all life began—and little wonder, considering the fertile valleys and plains and the clear rivers that abounded in this section.

Plate 7. THE TOWER OF BABEL, by Pieter Bruegel, the Elder (Flemish, about 1520–1569), Kunsthistorisches Museum, Vienna.

Men always wish to build their cities near rivers and in fertile places. That is why some of Noah's descendants went south into the land of the Nile River, and why others journeyed to the Jordan River plain and many more to the rich Eastern fields of the Tigris and Euphrates rivers. Here a busy civilization began. People dwelled in houses and had shops. They farmed, and lived in peace with their neighbors, since all men spoke the very same language. This situation was not to last.

Some ambitious people living in the area of the Tigris and Euphrates—in a place later to be called Babylon—decided to make their city the center of the world. It was their thought to build a tower so high that it would reach into Heaven itself and come upon the face of God.

"We shall be the most famous people in the world," they said, "and rivals to God Himself."

So they drew up their plans for the mighty tower. It would be made of bricks, held together by tar, and it would be so large that two teams of horses could pass each other on its ascending ramps.

Feverishly, the builders began, and, every day, the tower rose higher and higher into the sky. Apparently, it might accomplish the purpose of piercing heaven itself.

But God decided to teach these people that He could not be challenged by mere men. He cut short their foolish dreams by causing changes to come over their speech, until no one could understand anyone else. When a man asked for a pail of water, he received a bundle of bricks instead. Therefore, it became impossible to finish the tower, and, before very long, amid fighting and confusion, the too ambitious plans were abandoned. Soon, only the foundations of the tower remained. Later, these, too, were destroyed, and the place became called Babel, which means "confusion of many voices."

So it was that God brought many languages into the world and caused people to spread out into other areas and, thus, to fulfill His commandment: "Multiply and be fruitful."

Abram— the Idol Breaker

IN THE CITY of Ur of the Chaldees lived a family descended from Noah's son Shem. The father of this family, Terah, was one of the few good men in his city. There, the people worshiped little statues as though they were God. They had forgotten the one supreme Creator.

Terah had a son named Abram, who, from his earliest childhood, believed in the one true God. And it is said that one day, as a boy, Abram overturned many of the idols that were worshiped in his city, and condemned the people for being false to God. Perhaps because of this, Terah had to take his family and hurriedly leave.

In those times, when people moved from town to town, they formed what is called a "caravan." This is a procession of many camels and sheep. Such caravans may still be seen in the Middle East, wending their ways over the land.

Terah settled his caravan in a town called Haran, which was north of the land of Canaan. Abram liked the new surroundings; they were green and fertile, and seemed destined for great events.

One day he heard the voice of God in his heart, for God had remembered His faithful servant.

"Take your family and your goods," said the Lord, "and journey through Canaan. Some day, all of it will belong to you and your descendants—and it will house a great nation in the world."

Abram was profoundly moved by this vision, and immediately gathered his belongings and his family, which consisted of his lovely bride Sarai and a nephew, Lot. In addition, they took their servants and their camels and all their earthly goods to begin the journey.

For many days, they passed through green, sweet-smelling hills and across plains of many fine trees and streams. Abram was overcome by the beauty of what he found, and he paused and built an altar to the Lord near the city of Beth-el, which means "house of God."

There were, however, others who lived in this land. They were descendants of Ham, the son who had mocked Noah his father. At that time, Noah had cursed Ham, saying that he would always bear the scorn of his brothers. And so it was, even to Ham's descendants, for now they fought among themselves, brother against brother.

Because of the fighting, Abram and his caravan found there was not enough food to go around. He was a peaceful man, besides, and wished no trouble with the Canaanites. So he ordered his caravan southward toward the land of Egypt, where there was prosperity and food. Lot, Sarai, and all their servants joined in the expedition. For weeks, they passed through the southern desert, and, soon, they were at the borders of Egypt, where the king, known as Pharaoh, ruled with an iron hand.

Abram knew something of Egypt and, one day, before they crossed the border, he took Sarai aside:

"You are a beautiful woman," he said, "and in Egypt, if the Pharaoh likes you, he will have me killed and take you for his bride. If we pretend we are but brother and sister, he will not kill me, and I shall be able to fight and free you from his bondage."

"That is true," Sarai replied. "I will say that you are my brother."

With this plan in mind, they entered the kingdom of the Pharaohs.

In those days, Egypt was the greatest power in the world. The people were proud and strong, and they owned many slaves. For tombs they built themselves underground chambers, which they filled with gold and jewelry, believing that these would buy their way to paradise. The Egyptians did not believe in the one true God, but in many gods. They made statues in the likeness of these gods, and worshiped them.

In this strange country, Abram and Sarai were very much alone. They kept to themselves and went about their business. But, one day, spies of the Pharaoh saw Sarai as she was fetching water from a well. True to Abram's fears, they reported her great beauty to Pharaoh, and he sent for her at once.

She was taken to his splendid palace amid the swaying palms, dressed in fine garments, and given many jewels, for Pharaoh intended to make her his bride. Abram was spared since the Egyptians thought that he was merely Sarai's brother and not her husband.

But God would not forsake Sarai; and He sent sickness and plagues on the house of Pharaoh, so that Pharaoh soon grew afraid. Probably from his spies, he learned the true identity of Sarai and he sent for Abram at once.

"What have you done to me? Why didn't you tell me that Sarai was your wife and not your sister?" Pharaoh exclaimed. "I might have married her myself because of this untruth."

But Pharaoh relented and forgave Abram and even allowed Abram and Sarai to depart from Egypt with all their possessions and even with sheep and oxen and other gifts that Pharaoh bestowed upon them. He ordered that they be permitted to go on their journey out of Egypt peacefully.

Abram wanted no more of Egypt. He took Sarai and Lot and all his possessions, and once again turned his eyes toward Canaan—for he felt a yearning in his heart to return to the sweet-smelling hills that God had promised to him and his descendants forever.

God Speaks to Abram

BY THE TIME that the caravan reached Beth-el, it had grown very large with the presents of Pharaoh and the increase of the flocks. Beth-el was too small to hold such a vast community, and so Abram and his nephew Lot decided to separate. This would be very hard for them, since they loved each other dearly.

"You are like a son to me," said Abram to Lot, "and I want you

OPPOSITE: Plate 8. ABRAHAM AND MELCHIZEDEK, by Dieric Bouts (Flemish, about 1415–1475), Church of Saint Pierre, Louvain, Belgium.

to have the best. Therefore choose whether you wish to stay here in Beth-el, or whether you want to find a better settlement. I will abide by your decision."

Lot was very grateful, and told his uncle that he would take his part of the caravan and journey toward the Jordan, where he knew there were fertile cities.

And so Abram and Lot divided the land and parted as friends for the sake of the community.

Abram was sad. He wandered to a high point on the mountains so that he might watch as Lot departed. Slowly his nephew's caravan moved farther and farther away in the pale light of the evening.

Abram felt very much alone. But the voice of God came to him again, in the evening, and said:

"Banish this loneliness. There will come a time when your descendants will be as numerous as the pebbles in the sand. They will occupy this country north and south, east and west, as far as you can see from this high mountain. Go walk through the land; for unto you will I give it."

And so Abram set up his tents beneath the great oak trees of a place called Hebron, and his tribe increased.

At first this tribe was known as Habiru or Eberus, a word that, perhaps, derives from Hebron, where they lived—or from an ancient word meaning "stranger" (and strangers they were to the Canaanites). We can see how this word, "Habiru," came to be "Hebrew." In fact, Abram is known as the Father of the Hebrews.

Lot Is Made a Prisoner

LOT WAS ALSO a Hebrew, and, for this reason, he was considered a stranger in the city where he settled. This place was Sodom, a city of idol worshipers and many rich people. One day a jealous king of a small country decided to attack Sodom.

After a terrible battle, the city fell, and all the men were taken prisoner, including Lot. Fortunately, a young servant escaped and went directly to Abram to report the news. Abram immediately formed an army of his tribesmen and rushed off to free his beloved nephew.

His ability in warfare was very great, and he defeated the invaders and freed his kinsmen. One of the rulers of Sodom, who was a pious man named Melchizedek, gratefully bestowed his blessings upon Abram.

"You are truly a man of God," the old king said, and he handed Abram gifts of bread and wine, and other riches.

Taking the gifts, Abram divided them among the soldiers and the slaves. He wanted nothing for himself but freedom for Lot, which he had accomplished with the help of God.

But, as the years went by, Abram was sad. Rich and powerful though he was, he had no children of his own—and, therefore, if he died, his servant Eliezer would take his place in the tribe. Eliezer was a pious man, but still he was not a son of Abram.

God was aware of Abram's sorrow.

"Can you count the stars in the heavens?" said the Lord. "No one can—and yet I will make your descendants as numerous as the stars that fill the moonlit sky. Once again, I repeat to you, they will fill this land from the Nile to the Jordan, to the rivers beyond. You will have sons; they will fight their enemies; and, for a period, they will be slaves in a foreign country. But they will return, for I have chosen them as My people, to bear My blessings in the world. Do not despair; I have promised."

So ABRAM RESUMED his life and grew old with Sarai, whom he loved most dearly. She, too, was troubled that she bore no son. One day, she went to her husband when he was resting.

Abram Marries Hagar

"Do you remember Hagar, the girl we brought from Egypt?" she questioned. "She is young and healthy, but has no husband. Take her as another wife. Perhaps she will bear you a son, as I cannot."

In those days, many men had more than one wife, especially the leaders of a tribe—and so Abram was not against this idea. He called the slave girl to him and, with Sarai's consent, they were married.

At first Hagar was honored by her new position as wife to the chief of the Hebrews. But her gratitude soon turned to pride, and she began to assume an air of great importance. Then, when it was learned that she was expecting a child, Sarai became very jealous. She began to treat Hagar like a slave again. They argued and cried until, at length, Hagar could stand no more and ran away.

She hadn't gone very far when she heard the voice of an angel come from God.

"Why are you running?" the angel said.

"Because my mistress is cruel to me and is jealous of my child," Hagar answered.

"You must go back," the angel said, "for you are the wife of Abram, and God has promised that his sons shall be the leaders of great nations. You are to bear one of Abram's sons—call him 'Ishmael,' which means 'heard of God,' and he will be a great and powerful prince."

Hearing this, Hagar knew no fear and returned to have her baby in the tent of Abram.

The child Ishmael grew up and was loved by his father. But God had not intended this boy to be the true heir of Abram, and so He spoke again to His faithful servant:

"I know," said the Lord, "that you and your wife are very old, but, even so, you will have a son together, and he will be the leader of My people when you are gone."

"A son!" exclaimed Abram. "When I am one hundred years old? and when Sarai, my wife, is ninety years old?" And Abram laughed inwardly.

"Laugh," said God. "I am not offended. Your son shall be named Isaac, which means 'laughter.' I also wish you and your wife to change your names so that they will have new meanings. You shall be called 'Abraham' or 'father of a great multitude,' and Sarai will become 'Sarah,' which means 'princess.' In this way will the world know you. Besides, I will make a covenant, or a pact with you, that so long as your descendants worship Me—and Me alone—I will not forget them throughout eternity. As a sign of this pact between us, every one of your men must be circumcised as a ritual to God. That is what I ask of My Chosen People."

And Abraham obeyed, and was filled with joy and thankfulness.

Abraham and the Angels

BENEATH THE SPREADING oak trees, Abraham rested by his tent. The day was clear and warm, and all was peaceful. Down the road were coming three men dressed in flowing robes. Abraham saw them, and rose to open the flaps of his tent, for all were welcome in his home. These three were angels from the Lord; and their handsome faces and gentle smiles filled Abraham with a sense of joy.

He offered them water for washing and bread and fresh roasted meat, which he prepared and served himself. No one could be more hospitable than Abraham.

For a long time, the three guests sat at the table and enjoyed the

OPPOSITE: Plate 9. ABRAHAM ENTERTAINING THE ANGELS, by Rembrandt (Dutch, 1606–1669), Private Collection, Holland.

food while their host saw to their needs. Sarah had remained inside, as was the custom for women in those days. But she was interested in who these strangers might be, so she sat close to the tent flap and listened.

"We are come from the Lord," the angels said, "to repeat His pledge that, within a year, you will have a son with Sarah and that he will lead a great nation, as you have done."

Suddenly, there was the sound of laughter. The angels rose.

"Who laughs at God?" they questioned.

Sarah approached. She begged forgiveness but, like Abraham before her, she could not believe a son would be born to one so old. The angels reassured her, and, thanking their host for his hospitality, prepared to leave.

"We are going to the cities of Sodom and Gomorrah," they said.

"I know them well," Abraham answered. "My nephew Lot lives there. I will lead you if you wish."

One of the angels was, in fact, the Lord and now He spoke to Abraham and told him that He had long been angered by the wickedness of Sodom and Gomorrah. It was now His judgment to destroy them both by fire and hail. No one would be saved.

Abraham was in despair. "Surely you can save the cities if only fifty righteous men can be found?"

And God promised to do so, if there were fifty, or thirty, *or* twenty.

"Ten, even ten," Abraham begged. But God and the angels knew that not even ten good men were left in the wicked cities. And so the angels set out to destroy them.

The Destruction of Sodom and Gomorrah

IT WAS TRUE, sad as it may seem, that not even ten good men were left in Sodom and Gomorrah. This the angels were soon to prove. When they entered the city of Sodom, they were followed by gangs of men until they arrived at the house of Lot. Only Lot was pure of heart. He urged the strangers to enter his home and enjoy some refreshments. But they wished to remain outside, probably to observe the wickedness of the city. Seeing the crowds of idle men lurking about, Lot was more insistent. "Please come inside and rest," he said to them—and they finally accepted.

Minutes later the sounds of stones being thrown against the house alarmed Lot and his guests, and they rushed to the windows. Outside, the men of Sodom were gathered, shouting,

"Send those strangers out here. We have plans for them."

Lot tried to quiet the crowd and opened the door to speak. No sooner had he shown his face than a barrage of stones came flying at him, and the angels had to call on God to strike the evil men blind, thereby saving Lot from certain death.

Blinded and confused, the gangs departed, and the morning dawned gray and foreboding.

"You must take your family and escape from here," the angels told Lot, "for God intends to destroy these wicked cities before the night."

At first, Lot couldn't believe this news. But the angels insisted.

"The others do not believe us," they said, "and they will all be destroyed. You alone are a righteous man. Save yourself and your family.

"But heed this single warning," they continued. "Anyone turning back to look upon the great destruction will also be destroyed, for God does not wish any witness to His fury."

And so Lot and his family fled high into the mountains that bordered the wicked place.

By midday, the destruction began. Great fires started in the cities, and the smell of sulfur filled the air. High up in the mountains, Lot's wife paused by the road. Overcome with curiosity, she turned to take just one look at the raging terror—and, in that same instant, as the angels had warned, she was transformed into a pillar of salt!

Lot and his daughters, however, hid in the caves until the destruction was complete. Then they resumed their lives in other cities, and the daughters had sons who peopled the nations to the north of Abraham's dominion.

FOR WEEKS AFTER the destruction, ashes and smoke blew over the entire region; and Abraham decided to remove his people toward the south, so that they might be spared the sorrowful reminder of Sodom and Gomorrah. Taking up his caravan, he journeyed to a small kingdom ruled by a man named Abimelech.

Once again, Abraham and Sarah pretended to be brother and sister, because, like the Pharaoh of Egypt, Abimelech simply arrested whichever women he liked, killing their husbands as he did so.

Indeed, he arrested Sarah and had her brought to his palace. But, God was merciful. In a dream he came to Abimelech and told him the truth, that Abraham was Sarah's husband. Fearfully, Abimelech freed Sarah, gave her many gifts, and invited Abraham to settle wherever he wished in his kingdom.

In such a settlement, Isaac was born to Abraham and Sarah, as God had promised. Their joy was enormous. But there were also Ishmael and Hagar, who were jealous of the newborn child. One day, Sarah saw Ishmael, who was now a big boy, teasing the baby, and she became alarmed.

"Suppose he tries to do my baby harm," she thought. Then she rushed to Abraham and begged him to send Hagar and her son away to find another home. At first, Abraham did not wish to comply, but he remembered God's promise that Ishmael would also be the leader of a nation, and so he knew that the Lord would protect Hagar.

Then he gave Hagar and Ishmael food and water. At sunrise, they set out, the servant woman and her child.

Days passed, and it seemed to Hagar that she was wandering aim-

Isaac
Is
Born

Plate 10. THE DESTRUCTION OF SODOM (LOT'S WIFE),
by Jean Baptiste Camille Corot (French, 1796–1875),
The Metropolitan Museum of Art, New York.

OPPOSITE: Plate 11. THE DISMISSAL OF HAGAR, by Jan Steen
(Dutch, 1626–1679), Gemäldegalerie, Dresden.

lessly in the desert. The water ran out. Her food was almost finished.
Little Ishmael began to cry, and terror gripped his mother's heart. She
carried her son to a place in the shade and hid her head, awaiting death.

But soon, above her, she felt the beating of wings, and there stood
a glorious angel of God who led her to a well of cold, clear water, and
pledged to her that Ishmael would, indeed, become a prince as God had
promised. And so it was that, many years later, Ishmael established the
tribe of Arabians, who are considered, even today, descended from him
and from Abraham.

The
Sacrifice

MEANWHILE, ISAAC HAD GROWN into a fine young boy who was the joy of his aged parents. God loved him and wished him no harm. Yet, one day, He decreed to Abraham a strange and awesome thing.

"Take Isaac, your beloved child," said the Lord, "and bring him to the mountain. There you must slay him on an altar as a sacrifice to Me."

Abraham was overwhelmed with sorrow. Yet he knew that even such a heartbreaking request had to be obeyed—for it is easy to obey simple commandments. The true test of faith is to obey what seems impossible.

So, early in the morning, when Sarah was asleep, Abraham led Isaac through the thickets to the mountain with grievous sorrow in his heart. But Isaac, in his innocence, enjoyed the journey and talked of many things that he hoped to do in the future. How sad this was for Abraham to hear.

At last, they reached the sacrificial place, and Abraham took the boy to the altar.

"Where is the lamb for the sacrifice?" asked Isaac in his innocence.

"The Lord will provide," his father said. "We must trust in Him."

Then Abraham bound Isaac to a rock and produced a glistening knife which he held with a tremble above the poor child's head. Closing his eyes, which were filled with tears, Abraham began to lower the weapon when suddenly he felt a strong hand take hold of his arm. An angel of God had come to rescue Isaac!

"You are truly a man of God," the angel said, "and He is well pleased that you were prepared to offer your only son to Him. Once again, He repeats His pledge that yours shall be a mightly nation through which the entire world will one day be blessed and delivered."

Abraham was overjoyed. Taking Isaac in his arms, he said a prayer of deep thanksgiving. Then, looking around, he saw a ram that had been caught by its horns in a thicket. He now knew that God had provided a proper sacrifice, and he offered the ram in place of his son. Then, hand in hand with Isaac, Abraham joyously descended the mountain.

OPPOSITE: Plate 12. THE SACRIFICE OF ISAAC, by Rembrandt (Dutch, 1606–1669), Pinakothek (Picture Gallery), Munich.

A Wife for Isaac

THE YEARS WENT BY. Isaac grew to manhood and began assuming the duties of leadership. Then sorrow came to him and Abraham, for Sarah died. She was very old, and had seen a rich and happy life. Yet she was mourned by all. After a period of sorrow, Abraham purchased a field where he could bury his wife in dignity; and she was laid to rest.

Now Isaac would have to find a wife, a good woman like Sarah, who would be an example for the other women of the tribe. So Abraham summoned Eliezer, his faithful servant, and instructed him to go back to Haran, the town where Abraham's father first settled—and there find a bride for Isaac.

"She must be of our people," said Abraham, "and she must be gentle and kind. When you find such a girl, bring her here so that she may marry Isaac and settle in this Promised Land."

Eliezer packed his camels and set off.

After many days the faithful servant came to the town of Haran, which was many miles north of Abraham's home. There he prayed to God for guidance in choosing the proper wife for his young master. It was a great responsibility.

In those days, the center of every town was the well, where people came for precious water. Here Eliezer rested and prayed, saying, "I will ask the maidens who come here for a drink of water. The one who complies may well be the proper wife for Isaac."

Then he lifted his eyes and saw a lovely girl approaching the well.

"May I ask you for a drink?" said Eliezer.

The maiden smiled and eagerly offered her pitcher to Abraham's servant. Then she asked permission to water his thirsty camels, as well. Eliezer was amazed.

"Surely," he said to himself, "this woman would make an ideal wife for Isaac."

And so it was arranged that the girl, Rebekah, was asked to be Isaac's bride. She was truly the perfect choice. Not only was she kind and gentle, but she was also of the very same family as Abraham. Eliezer placed Rebekah on a camel, and they began the long journey to the south.

When, after many days, they approached the home of Abraham, Isaac was walking in the fields. Rebekah immediately fell in love with him and he with her. Together, they made a happy couple, and Abraham was content to see his son established as head of the tribe.

Then, one quiet morning when there was not a sound to be heard, Abraham closed his eyes and joined God in heaven. He passed from the earth as peacefully as a feather floats on a breeze and was buried beside his wife while many mourned and honored his greatness.

Now isaac was the leader of his people, and Rebekah was his wife. Though they were prosperous and happy, they had no children. Sadly, Rebekah prayed to God and God answered her. She would have two sons—twins. The younger would be master over the older. Each son would lead a great nation that would spread far into the world.

And so it was that Jacob and Esau were born. Esau was the older—by a few minutes. And he was a rugged little baby, covered with auburn hair. In fact, Esau means "hairy."

Jacob followed right on his brother's heels, and, for that reason, his name means "the one who takes"—it was as though Jacob wanted to take his brother's place. Indeed, some day he would, as God had promised.

The boys were very different. Esau loved to hunt and roam about the woods. He was also an excellent cook, and the deer meat that he prepared was a favorite dish of his father's. Jacob stayed at home in the tents and tilled the soil.

God had decided that Jacob would be the greater man, because Jacob loved God, whereas Esau was more concerned with hunting. Nevertheless, Esau, as the older brother, had first claim to Isaac's property and blessings. One day, he sold those rights for a bowl of soup. This is what happened:

Esau was hunting and lost track of the time. He became very hungry. Returning to the tent, he smelled delicious lentil soup cooking on the fire. There was Jacob stirring the soup.

"I'm so hungry," said Esau. "Would you give me some of that soup?"

"If you will give me your birthright," answered Jacob.

"My birthright?" his brother replied. "What do I care about that? I'm dying of hunger."

"Then you'll swear it over?" asked Jacob, holding back the bowl.

"Yes, yes," Esau answered, and he grabbed the soup and consumed it all in one gulp.

Thus, simply because Esau was hungry for a bowl of soup, Jacob fulfilled God's prophecy that he would one day be greater than his older brother.

The years went by and food was scarce in the land. So Isaac took his family to the kingdom of Abimelech in the nation of the Philistines. There Isaac and his sons were prosperous, for they were favored by God. But their neighbors became jealous.

*Jacob
and
Esau—
the
Twins*

*A
Feud
with
Abimelech*

"Isaac is too rich," they said. "Let's pour sand in his wells. Then he won't be able to get fresh water."

And this they did. But Isaac was patient, and ordered his servants to dig new wells. Unfortunately, the jealous neighbors were also persistent—they filled the new wells, too, and quarreled with Isaac's men.

Finally, King Abimelech asked Isaac to leave the country for the sake of peace. This was the fate of the Hebrews, to wander from one place to another, year after year, and, because of it, Isaac became despondent.

"Will it always be this way?" he wondered.

One day, God came to him in a vision and repeated the promise He had made to Abraham.

"Your descendants will be as numerous as the stars and they will have My blessings," said the Lord.

Isaac was inspired. He settled peacefully, and continued to lead his people. Eventually, King Abimelech apologized for sending him away, and they became good friends once more.

The Blessings

WINTER CAME, followed by spring, summer, and fall. One by one, the years slipped past. Isaac was very old and blind. He felt the call of God in his soul, and knew that he would die before long.

"I must bless Esau," he said to Rebekah. "He is the elder; he must have his blessings and his rights. Call my son Esau to me."

When Esau arrived, Isaac made a simple request of him.

"Go slay a deer for me and prepare my favorite dish, which you do so well. Then I will give you your rightful blessing."

Eagerly, Esau took up his bow and arrows and went into the woods.

Now, Rebekah knew that Esau had sold his birthright, and so she quickly went to Jacob to prepare him.

"It is God's will that you have the blessing and the property," she said, "even if it means that we must be unfair to your brother. Listen to my plan. I shall prepare some meat the way your father likes it. We

shall dress you in Esau's clothes and *you* will go to receive the blessing in his place."

"But suppose my father discovers our plan?" said Jacob. "He will curse me, not bless me."

"I will take the blame," his mother answered. "Let us not waste time."

"One more thing," Jacob said. " My brother Esau is a hairy man; and, if our father touches my hand, he will know that we have tricked him."

But Rebekah was prepared. She covered Jacob's hands with fur, and sent him into Isaac's tent. There the old man lay in darkness.

"Who has come?" he asked.

"Esau," answered Jacob, disguising his voice.

"Esau?" said Isaac. "So quickly?"

"Yes," Jacob replied. "God led me to a deer as soon as I stepped into the woods. Here is your favorite dish."

Isaac was suspicious. "Come closer, my son," he said.

And Jacob knelt before his father.

"It is strange," Isaac whispered, caressing Jacob's hand. "The voice is the voice of Jacob, but the hands are the hands of Esau."

"Of course, I am Esau," Jacob replied. "Here, eat the food and enjoy it; then give me your blessing."

Isaac ate. When he had finished, he raised his hands above Jacob, and, believing him to be his older son, he said:

"You were the firstborn, my son. Therefore, to you go my land and my flocks and my blessings for prosperity. Above all, remember, you will be the leader of our people. Your brother must serve you, for you alone are the favorite of God."

Then Jacob rose, kissed his father, and quickly, knowing that Esau was about to return, he left and hid with his mother.

Esau entered the tent. He had hunted a deer and prepared a good stew with its meat. Now he approached his father in the darkness.

"Who is there?" said Isaac.

"Esau, your son," the hunter replied. "Here is your favorite dish. I have come for your blessing."

Isaac cried out, "Oh, I have been deceived and you have been betrayed. Your brother has stolen your blessing!"

Esau was bitter and in despair.

"Is there nothing left for me?" he cried. His father felt pity in his heart, and said:

"I cannot give you your rightful blessing, for another one has taken it. But I will pray for you. Even though you must serve your brother, I will pray for your prosperity."

Then Esau rushed from his father's room, and in a loud voice for all to hear he shouted:

"I will kill my brother Jacob for his treachery!"

Rebekah heard these vengeful words, and ran to the place where Jacob was hiding.

"You must leave here, for Esau will kill you. Go to my brother's home in Haran. There you will be safe. I shall tell your father that I sent you to find a wife among my people. It is true, I do not wish you to marry one of these strange women, as your brother has done. Go, then, and take my blessing."

Isaac agreed that Jacob should seek a proper wife and he blessed his son before he departed for Haran.

THE NIGHT WAS DARK and the journey long, so Jacob decided to rest in the wilderness. His bed was the hard earth, his pillow a stone; and, above him, the star-filled sky stretched out like a blanket.

Jacob had a beautiful dream while he slept. Golden light seemed to flood the sky, and a great gold staircase, or ladder, appeared ascending to Heaven. On this ladder, angels walked up and down in flowing robes. At the top of the ladder, miles and miles away, God sat on His throne, and He spoke to Jacob.

"Remember My promise to Abraham," He said, "and do not forget the land that I have pledged to you and to your people."

It was a wonderful dream, and Jacob awoke filled with the majesty of God. He called the place "Beth-el," or "house of God," and, thus inspired, hurried along on his journey.

Several days later, Jacob came to the outskirts of Haran, where his uncle lived. There he saw a beautiful maiden trying to roll back a stone that covered the mouth of the well. He quickly went to her assistance. When he had drawn some water for her, he asked:

"Do you know Laban, who lives in this village?"

"Indeed I do," she answered with a smile. "He is my father."

Jacob was overjoyed. "He is my uncle," he said, "for I am Jacob, and I have come many miles to stay with him."

"Rachel is my name," the maiden answered. Already, Jacob felt great love for Rachel and he kissed her and wept for happiness. She too was overjoyed as she escorted Jacob to her father's house.

There, Laban greeted his nephew and prepared a feast for him. It was decided that Jacob would tend the flocks on his uncle's land.

After a few years of life as a shepherd, Jacob wished to begin a family of his own. He was deeply in love with Rachel, and went to his uncle for permission to marry her. His uncle agreed, but on the one condition that Jacob would work for him for seven years before the marriage; he was anxious not to lose his faithful nephew. This Jacob promised, and seven years went quickly by.

At last it was the day of Jacob's wedding to Rachel. Joyously, the bridegroom waited to receive his bride as she came down the path to meet him.

The marriage ceremony was performed, and Jacob drew close to kiss his bride. But when he lifted her veils, he saw, to his amazement, not Rachel but Leah, her older sister.

Laban stepped forward and said, in a solemn voice:

"Leah is the older of my daughters and she must marry before the younger. It is the law of this land. Therefore, if you wish to have Rachel, you must work another seven years."

Jacob's Ladder

ABOVE: Plate 14. ISAAC BLESSING JACOB, by Gerbrandt van den Eeckhout (Dutch, 1621–1674), The Metropolitan Museum of Art, New York.

OPPOSITE: Plate 15. JACOB'S DREAM, by Domenico Feti (Italian, 1589–1623), Kunsthistorisches Museum, Vienna.

Jacob loved Rachel enough to work twice as long for her as he had originally agreed. A week later, he married Rachel, and began seven more years of service to her father.

Jacob Makes a Bargain

THE YEARS WENT BY, and eleven sons were born to Jacob. He began to think of returning to Canaan, where his father and mother still lived. One day, he went to his uncle Laban, and said:

"I wish to leave your village with my wives and children and return to Canaan."

"I'm sorry to hear this," Laban answered. "We have done well together over the years, you and I. Can't I persuade you to stay?"

At first Jacob refused, but Laban continued to urge him, finally asking him to name his own price.

Jacob thought a while and said:

"Very well. Let us go through your herds and flocks and pick out all the speckled and spotted cattle, all the brown sheep, and all the speckled and spotted goats. These your sons will take away. Then your herd will consist entirely of unspotted cattle, white sheep, and unspotted goats. They will all belong to you, none to me."

"But what do you want for yourself?" Laban asked.

"I want all the speckled and spotted calves and kids and brown lambs born to your herds from now on," Jacob continued. "These will be mine and my family's in the future, just as the presently spotted animals belong to your sons now."

It seemed like a good bargain. Laban agreed. All the speckled and spotted cattle, all the brown sheep, and all the speckled and spotted goats were taken away by his sons.

Then Jacob took some sapling trees with the bark on. He cut off the branches, leaving white spots where the raw wood showed underneath. He peeled bark away in places, leaving stripes and speckles. When he watered Laban's herds, Jacob set the rods before the stronger, fatter animals, but not before the weaklings. Thus, when the animals gave birth, the strong calves and kids were spotted and speckled, and the strong lambs were brown. In six years, Jacob built himself a splendid herd.

Laban's sons were jealous. They said that Jacob had taken all the good sheep and cattle and left them with the weaklings. Quarrels and trouble began. Jacob knew what this could lead to. One day, he called Rachel and Leah to him, and they decided to pack their caravan quietly and move out of the village at night.

This they did with all their children and servants and cattle. Rachel also took her father's precious idols, for she did not think it proper that he worshiped them. When Laban discovered this, he was very angry and followed Jacob with his own caravan.

AT A PLACE called Gilead, Jacob and his large family made camp. Once again, he heard the voice of God bidding him to return to Canaan, and he was more determined than ever to reach his father's home.

When the angry Laban reached Gilead, he made a thorough search for his idols. But Rachel had hidden them under the saddle of her camel. Finally, after searching to no avail, Laban relented. He realized that the time had come for his daughters to leave home, so he extended his hand to Jacob and made peace. The two caravans parted at a place called Mizpeh, which means "pledge of friendship."

But danger lay ahead, for Jacob was entering Edom the land where Esau lived. Had twenty years softened Esau's heart, he wondered, or did he still wish to kill Jacob for the trick played on him? No one could tell. Only God in heaven knew, and He sent a group of angels to meet Jacob on the road and comfort him.

With such encouragement, Jacob wished to make peace with Esau. And so he sent messengers with gifts to his brother, and anxiously awaited their return. When the messengers arrived back at his camp, Jacob questioned them eagerly. But all they could say was that Esau intended to meet him with four hundred men the very next day. Jacob didn't know whether that meant peace or war. So he left his wives and children and cattle on one side of the river, and with a few men he crossed to the other, prepared for whatever God decreed.

The night was very still. Jacob could not sleep. He rose and went wandering in the field, when suddenly he came face to face with a stranger in the dark. Was it Esau come to kill him?

Panic filled Jacob's heart and he grabbed the stranger and wrestled with him. Until morning, the two men tugged and rolled in the dirt. When the sun rose, Jacob saw that he had been wrestling, not with Esau, but with an angel of God and because the angel could not overpower Jacob, he grabbed his thigh and put it out of joint. Still Jacob would not let go; the angel pleaded for his release.

"You must bless me," cried Jacob, "before I release you. I have done my brother wrong and I am afraid of him."

The angel then blessed Jacob, and told him that thenceforth he would be called "Israel," which means "chosen by God."

The Journey Home

Jacob fell down exhausted from the fight, but now, at least, his conscience was clear, for the pain in his leg would always remind him of his guilt toward Esau. He was, therefore, not afraid when his brother came with four hundred men and confronted him.

Instead, Jacob fell to the ground and bowed seven times in repentence.

Seeing this, Esau's heart was softened and he embraced his brother; and they made peace again.

There was a great celebration over this reunion. Then Jacob proceeded to Canaan with his caravan.

But all was not easy on the way. Passing through a town called Shechem, Jacob's sons engaged in war against the local prince, who, they said, had insulted their sister.

There was also sorrow. Rachel, the beloved wife, had borne Jacob only one of his eleven sons, the boy named Joseph. Now she was to have another child, and Jacob was utterly happy. But the birth of the baby, Benjamin, was too much for Rachel, and she died. Sorrowfully Jacob buried her near the place called Bethlehem.

And so it was that Jacob returned to his father Isaac, and was there when Isaac died at the age of 180. Esau also came to mourn. In time, a new generation was to arise among the sons of Abraham.

Joseph and His Brothers

JACOB GREW OLD. His fame was great and his tribe increased. He had twelve fine sons who helped him with the flocks and with the harvests. Reuben was the eldest; the youngest was Benjamin, Rachel's second and last child. But, of them all, Jacob loved Joseph best, for Joseph was Rachel's firstborn son, and he was clever, gay, and very handsome.

The brothers did not love Joseph. For one thing, he often reported their wrongdoings to Jacob and they thought he was a tattletale. For another, Jacob had given Joseph a beautiful coat of many colors, and he was always wandering around the fields showing off.

He also had many strange dreams, which he often related to his father and brothers.

"Last night I dreamed that we were all gathering wheat," he said once, "and my bundle was very big and your bundles all bowed down to mine . . ."

His brothers were furious.

"So you are to reign over us!" they said. "And we are to bow down to you! Go away! We don't want to hear any more of your dreams!"

But he continued:

"Last night I dreamed there were eleven stars in the sky, and they all bowed down to me—even the sun and the moon bowed down to the ground before me."

Joseph was very young, and he thought these stories interested his brothers. But they assumed that he was just bragging; and they complained to their father.

"You mustn't make your brothers angry," Jacob said to his favorite son. "They are older than you."

And so Joseph stayed by himself while his brothers went to pasture with their flocks.

The Dreamer Becomes a Slave

ONE DAY, JACOB DECIDED to send Joseph in search of his brothers to see how they were, for they had been gone many months. Joseph put on his colorful coat and began the journey. He was about seventeen years old.

He had trouble finding his brothers, for they had wandered far afield. At last, he saw their camp, and ran joyously to meet them. But the brothers were not at all pleased to see this "dreamer," as they called him. In fact, they began to plot a way to get rid of him.

"We'll kill him and throw him into a pit," they said. "We can say that a lion has eaten him."

Reuben, the eldest brother, would not agree. There was a discussion over what to do with Joseph, and it was decided not to kill him, but to leave him in the pit to starve. Reuben actually intended to rescue him later, for he knew that Joseph's death would be a cruel blow to Jacob. Then Reuben went to the hills to tend his flock.

The other brothers immediately grabbed Joseph while he slept, stripped him of his pretty coat, and lowered him into an empty pit. Afterward they sat down as though nothing happened, and had supper.

While they were eating, an Arab caravan came wending its way across the field.

"Where are you going?" the brothers asked.

"To Egypt selling slaves," the Arabs answered.

"Slaves," the brothers thought. "This gives us an idea. Why should we kill Joseph when we can sell him to these Arabs? We'll be rid of him just the same."

And so they lifted Joseph out of the pit and handed him over to the Arabs for twenty pieces of silver.

The evil deed was done. But there was more. The brothers took Joseph's many-colored coat and dipped it in the blood of an animal, so that it would look as though a lion had attacked "the dreamer." Then these wicked men brought this coat to their aged father, who fainted in grief when he was told that his beloved son was dead.

But God had greater plans for Joseph. Indeed, his dreams of glory were all to come true, and even his father's great sorrow would change to joy.

Joseph in Egypt

FOR A THOUSAND YEARS and more, Egypt had been the most glorious nation in the world. Gleaming pyramids rose into the clear blue sky. Mighty temples lined the flowered banks of the Nile. And Pharaoh, the king, lived in a palace paved with gold.

Into this strange land, the boy Joseph was brought as a slave. He was sold to a rich man named Potiphar, who owned a great house near Pharaoh's palace. At first, Joseph did lowly chores for his master. But his intelligence won him favor, and he was soon promoted to a high position in Potiphar's household.

He was a good servant and faithful to his master. Unfortunately, Potiphar's wife had evil designs on her youthful servant. She often tried to trick him and tempt him when her husband was away.

"Am I not beautiful?" she would say to him. "Then kiss me; my husband will not see us."

But Joseph resisted her, in loyalty to his master, and she grew angry and bitter.

One day, Potiphar's wife tried to embrace Joseph, but he pushed her aside and left the room. At the same time, she held onto his cape and pulled it from his shoulders. Later, in order to avenge her disappointments, she told her husband that Joseph had forced his attentions upon her. She showed him Joseph's cape as proof. Her story, of course, was the exact opposite of the truth, but Potiphar believed his wife; and Joseph was cast into Pharaoh's prison.

Once again, Joseph was betrayed, but God was with him. He soon became an assistant to the jail keeper and, as such, he made the rounds of all the prisoners every morning.

ON ONE INSPECTION of the prisoners Joseph saw two men who had recently been arrested by Pharaoh's own command. One of these men was the royal cupbearer, the man who carried Pharaoh's wine cup to the table. The other was the palace baker, who made Pharaoh's breads and cakes.

They were both despondent. The night before, they had dreamed disturbing dreams and could not understand them.

Joseph told them that, with the help of God, he was able to interpret dreams, and would do so for them.

The cupbearer began:

"I dreamed that I saw a grapevine with three branches, and, as I watched, the branches became ripe with delicious grapes. I pressed these grapes into wine and brought the wine to Pharaoh in his golden cup. What does it mean?"

Joseph pondered a minute and then he said:

"The three branches mean three days. In three days, you will be free and you will carry the wine to Pharaoh in his cup, just as you have dreamed.

"But I beg of you," Joseph continued, "when you are free, re-

Joseph Interprets Many Dreams

OPPOSITE: Plate 18. JOSEPH ACCUSED BY POTIPHAR'S WIFE, by Rembrandt (Dutch, 1606–1669), State Museums, Berlin.

65

member me in prison. I have been falsely accused and I am far from my home, where no one can help me."

The cupbearer was overjoyed, and promised to help Joseph.

Now the baker told his dream:

"I had just baked three loaves of bread and was carrying them in a basket on my head. As I was walking, many wicked birds descended on me and ate the breads. What does it mean?"

Joseph was reluctant to answer.

"I am sorry to tell you," he said. "The three loaves mean three days. In three days you will be sentenced by Pharaoh to hang, and the birds will fly around your gallows when you are dead."

Three days later, as Joseph said, the baker was hanged and the cupbearer was freed to attend Pharaoh's birthday. But Joseph remained in prison, for the selfish cupbearer did not remember him.

Then, one night, Pharaoh himself had a strange and disturbing dream. He stood by the River Nile, and, as he stood there in his dream, seven fat cows came out of the river and went into the meadows, where they grazed. After them came seven skinny cows eagerly looking for food. And these cows went into the meadows and ate the fat cows.

Pharaoh was so astonished that he awoke. Convinced it was but a dream, he returned to sleep. But he dreamed again. This time he saw seven ears of corn on a stalk, and they were golden and rich. Next to them there grew seven spoiled and rotten ears of corn, which leaned over and devoured the fat ears.

Pharaoh was still disturbed, and, in the morning, he called his wise men and magicians to interpret his dreams. But all that they could do was to quarrel and make fools of themselves, until Pharaoh angrily dismissed them and called for his wine.

The cupbearer entered with the wine, and overheard the discussion about the dreams. Then, at last, he remembered Joseph in prison, and told the Pharaoh.

Pharaoh immediately sent for Joseph, who came to him beautifully dressed and filled with the inspiration of God.

"I understand that you can read my dreams," said Pharaoh.

"Not I," Joseph answered, "but God, through me, for it is God who does all good things."

"So be it," said Pharaoh, and he related his two dreams to Joseph, whom he ordered to interpret them.

Joseph pondered a while and said:

"God has given you a glimpse of things to come. First, Egypt will have seven good years, like fat cows and golden ears of corn. There will be plenty to eat, and the crops will grow well. But after that, there will follow seven years of famine, like the skinny cows or the rotten ears of corn. Both of your dreams have the same meaning."

"What shall we do?" asked Pharaoh in alarm.

"You must seek a wise man," said Joseph, "who can prepare for the famine as God instructs you in your dreams. For, if you store up food and supplies during the good years, you will be ready when the famine comes."

Pharaoh was so impressed that he put Joseph himself in charge of this project. Soon Joseph rose to great heights in Egypt. He became a favorite of the king, very much like a Prime Minister or a Secretary of State. For seven years, Joseph instructed the Egyptians to store great quantities of food in granaries, and he traveled throughout the country in his fine chariot, while everyone bowed down to him.

Joseph the Governor

SO GREAT WAS Joseph's fame throughout the land that he married a highborn lady and had two fine sons, Ephraim and Manasseh. His house was paved with gold, and only the Pharaoh wore garments as fine. Surely, God had delivered him.

Then, as Joseph had predicted, the famine set in. Crops failed and the wheat shriveled. The cows grew skinny and the corn was spoiled. But no one went hungry in Egypt. The people opened the warehouses where Joseph had stored food, and they ate in plenty as before. Joseph's power and glory were enormous, and his reputation spread to other lands where the famine was also serious.

One of these stricken countries was Canaan, where Joseph's brothers lived. Twenty years had passed since they had sold their brother into slavery. But this they had forgotten. Only one thought now occupied their minds: how to find food to feed their people.

Jacob spoke to them.

"My sons," he said, "I have heard that there is food in Egypt, and that the Egyptians are willing to sell us corn and wheat. Go, then, and buy enough for our people."

The brothers agreed, and packed their caravans; then, after Jacob blessed them, they set off. Only Benjamin, the youngest, remained behind, for he had become the favorite now, and Jacob, remembering the sad fate of Joseph, was afraid to lose him.

The ten brothers entered Egypt and went to the palace of the great governor, who was in reality their brother Joseph. He recognized them at once. But they had no idea who he was, for he was dressed like an Egyptian lord.

As was the custom, the brothers fell on their knees before the mighty governor—just as Joseph had once predicted in his dream! They remained that way, with their faces to the floor, and Joseph thought to himself:

"I must test their courage."

Then he spoke out in a loud, harsh voice, and said:

"You are spies who have come to Egypt to make plans for war!"

"No, no," the brothers protested. "We are peaceful men. We have come from Canaan where we left our aged father and our little brother Benjamin."

Joseph's heart leapt in his breast when he heard the name of his younger brother, for he loved him best.

"I shall see whether you are spies," he said. "One of you will go to Canaan and bring your youngest brother back to me. The rest will wait in prison."

After three days, Joseph feared that Jacob might grow ill if he thought his sons were in danger, so he released all the brothers except one, and had them brought before him.

"You may all go home with the food," he said, "except for one. He will be my hostage until you return with Benjamin, your youngest brother."

The brothers huddled together to make plans, and spoke only in Hebrew, which they thought the royal Egyptian would not understand.

Reuben, the eldest, spoke:

"We are being punished," he said, "for the crime we committed against our little brother Joseph many years ago. Remember how I begged you not to harm him?"

When the brothers realized that this was true, they repented, and prayed to God to forgive them for that crime. Joseph overheard everything, and was so deeply moved that he began to cry. Not wishing his brothers to see him, he left the room. Calling his servants, he instructed them to fill the brothers' sacks with grain, and with money as well. Then he chose one of the brothers, Simeon, to remain as a hostage while the others returned to Canaan.

"Remember," he said to them, "I will kill Simeon if you do not return with Benjamin as you have promised."

And so the brothers went home, full of remorse, and told Jacob what had happened. But he refused to let Benjamin go to Egypt.

"Simeon will die!" the brothers begged him.

But Jacob refused again. He feared the loss of his youngest son.

When the brothers unpacked their sacks and found the money with the food, they became more alarmed.

"Now the Egyptians will say we are also thieves!" they exclaimed.
"We must go back!"

But, again and again, Jacob refused.

The famine grew worse, and the brothers saw their children starving. Once more, they went to Jacob.

"Our brother Simeon rots in prison," they pleaded. "Our food is
gone. Let us take Benjamin and go to Egypt."

But Jacob seemed not to hear them. Finally, Reuben stepped
forward.

"Father," he said, "I will let you have my own children in exchange for Benjamin. And if any harm comes to him, you may kill my
children or make them slaves."

This offer seemed so desperate in Jacob's eyes that he relented and

finally said that he would allow Benjamin to go. He made the brothers promise that they would protect his favorite son. Then, blessing Benjamin, he bade the brothers pack their caravan for Egypt.

Loaded with gifts and money, the brothers set out, carefully safeguarding Benjamin as they had promised.

JOSEPH WATCHED from his window as the caravan entered his grounds. When he saw Benjamin, he could not control his tears, and he told his servants to prepare a feast in his house.

When the brothers approached the palace, a soldier came to meet them. They feared that they would be arrested, because of the money that they had found in their sacks. But the soldier put their fears to rest, and told them to prepare to dine with his master.

Bewildered, the brothers entered Joseph's dining hall. There they saw Simeon, well and safe. When Joseph entered, they bowed to him again, and he inquired:

"How is your father? Is he well?"

The brothers assured him that he was, and bowed again. Then they introduced young Benjamin; and Joseph wept with happiness, but hid his tears from his brothers.

When it was time to dine, they all sat down at separate tables, for the hall was very large. At the brothers' tables, the seats were arranged by name, and the brothers wondered how Joseph knew them. But their fears were allayed, for, during the meal, Joseph frequently sent delicacies from his table to his brothers' tables. The best and the most went to Benjamin.

When the feast was over, the brothers prepared to leave. Once again, Joseph instructed his servants to put money secretly in the sacks of grain and—this time—to place his own silver drinking cup in Benjamin's sack. When this was done, the brothers, none the wiser, set off for home. They had not gone more than a few miles when Joseph's soldiers came after them.

"The master's silver cup is missing," the soldiers said.

"We did not take it," the brothers protested. "Search us, and, if you find that cup in our possession, you may kill the guilty man or make him your slave."

The soldiers began to search, and, when they came to Benjamin's sack, there was the silver goblet—as Joseph had planned! The brothers were grief-stricken. Remembering their pledge to Jacob, they all returned with Benjamin to accept their fate.

Joseph awaited them. He was anxious to test his brothers' faith. When they entered, he pretended to be very angry, and ordered Benjamin made a slave for stealing his precious cup. The brothers moaned and begged; and then one of them named Judah stepped forward and exclaimed:

"Take me instead as your slave."

Joseph was surprised, and urged Judah to explain himself.

"When you told us to bring Benjamin to Egypt," said Judah, "our father was afraid, and would not let him go. You see, many years ago, one of our brothers died and he was a child of Benjamin's mother, one who was dearly loved by our father. Now we must protect our youngest brother. If we return without him, our father will grieve for the boy and will surely die.

"Have mercy!" Judah continued, "for the sake of our aged father. We do not wish him to suffer more than he has already suffered."

At these words, Joseph could no longer hide his real identity, and he sent the servants away.

Weeping, in a loud voice he cried:

"I am Joseph, your brother, whom you sold as a slave. But God has made me a great man in Egypt, and I forgive you."

Hearing this, the brothers fell on their knees, weeping and praising God. And Joseph embraced each brother, and, especially, Benjamin.

When Pharaoh learned that Joseph's brothers were in Egypt, he ordered a feast, and sent chariots and gifts to Canaan, so that Jacob could join his sons and live with them in Egypt. And so it was that the Israelites came into Egypt during the time of Joseph, and the sons of Jacob were united once again.

The Hebrews in Egypt

ABOUT SEVENTY PEOPLE joined Jacob in his journey to Egypt, where they were greeted by Joseph and the Pharaoh. Because the Israelites were skilled shepherds, they were allowed to settle in Goshen, which was very good farm country. Here the people prospered, and Jacob lived for nearly twenty years, enjoying the fame of his son Joseph and the happiness of all his children.

But soon it was time for Jacob to join his ancestors in heaven, and he called Joseph to him and said:

"God has been very good to me. Not only did I find you again, but I have also seen your children, whom I love. Bring them to me, and I will bless them."

And so Ephraim and Manasseh were brought to their grandfather, who laid his hands upon them and blessed them. Perhaps Jacob remembered when he had received such a blessing from his father Isaac.

After this Jacob called all his sons, and told them to lead the Israelites as God had commanded. In this way, he established the Twelve Tribes of Israel; later these tribes became very large and peopled the land of Israel. Then peacefully, Jacob died, and soon he was buried in Canaan, near his father, Isaac, and his grandfather, Abraham. Joseph led the mourning, which lasted for forty days.

Now that Jacob was dead, the brothers feared that Joseph would be cruel to them. When he assured them they were truly forgiven, they prospered in Goshen. At the same time, Joseph's fame increased. He saw to it that no one went hungry in Egypt, and he made Pharaoh very rich and powerful. The tribes of Israel grew in population, and many years went by.

Then Joseph knew that he, too, would die, for he was very old. He called his sons to him and said:

"I die; but God will surely remember you, and bring you up out of this land unto the land which he promised to Abraham, to Isaac, and to Jacob. And when God thus remembers you, you shall carry my bones from here into the Promised Land."

Then Joseph died and was mourned by all.

THE BOOKS OF EXODUS, LEVITICUS, NUMBERS, AND DEUTERONOMY

The Story of Moses, Who Freed His People Israel from Bondage in Egypt; of Miracles and Plagues; of the Long Journey in the Desert to the Land of Canaan; of the Holy Tabernacle and the Commandments of God.

FOR ALMOST four hundred years, the Israelites lived in Egypt and their numbers increased. Many, many years before, God had prophesied to Abraham that his people would be slaves in a foreign land. This ominous prediction was about to come true, for, as the Hebrews grew in number, the Egyptians became fearful that, some day, they might overrun the country. Furthermore, a new Pharaoh was on the throne of Egypt, and he did not remember, or care to remember, the good work of Joseph.

Instead, he ordered all the Children of Israel into slavery, and assigned to them the building of granaries and temples. Above all, to make sure that the Israelites would not grow in population, Pharaoh issued a terrible decree.

"All baby boys of the Hebrews must be killed," he said. "They must be thrown into the Nile to drown."

What a terrible decree! Even the Egyptians were shocked. But, nevertheless, Pharaoh's soldiers carried out his orders.

One Hebrew family living near the Nile decided to resist the Pharaoh's evil decree. There were at first two children in that family, a boy named Aaron and a girl named Miriam. Aaron was old enough to escape the Pharaoh's order, and Miriam was safe, because Hebrew girls were allowed to live. But now there was a baby boy in the family, and his mother feared for his life.

In order to save her child from the Pharaoh's soldiers, the baby's mother lined a small straw basket with a blanket and put the baby inside. Then she lowered baby and basket together gently into the Nile, among the tall reeds and bulrushes. She told Miriam to watch the basket and to see that no harm came to the infant.

As Miriam watched, the basket started to float down the Nile. Un-

The Birth of Moses

able to stop it, the little sister ran along the shore to a place where some Egyptian ladies were bathing. Suddenly, Miriam stopped in her tracks —there among the bathers was the Princess of Egypt herself, daughter of the Pharaoh.

"What is that floating there?" the Princess asked her maids, pointing to the basket. "Bring it to me at once."

The maids quickly lifted the little basket out of the water, and handed it to the noble lady. At this moment, the baby inside began to cry, and the Princess was deeply moved.

"This must be one of the Hebrew babies," she said. "How beautiful he is. Since I have no son of my own, I will keep him and raise him in the palace."

When Miriam heard this, she stepped forward and said, "Mighty Princess, I know a Hebrew woman who will be a very good nurse for this baby. May I fetch her?"

The Princess guessed that this "nurse" was probably the baby's own mother, but she was kind, and she agreed.

And so it was that the baby was raised by his very own mother under the protection of the Princess of Egypt. When the child was old enough, he went to the palace to live and study. And the great Princess called him Moses, which means "child drawn from the waters." Yes, this was Moses, the man whom God had chosen to save his people.

Moses Leaves Egypt

IN SPITE OF the fact that Moses was raised in Pharaoh's palace, he remembered that he was an Israelite. His mother and sister Miriam taught him all about Abraham and the one true God. It therefore caused Moses much pain to see his people forced into slavery.

One day, when he was about twenty-five, Moses witnessed an Egyptian soldier beating an old Hebrew slave. Anger filled his heart, and he grabbed the Egyptian and killed him with one blow. Then he buried him in the sand.

A few days later, word spread that the son of the Princess had killed an Egyptian. Moses knew that Pharaoh would send soldiers to arrest him. So he fled from Egypt, and crossed the desert into a land called Midian.

Tired and thirsty, he sat down by a well. A few minutes later, several young women came to fetch water. No sooner had they lowered their pitchers, when a group of rough shepherds rushed upon them in order to drive them off.

Moses leaped to his feet and, single-handed, chased the bullies away. When the girls returned to Jethro, their father, they told him of this brave Egyptian who had protected them at the well.

"Invite him to dinner," said Jethro, "for he must be a good man."

That evening Zipporah, the eldest daughter, saw Moses on the road and invited him, as her father had suggested. Moses was very pleased.

After dinner, Jethro asked his guest to remain in Midian and help tend his flocks. Moses agreed to do so. Besides, Zipporah was very pretty, and Moses fell in love with her. They were soon married, and, later, had a son named Gershom. So it was that Moses became a peaceful shepherd and lived in Midian with his family.

IN EGYPT, the old Pharaoh died. But the new king was just as evil, and the Hebrews were beaten, killed, and forced to suffer many hardships.

Moses was far away from this misery. He led a quiet life, tending the flocks and walking alone among the mountain trees. One day, he was leading his flocks to a place called Mount Horeb when he saw a fire burning in the bushes. As he watched, the flames did not seem to burn the bush at all.

"This is very strange," he said, and, cautiously, moved a little closer.

Suddenly, a powerful voice was heard from amid the burning bush.

"Moses," it said, "do not come near this bush, for God is here. This is holy ground, remove your sandals and come close."

Moses was overcome. He removed his sandals, out of respect, and knelt before the fire.

"I am the God of your fathers," said the voice. "In Egypt, My people, the Israelites, are suffering under Pharaoh's cruelty. They have prayed to Me for help. Now I will deliver them out of Egypt and bring them back to the land of Canaan, which I promised to Abraham.

"You, Moses, must lead your people," the Lord continued. "You shall bring them out."

Moses was amazed.

"I!" he said. "Oh, Lord, you must find another, for I am unworthy of this great responsibility."

But God was firm. "I promise to help you in your mission," He continued.

"Well and good," Moses replied. "But suppose the Hebrews have forgotten You. What shall I say?"

The
Burning
Bush

ABOVE: Plate 22. MOSES SAVED FROM THE NILE, by Nicolas Poussin
(French, 1594–1665), The Louvre Museum, Paris.

OPPOSITE: Plate 23. MOSES BEFORE THE BURNING BUSH,
by Domenico Feti
(Italian, 1589–1623), Kunsthistorisches Museum, Vienna.

"Tell them that you have spoken with the Lord," God answered, "the one true God. Gather them together and bring them into the wilderness, and there build an altar to Me. Then they will believe again."

Moses was unsure.

"I know Pharaoh," he said. "He will not let us go."

"That is true," said God. "Many times he will refuse. But after I have shown My power in Egypt, he will finally obey."

"But I myself am powerless," Moses declared in a trembling voice.

"I will give you great powers," answered God, "and with these you shall succeed."

To prove His words, the Lord transformed the staff of Moses into a snake, and Moses was afraid. But, at His will, God made the snake change back into a staff, as it had been before.

"Now place your hand on your chest," God commanded Moses. And when Moses did so, his hand became white and full of scabs.

"Now remove your hand," God continued, and Moses obeyed. Now his hand was normal once more!

"These are the signs of My power," said God. "And, if you need further evidence, I will change the waters of the Nile to blood. The Egyptians will learn who is powerful."

Moses was trembling, and his heart was heavy. He wanted to see his people freed, but still he felt unworthy of the task, and so he said:

"My Lord, you know that I am hesitant of tongue, a stammerer and I cannot speak very well. How should I convince the mighty Pharaoh?"

The Lord was angry.

"Moses," He said, "I can give you speech if I choose or I can send someone to help you. You have a brother named Aaron. He will join you here in three days, and he will speak before Pharaoh at your command. Now rise, and do as I tell you."

At last, Moses realized that he could not evade his mission—he had to obey! Gathering his flock together, he returned to Jethro's house.

"Let me go back to my own country," said Moses to his father-in-law, "and let me take with me my wife and son."

OPPOSITE: Plate 24. MOSES AND AARON BEFORE PHARAOH,
by Félix Chrétien (French, about 1510–1579),
The Metropolitan Museum of Art, New York.

Jethro knew that Moses had a great mission to do, and he bade him leave for Egypt, saying,

"Go in peace."

On the way, Moses met his brother Aaron, as the Lord had promised; and he was overjoyed. God had already told Aaron of the mission, and, so, the two brothers went heroically toward Egypt.

The Hard-Hearted Pharaoh

WHEN MOSES and Aaron arrived in Egypt, they went directly to the Hebrews in Goshen. There Moses told the elders of the city what God had commanded. He showed them the miracles of the Lord, and they believed in His promise. Moses and Aaron next turned toward the Pharaoh's palace.

To Moses this was a familiar place, for he had grown up in the royal house. Now he waited with Aaron outside Pharaoh's chambers.

After a long delay, they were admitted and stood before the golden throne of the mighty king.

"The Lord God of Israel," said Moses, "commands that you free His people, the Hebrews, so that they may worship Him."

"Who?" said Pharaoh. "What God is this?"

Aaron spoke. "He is the one true God, and even you must obey His commandments or you will surely be punished."

The Pharaoh was not impressed. He immediately ordered Moses and Aaron to leave his presence. When they were gone, he called his guards.

"These Israelites are complaining," he said. "I will show them! Give them no straw for their bricks. They must find their own! That will keep them busy and they will have no time to complain."

In those days, bricks were made of clay mixed with straw so that they would not crumble. To find one's own straw was very difficult indeed. But this was the task that Pharaoh set.

Now, because the bricks crumbled, the soldiers beat the slaves worse than before. With all this suffering, the Hebrews thought they had been badly advised by Moses and they bewailed their fate, but Aaron told them to have faith and to pray.

Moses himself was discouraged, until the Lord came to him and commanded him to appear once again before Pharaoh.

This time, the Pharaoh wanted proof of God's greatness, so he ordered Moses to perform a miracle. Moses remembered God's instructions and told Aaron to cast his rod to the floor, where at once it turned into a snake.

Pharaoh laughed. His magicians could do the same, he said. And he ordered them to change their staffs into snakes. This they did, at his command. But Aaron's snake was larger, and gobbled up the others. Then it changed itself back into a staff. Pharaoh thought that this was nothing but a clever trick, and he ordered Moses and Aaron to leave. He would not allow the Israelites to go free.

The next morning, Moses and Aaron awaited the Pharaoh at the banks of the Nile, where he was coming to bathe. God had strengthened Moses' heart. He promised that He would send a series of plagues against Egypt until the Pharaoh obeyed and freed the Hebrews. These plagues were terrible things. God wanted to prove His power to the world and to make the Israelites truly grateful for their freedom. Freedom too easily won seems unimportant, but a struggle that results in victory is a wonderful achievement.

THE FIRST PLAGUE turned the rivers and the waters of Egypt into blood. It happened as Pharaoh approached the Nile for his bath. Moses confronted him.

The Plagues Begin

"Let my people go," he said. Pharaoh laughed. Then Aaron waved his staff over the Nile, which was instantly turned into a sea of blood. All the fish died, and a terrible odor filled the nostrils of the Egyptians.

Desperately Pharaoh called his magicians; and they, too, could turn water into blood—or it seemed as if they could. This convinced Pharaoh that Moses was only a magician, and he would not let the Hebrews go. For seven days, the water of Egypt remained undrinkable. But Pharaoh didn't care. His heart was cruel.

Moses came to Pharaoh again in his palace. "Let my people go!" he cried. But Pharaoh turned aside.

Then Moses commanded all the frogs of Egypt to leave the seas and come up on the land. Millions and millions of frogs jumped out of the waters and into people's houses, into their beds, and even onto their dinner tables.

Pharaoh was annoyed. Again he called his magicians. They, too, could make frogs do as they wished. But that did not relieve the situation. Finally, Pharaoh cried to Moses:

"Take these frogs away, and I will free your people."

On the next day, the frogs disappeared, and all was normal in the land. The Pharaoh smiled to himself.

"I've got rid of the frogs," he said. "I don't have to keep my word. The Hebrews will stay as slaves."

36.
The
Plague
of
Insects

AARON WAS ANGERED. He struck his staff into the sand, and every grain turned into a nasty bug that crawled all over the palace. This time, Pharaoh's magicians were powerless, for God had taken their magic away. But Pharaoh was angry, and this made him very cruel. He would not let the Hebrews go.

Moses was losing his patience. He cried to God, and God commanded him to await Pharaoh at the river once again.

When Pharaoh came, Moses said, "Let my people go." Pharaoh refused as before. Now Moses called upon God to send another plague, and this time the air was filled with flies. Millions and millions of flies descended on the Egyptians, clinging and stinging and getting into their mouths, ears, and eyes. Pharaoh was horrified. He called Moses and said to him:

"If you want to worship your God, you may do so, here in Egypt, but you must take away these flies."

Moses reminded the king:

"Your people will not permit us to worship here. Let us go for three days into the wilderness, and God will destroy these insects!"

Pharaoh agreed. Then Moses warned him:

"But do not play tricks on us, mighty Pharaoh, for God is watching."

"Take away these flies and you may have what you want," answered Pharaoh. But he lied. When the flies disappeared, he ordered his soldiers to prevent the Hebrews from leaving Egypt.

The
Plagues of
Sickness
and Hail

GOD WAS PREPARED with many more plagues for Egypt. He commanded Moses to make another appeal. When Pharaoh refused, a terrible sickness descended on the land, and all Egyptian cattle died. But Pharaoh was safe in his palace, and he would not let the Hebrews go.

Moses stormed into the palace again.

"Let my people go!" he cried.

"No, they shall remain!" said the arrogant Pharaoh.

Then, by God's command, Moses scooped up some ashes from the ground and threw them into the air. They descended upon the Egyptians and caused boils and pimples to break out all over their skins. Even the court magicians were afflicted and could not perform their tricks for Pharaoh. He was angered and embittered, but he was too stubborn to let the Hebrews go.

Now God brought a violent hailstorm upon Egypt, for again, Pharaoh had refused His commandment. Great lumps of hail fell from the sky and destroyed the Egyptians' houses and their crops. Thunder and lightning crashed in the skies. The people were terrified. Only the land of Goshen, where the Hebrews dwelled, was spared.

Pharaoh had never seen such a storm in his life, and he fell on his knees before Moses.

"Take your people. Do what you want," he said, "but end this awful storm."

Moses went from the palace and raised his arms to Heaven, and the hailstorm ceased.

Pharaoh looked into the skies. The sun was shining.

"That's all I want," he said; and he once more refused to let the Hebrews go.

Courageously and patiently, Moses and Aaron again stood before the king.

"Let my people go," cried Moses.

This time, the court magicians and ministers agreed. "We're sick of these plagues," they cried to Pharaoh. "Let these dreadful people go."

But Pharaoh would not relent. "Only the men may worship in the desert," he decreed. "The women and children will remain as slaves."

Moses would not accept this, and he called upon God to bring forth still another plague.

THIS TIME, millions and millions of fat green locusts came out of the skies and ate everything in sight—every leaf, every blade of grass, and every piece of paper. They were so numerous that the sun could not be seen as they flew past.

"Take these locusts away," cried Pharaoh, "and you may have your freedom!"

So Moses prayed and the locusts all were blown into the sea and drowned. When the air was clear, Pharaoh smiled and said,

"That's all I wanted. The Hebrews may not go free."

Time was growing short. Moses was becoming more impatient and angered. He approached Pharaoh once again.

"Eight plagues have been sent against Egypt," he said. "Relent for your own sake." But Pharaoh refused as before.

This time, God blotted out the sun from the sky, and deep darkness fell over Egypt. Only the Hebrews were spared. Egyptians stumbled and fell in the blackness. Their candles would not burn; not even a tiny star shone in the boundless night. Pharaoh was enraged. He ordered Moses killed if he came once more into the palace.

*Locusts
and
Darkness in
Egypt*

The Passover Feast

NOW THE TIME had come for the tenth and most dreadful plague, for God was determined to make Pharaoh relent. He called Moses and said:

"Tell all the Hebrews to prepare a feast in their homes. Each one must kill a lamb for roasting, and, from this lamb each must take blood and sprinkle it over the door post of his house. For, this night, I shall descend upon Egypt with the Angel of Death, and strike down the oldest son of every Egyptian. Only those who sprinkle blood upon their houses will be spared, for I shall pass over those places and spare them."

In spite of Pharaoh's threat, Moses again approached the palace.

"Listen to me, Pharaoh," he said. "If you love your son, you will relent. For, tonight, the Angel of Death will come to Egypt and slay every firstborn child of every man and beast in your land. Only the Hebrews will be spared. This will happen if you do not free my people."

"I am not afraid of such threats," shouted Pharaoh. "Get out of here or I will have you put to death."

Moses left the palace for the last time, and called upon God to fulfill His frightful plan.

And so it happened that night, God descended on Egypt, and, when He saw a Hebrew house sprinkled with blood, He passed over and went on to the Egyptian homes. There, each firstborn son fell dead, even the Pharaoh's eldest son.

The Hebrews stayed in their homes, fully dressed and ready for the great escape from Egypt, the Exodus. They celebrated the glory of God at their supper, and, because God had passed over their homes, they called it the Feast of the Passover. To this day, this sacred feast is held by Hebrews every year to commemorate the power of God.

But the Egyptians had no cause for celebration. Their sons lay dead. Their cattle had perished. Now, even in the great palace a cry was heard, for Pharaoh had found his own dear child lying dead on the floor. In agony he called for Moses and Aaron.

"Rise up, go and take your people out of Egypt," cried the Pharaoh. "I want no more of them. Let them go! And let them take their flocks. I now know the power of your God."

At last, the Hebrews would be free. They quickly gathered their belongings and cattle and the gold and silver that the Egyptians gave them on demand, and, with great excitement, they herded together in the streets.

Moses and Aaron stood at the head of the enormous throng.

"We are free," they cried. "God has delivered us! Now we will head toward the Promised Land, which flows with milk and honey. Our days of slavery are ended!"

PEOPLE WERE EVERYWHERE gathering their belongings and their cattle, all in haste to leave the land of slavery. There was so much excitement that the women had no time to bake their bread; instead, they carried the unleavened dough into the desert. Today, such bread is called "matzo," and is eaten at the Passover feast along with the paschal lamb and many herbs and greens. From this time forth, Passover would be a time of rejoicing for Israel.

When the journey began, the people seemed determined to keep on walking without a stop. They were proud of their freedom, and they carried with them the bones of Joseph, their ancestor. But, as the days passed, they grew tired and needed rest. For a time they camped near the great Red Sea that separated Egypt from the wilderness of Sinai— a desert region that lies south of the Holy Land. Here, the people awaited instructions from Moses, their leader.

He told them:

"God will lead us in a fiery cloud that will hover above us night and day and direct us to safety. No one need fear so long as God is with us."

And, true to his word, a great cloud formed in the sky, like a beacon to guide the Israelites out of Egypt.

EVERY DAY the people came closer to the Red Sea; and the cloud always led the way. All seemed well and safe when behind them, suddenly, the sounds of hoofbeats and soldiers were heard.

"Pharaoh's armies are coming," someone cried. "We'll all be killed."

It was true! The wicked Pharaoh had once again decided to prevent the Hebrews from leaving Egypt. And, soon, the Egyptian hordes could be seen racing toward the Israelites as they approached the water. What could they do? They were caught between Pharaoh and the sea.

Now fear and shouting spread through the camp. The people blamed Moses. "Did you take us out of Egypt because there were no graves there? Let us surrender rather than die!" they cried. God then spoke to Moses.

"Go to the water's edge," He said. "Moses, lift your staff, and I shall save you."

Then Moses raised his staff over the sea, and, suddenly, the waters parted right down the middle from one shore to the next. A wide, dry path spread out before the hurrying throng. Upon this miraculous path, between two great walls of water, the Children of Israel crossed safely into freedom.

BELOW: Plate 26. THE PASSOVER MEAL, by Dieric Bouts
(Flemish, about 1415–1475), Church of Saint Pierre, Louvain, Belgium.

But were they free? Pharaoh's army followed close behind. They, too, were using this miraculous path to pursue the Children of Israel and bring them back as slaves.

Closer and closer they came. The entire Egyptian army had almost reached the shore when God sent the waters crashing back into place. Every soldier, and every horse, were drowned in the roaring waves. Only the Pharaoh, it seems, escaped.

From the other side, the Hebrews watched as the waters closed in over their enemies. Then they sent up a mighty hymn of joy to God for having saved them:

"Sing ye to the Lord, for He hath triumphed gloriously: the horse and his rider hath He thrown into the sea."

Manna from Heaven

NOW THE JOURNEY resumed. With the cloud of God ever above them, the Israelites passed from one place in the desert to another. They no longer feared the Egyptian army, which had drowned by God's command. But they did fear hunger and thirst.

So they paused in an oasis where there was water to drink. But it was bitter water, and the people did not like it. They began to complain.

God then commanded Moses to cut down a tree that grew near the lake and to throw this tree into the waters. When Moses did this, the bitter water grew sweet, and everyone drank with pleasure. But the people were also hungry. As they traveled, they complained.

"In Egypt we were slaves," they said, "but, at least, we received food when we were hungry."

Moses could not answer them, but he prayed to God to bring food from Heaven. The next day, a great flight of quails came winging over the camp and dropped into the laps of the people. What a delicious feast they had!

Having eaten meat, the people wanted bread, and Moses prayed to God again for assistance.

The next day, tiny white droplets began falling over the camp, and the Israelites rushed out to see what they were.

"This is bread from Heaven," said Moses. And, indeed, when the people rolled this substance all together it formed little loaves of sweet-tasting bread, which they called "manna."

"Each man gather enough manna for one day," instructed Moses. "Trust to God for the next day's supply."

But selfish people didn't obey this command and gathered more than enough for their needs. The following day they found the manna had spoiled and was useless. So they knew that they had to obey God's wish. And when He told them not to gather manna on the Sabbath, those who tried found nothing at all. But, on the next day, when the Sabbath had ended, the sweet white manna drifted down again from Heaven, and the people could eat.

ONCE MORE, the Israelites journeyed onward, led by the cloud of God. Now they approached Mount Horeb, where Moses had seen the burning bush. But they were thirsty, and again they complained.

"Why did you bring us out of Egypt?" they cried to Moses. "Did you want to kill us with thirst?"

Moses was at his wit's end. "What am I to do with these people?" he called out to God. "They're almost ready to stone me!"

"Strike the great rock of Horeb with your staff," God commanded, "and water will spring forth."

This Moses did, and clear, cold water gushed from the rock. The people drank, and then continued their journey.

Now trouble loomed on the horizon. Nearby, a band of warlike tribesmen, the Amalekites, were preparing to attack the Hebrews. Moses learned of this, and decided to raise an army. He chose a brave young man named Joshua to be commander-in-chief, and sent him with his army into the field against the invaders.

When the fighting began, Moses and Aaron and a man named Hur went to a hilltop overlooking the battle. God instructed Moses to raise his arms above the field so that Israel would win. Moses obeyed, but soon his hands grew weary and he let them fall. At that same moment, the Amalekites began to gain the upper hand. Realizing that he could not afford to lower his hands, Moses told Aaron and Hur to hold his arms above his head, no matter how long the battle raged. In this way, the Israelites conquered their enemies as God wished.

When the battle was over, the joyous Hebrews rested, and sang their praises to God.

Then Moses had a pleasant visitor. His father-in-law, Jethro, came to the camp. There was much conversation, and good cheer. Moses told Jethro about the plagues and the miraculous crossing of the Red Sea; and Jethro was proud of his son-in-law.

He was also worried, for he knew that Moses was heavily burdened by his task of leadership. Every day hundreds of people lined up outside Moses' tent with complaints and questions. By the end of the day, Moses was weary and exhausted.

Water from the Rock

ABOVE: Plate 27. THE DELIVERANCE OF THE ISRAELITES,
by Bernardo Luini (Italian, about 1475–about 1532), Brera Gallery, Milan.

OPPOSITE: Plate 28. GATHERING OF THE MANNA, by Dieric Bouts
(Flemish, about 1415–1475), Church of Saint Pierre, Louvain, Belgium.

"Why not have some assistants?" said Jethro. "If you divide your camp into groups—groups of a thousand, a hundred, fifty, and ten—putting a leader over each group, the leaders can take some of the burden off your shoulders."

Moses agreed, and arranged his camp into a government with many assistants; and he found it was easier to handle his vital work.

The Giving of the Law

THE ISRAELITES CAMPED near Mount Horeb for many days. Then Moses was commanded by God to move the camp to nearby Mount Sinai. There, three days hence, God Himself would appear to the people in a cloud of thunder.

There was great excitement when this news was announced. Everyone prepared himself for the awesome moment. New clothes were made. People washed themselves, their children, and their animals. Then, three days later, they gathered at the foot of Mount Sinai, with Moses and Aaron standing before them.

Suddenly, a great black cloud of smoke rolled over the mountain, and stayed suspended there. Thunder and lightning broke out from the cloud, and a column of fire and smoke rose up to the sky. The mountain shook. A loud trumpet was heard. The people drew back from the mighty sound, fearing that God's tremendous voice would shatter them. But Moses cried out, as the trumpet sound became louder and louder, "This is our God! He will not hurt us! He has come to give us the Law!"

The fearful people nevertheless huddled together and watched in amazement as Moses and Aaron ascended the shaking mountain at God's command and disappeared into the smoke.

There, standing with God, Moses received the highest laws of the world, the Ten Commandments. He wrote these down, descended the sacred mountain, and came before all the people so that he might read them the Law.

In a booming voice, Moses announced:

"These are the Laws of God that He proclaimed to me on the mountain. Listen, and obey them forever:

There is only one God over all the earth. God is the Lord. You must not worship any other gods but Him.

You must not make idols of stone or wood or metal.

The name of God is sacred, and must not be used for profanities.

The seventh day, the Sabbath, is sacred, and you must not work on that day, though you may work on the other six days.

You must honor and respect your father and mother.

You must not murder.

A man and wife must be faithful to each other. They must not commit adultery.

You must not steal.

You must not lie.

You must not desire another person's house or his goods or his wife—or any of his possessions."

Then Moses read many more laws that God had given him. But the first Ten Commandments were the most important laws of all. God wished them to be remembered forever, so He called upon Moses to climb the mountain again and to receive the Ten Commandments written out on two great tablets of stone by the finger of God Himself. The Lord instructed Moses to bring Joshua, the soldier, as an assistant.

Once again, the mighty cloud descended on Sinai, and Moses, with Joshua, made his way through its midst. For forty days, Moses learned the law from God, and a brilliant fire burned on top of the mountain.

FORTY DAYS—little more than a month—yet the people grew restless, and strayed from the path that Moses had laid out for them.

"Moses will never return," they muttered. "We have been led here to die. Now we need the gods of Egypt to protect us." And they called on Aaron to become their new leader and guide.

Aaron, indeed, was disturbed when he heard the people express these ideas. Without Moses, he was not brave enough to insist that they follow the path of the Lord. So he said:

"Give me your gold and your precious stones, and I will make a Golden Calf for you to worship."

The people were delighted. They brought their gold to the fire, and Aaron made a large statue of a calf just like those he had seen in Egypt. All this he did in spite of God's commandment, "You shall not worship any gods but Me."

When the calf was finished, some people carried it to the center of the camp and placed garlands of flowers on its neck. How it glistened and gleamed, and how its bright red eyes sparkled in the light of the fire.

The Golden Calf

"This is our god!" shouted the people. "This Golden Calf led us out of Egypt."

Aaron went along with the crowd, and he ordered a celebration to be held on the following day.

But, high up on the holy mountain, amid the smoke and fire, God knew of the Golden Calf, and He said to Moses:

"The people have sinned greatly against Me. They have built an idol and are worshiping it. For this, they all must be destroyed."

Moses was angry with the people, but, nevertheless, he prayed for them.

"We've come too far," he said, "for You, O Lord, to destroy them now. Spare them, and I will see to it that they repent."

So God allowed the Israelites to live, and sent Moses back to the camp.

As Moses descended from the mountain, the people below began their celebration of the Golden Calf.

"What is that noise?" said Moses to Joshua who was by his side.

"It is singing," said Joshua, "singing to a golden calf. I can see it below in the center of the camp."

In Moses' hands were the holy tablets of stone upon which God had inscribed the Ten Commandments. Lifting them high into the air above his head, Moses suddenly stood before the people and cried:

"You are all wicked sinners and you do not deserve the Law of God!"

Then he threw the tablets over the side of the mountain, and they broke into many pieces with a crash!

The people were terrified. They ceased their singing and hurried back to their tents. In great wrath, Moses and Joshua threw down the Golden Calf and smashed it to powder. Then they sprinkled the powder in the drinking water, so that the guilty people would cough and choke when they drank.

Now Moses came before Aaron. He was very angry, indeed.

"Why did you make that idol?" he asked his brother.

And Aaron said, "I was weak. I was afraid of the people, so I gathered their gold and made them this calf."

"I must punish the evildoers," Moses said. He called the men of the tribe of Levi, who were faithful soldiers.

"Go throughout the camp," he told them, "with your swords drawn. God will lead you to the guilty. Kill them, or they will poison the minds of innocent people. Do as God commands!"

And so the guilty were punished, and Moses prayed to God to forgive all the other sinners of Israel.

God was merciful. He ordered Moses to return to the mountain and, once again, to receive the Ten Commandments written on stone. This time, Moses went alone and ascended into the smoke and fire of God's presence. There he heard many laws that were to govern Israel. He was told of the future and of the evil of idol worshipers. For forty days and forty nights, Moses was instructed by God, and the Ten Commandments were written afresh upon the tablets of stone.

Now, for the last time, Moses was to descend the mountain with the Commandments under his arm. Filled with the majesty of God and with the sacred laws that he had learned, Moses was indeed different from other men. And, because of this, his face glowed like a flame, so that the people were afraid to look at him, and drew back as he approached.

"Why do they fear me?" he asked as he came into the camp.

"Because your face is shining like a fire," said Aaron, "and they know you are the special friend of God."

So Moses put a veil over his face, and the people were no longer afraid. This time, they celebrated and rejoiced over his return, and promised to obey the Holy Law that he had received from God.

The Tabernacle

ONE OF THE THINGS that the Lord told Moses on Sinai was that the People of Israel needed a central place of worship where God Himself could dwell. He no longer wished to appear in a cloud on the mountain.

This place would be called the "Tabernacle," or tent, and it would be made so that the Hebrews could assemble it and take it down whenever they moved. God gave Moses careful instructions about how the Tabernacle was to look.

When Moses returned to camp, he called together Aaron and his sons and several of the leading craftsmen of the tribes. They would be in charge of the building and decorations of the holy Tabernacle.

The people would help, of course. For one thing, they were asked to donate all their precious gold and silver and many varieties of fine cloth and animal skins. They did this willingly.

For two years, everyone worked to complete the Tabernacle. Those who could weave prepared the tapestries. Brass workers and goldsmiths fashioned candelabra and objects for the sacred altar. Other craftsmen built the frame and furniture.

Then the day came when the beautiful shrine was finished. It had been made just as God had instructed. Outside, all around it, was an open court. In this court was the great altar where cattle and sheep

Plate 29.
THE ADORATION
OF THE
GOLDEN CALF,
by Nicolas Poussin
(French, 1594–1665),
The National Gallery,
London.

would be offered to God. Made of brass and beautifully ornamented, this altar could be carried from place to place by poles attached to its sides. Near the altar there was also a large fountain made of gold, where the priests could wash their hands and feet before attending to the rituals.

Inside the shrine were only two rooms separated by a purple veil or curtain. In front of this veil was the "Holy Court." Here stood a small altar, a table, and a seven-branched candelabrum, which was always lit. On the table were twelve loaves of bread representing the twelve tribes and meant as symbolic offerings to God. The table stood near the altar, which was small and always kept burning with sweet-smelling incense and spice.

The room itself was made of wood, covered with gold leaf. Heavy skins and curtains formed the roof. The skins kept out rain and cold; the curtains were beautifully woven, and were colored purple, red, and royal blue.

The other room of the Tabernacle was behind the veil. This was called the "Holy of Holies." No one was allowed to enter this sacred room except the priests and Moses. Here, only one precious object was placed, the Holy Ark of the Covenant, which God had commanded to be built. This was a large chest of solid gold. It was hollow inside and had a lid on top called the "Mercy Throne," meant as a resting place for God. On either side of this lid, two angels of gold were placed to guard the sacred contents inside, for God had instructed Moses to place the original Ten Commandments within the box.

The Ark was also portable, and could be carried from place to place by the sacred priests. For many centuries, it was to be the most important religious object of the Hebrews.

God was pleased. At night, His brilliant fire lit up the "Holy of Holies." During the day, He hovered in a cloud above the Ark for all to see. There was never such a holy place as the Tabernacle that the Israelites built in the desert.

The Priests

GOD INSTRUCTED MOSES to place Aaron and his sons in charge of worship at the Tabernacle. No longer would people build separate altars and offer sacrifices by themselves. Now they would meet together and, through the priests, make their offerings to God.

When all the details were arranged, Moses summoned the people to the Tabernacle for the first day of worship. At this ceremony, Aaron and his sons were to be anointed, as a sign of their high priestly position. Moses took a cup of pure oil and sprinkled it on Aaron's forehead. The same was done to Aaron's sons. This was the anointing.

For his duties as the High Priest, Aaron was dressed as God had commanded. He wore the finest linen garments, woven with gold. On his chest was a breastplate of twelve precious stones. On his head was a miter or crown. The hems of his garment were tassled, and tiny silver bells hung from each thread. When Aaron walked, these bells tinkled, and were very beautiful to hear.

Now that he was the High Priest, Aaron approached the altar, placed a lamb upon the grate, and called upon God to forgive the people all their sins. Then, suddenly, while everyone was watching, a flame rose on the altar by the will of God and consumed the lamb. This was the sacred fire, which was meant for all the sacrifices. This fire was to be kept burning by the priests, and, though they might add fresh coals and wood, they were told never to extinguish the flame. Even when they moved, they were to take a shovelful of burning coals and place them in a golden censer, so that the fire might also go from place to place.

When the people saw this sacred fire flame out on the altar, they were overjoyed. They knew that God had forgiven them and was truly in their midst.

Thus it was that the people brought their sacrifices to the Lord. Some sacrifices were burnt completely in the sacred fire; these were sin offerings. Some were only partly consumed, and the remainder given back to the priests and to the people. These sacrifices were known as peace offerings; they were given not for the purpose of atoning for sins, but, rather, in thanks to God for some blessing or happiness.

TWO OF AARON'S SONS who were priests were not very careful about the manner in which these sacrifices were burned. They had been told never to use any fire other than the sacred fire lit by God. But they were disobedient. One day, they lit the incense burner with a fresh fire that they had kindled themselves. God could not allow His priests to disobey, so He sent down a bolt of lightning to destroy these sons of Aaron. Moses ordered that the sinful priests be buried far outside the camp; and he urged Aaron not to mourn for them, lest God be further offended.

Then Moses came before the people and instructed them in many new laws of God. He began:

"God prohibits the eating of certain foods to all Hebrews. For

Aaron's
Sons
Are
Slain

example, you may eat beef and lamb, but never pork or ham or rabbits. You may eat fresh-water fish and salt-water fish so long as they have scales and fins, but not crabs, lobsters or eels. Chickens can be eaten and ducks and pigeons—but you cannot eat any bird that kills other birds, such as eagles or ravens.

"God wants His people to be healthy and clean," Moses continued. "You must always wash and keep away from filth. Sick people must be separated from the others until they are cured. Above all, we must be kind and generous and do things with dignity and justice.

"Never cut down all your wheat and leave nothing," said Moses. "Think of the poor; allow a little for them. Never cheat a man of his wages or keep someone waiting a long time to pay a debt. Don't talk ill of a man because he cannot hear you, or mock a blind man because he cannot see. Be kind to strangers and poor people and sick people, and especially to children. Remember God's Golden Law, which is: 'Thou shalt love thy neighbor as thyself.' In this way, we may all live in peace, and thus fulfill God's great commandments."

ONE WHOLE YEAR had passed since the Israelites escaped from Egypt across the Red Sea. One whole year since the Lord had passed over the Hebrew homes and spared their firstborn sons. For this reason, God instructed the people to hold a celebration called Passover. At this feast they were to eat roasted lamb and unleavened bread, just as they had done that first time. For centuries, this holiday has been celebrated by the Jewish people.

God also described other holidays He wished the people to keep. There was to be a Day of Atonement for sins, on which all were to fast from eating. There was to be a celebration of the harvest and of the spring. Furthermore, God instructed the Israelites that, every seventh year, they were to rest the soil from planting, just as people rested every seventh day. He also told them to celebrate every fiftieth year as a Jubilee. God wanted the people to appreciate their blessings.

When the Passover feast had ended, God beckoned Israel to move

*The
Feasts
and
Holidays*

OPPOSITE: Plate 30. MOSES SHOWING THE TABLETS OF THE LAW, by Rembrandt (Dutch, 1606–1669), State Museums, Berlin.

onward in the desert. The Tabernacle was taken apart very carefully and the Holy Ark, covered with fine tapestries, was carried by the priests. These priests, the Levites, were to lead the great procession, with Moses and Aaron beside them. Behind these leaders were to come the tribes of Israel carrying their banners and all their belongings.

It was estimated that there were over 600,000 men in these tribes, not including women and children. They all marched eastward toward Canaan, led by the Cloud of God. In their midst were the Holy Ark, the sacred fire, and all the many precious objects of the Tabernacle. As they marched, they sang the praises of God; and music from their silver trumpets pierced the air.

What a glorious sight this must have been!

Troubles in the Camp

PEOPLE ARE PEOPLE, and there were the usual troubles along the way. At one point, certain men refused to march unless they could taste meat. They were tired of the manna-bread that they had been eating for a year.

Moses begged God for fresh meat as he had done before.

"I know that these people are always complaining," said Moses to the Lord, "and I am sick of them. But what can I do when I know that it is Your commandment that I bring them to the Holy Land?"

God told Moses not to despair and sent a great flock of quails upon the camp. Greedy people grabbed these birds and cooked them and devoured them like wolves; but, because of their haste and gluttony, many took ill and died.

Moses had other worries as well. His own sister Miriam, who had watched him when he was a baby floating in the Nile, now became jealous and spiteful.

"Why should Moses be our leader?" she said to Aaron. "We have as much right to rule as he does. Come, let us ask him," she said.

With his sister by his side, Aaron confronted Moses with this question:

"Why should you lead us, Moses? Why not someone else—a priest perhaps?"

Moses turned his eyes toward heaven, and God angrily descended in His cloud. Miriam and Aaron fell to their knees. They realized that God wished Moses and only Moses to lead the people.

Miriam was afraid. When she lifted her head she noticed that her skin had turned white and scabby.

"Oh, I have been sorely punished," she wept. "Please forgive my foolishness."

"Forgive her, Moses," Aaron implored, and Moses prayed to God to relieve his sister of her pain.

After seven days she was cured, and God commanded the people to pack their belongings and head farther toward the Promised Land.

51.
Spies
Are Sent
on a
Mission

THE ISRAELITES were only a few days from the border of Canaan. At last, it seemed, the journey was ended. But Moses decided to take all precautions before the Children of Israel crossed into the Holy Land. He called one man from each tribe, and instructed them as follows:

"Go as spies into Canaan. Look around. See what you can learn. Find out if there are many people. What kind of houses do they live in? Are they weak or strong? Find out all these things.

"Besides this," he said, "bring us back some of the fruit of Canaan, so that we may see if the soil is good. We will await you in the desert."

So the twelve spies set off and entered Canaan. They did as Moses instructed and inspected the land. When it was time to return, they went to the vineyards and cut off a large cluster of grapes as a sample of the fruit of Canaan. This bunch of grapes was so big and juicy that it took two men to carry it on a pole.

These two men were Caleb and Joshua. Joshua was the same brave man who had accompanied Moses to Sinai. He and Caleb were delighted with what they found in Canaan, and advised Moses to enter the land without fear.

But the other ten spies were cowardly.

"Do not go into Canaan," they said. "The people there are like giants, and we are like tiny grasshoppers compared to them. Their cities have large walls about them and there are soldiers on every wall. Don't go, we beg you."

Many other people heard this report, and spread the word throughout the camp. Before long, there was a great outcry against Moses.

"We do not wish to go to Canaan," they said. "We shall all be killed if we do. Take us back to Egypt, where we belong."

Joshua and Caleb tried to reassure the people.

"God will protect us," they said. "Have faith in the Lord."

But the people were afraid, and began throwing stones at the two brave spies.

Then God descended in the cloud with a mighty roar. He was very angry.

"You are cowards and wicked people," He exclaimed. "I have commanded that you enter Canaan, and you do not wish to obey. Now you will suffer.

"For forty years," the Lord continued, "you will roam about in the desert until every man who refused to enter Canaan is dead. This is My punishment for your lack of faith in Me."

The people were terrified. *Now* they said they would go, they would obey. But God had made His decree.

"You will turn back," said Moses as he stood before the crowd. "Take all your belongings and head back, all the way back into the desert. Thus is cowardice rewarded!"

And so the people turned again toward the barren wilderness. In the confusion of this move, some soldiers tried to make a run into Canaan. They were killed by the Canaanites before they had a chance to lift their swords.

CAANAN HAD SEEMED so close. Now it would take another forty years to return. This disappointment, which the people had brought upon themselves, caused many to grumble and rebel.

Three men of the Levi tribe were especially anxious to replace Moses and lead the people themselves. They were namd Korah, Dathan, and Abiram.

"We are Levites," they said. "We can offer sacrifices as well as Aaron, and we can lead the people as well as Moses. Let us take command."

So they gathered some followers and approached the sacred altar with rebellion in mind.

When Moses saw this happening, he called many people to witness God's choice of who should lead.

"If the earth swallows me up," said Moses, "then these men may lead. But if they are swallowed, you will know the choice of the Lord."

And in that instant a great hole opened up in the earth beneath the feet of Korah and his followers. Everything they owned, even their houses, fell into the pit with them. The earth closed on them and they perished. The people ran from the place in fear.

Yet many of them still plotted against Moses. The Lord was angry, indeed.

"I will destroy these wicked people once and for all," He said. "Only Moses and Aaron will be saved."

But Moses knelt before God—as he had done so many times—and prayed for the sinful people. Finally, God agreed, though He did destroy many thousands who wished to do Moses harm.

Later, He caused the staff of Aaron to bloom with leaves and flowers as a sure sign that He intended Aaron and Aaron's children to be High Priests. This staff was placed in the Tabernacle with the other wondrous objects.

Over and over again, God forgave the people their wickedness and showed them His miracles. But still they sinned—not all of them, but enough to cause pain and suffering among the others.

Rebellion against Moses

107

Moses Smites the Rock

THE CHILDREN OF ISRAEL came to the desert of Zin and dwelt in Kadesh. Miriam died there and was buried.

As usual, the people were complaining. This time they wanted fresh water, for their wells were running dry. Again and again, they wished that they were back in Egypt, where water, meat, and fish were plentiful. They seemed to forget the beatings that they had received and the bricks that they had been forced to make.

Moses and Aaron went to the Tabernacle and fell upon their faces. The glory of the Lord appeared to them and spoke to Moses.

"I will bring water from the rocks," said God. "All you need do is to take your rod and command the rocks to send forth water and water will come."

Moses led the people to a large rock. Still they complained and his patience grew short. Speaking to the rock as God commanded, Moses struck it with his rod twice and shouted:

"You are always complaining! Well, here . . . I have brought you water. I hope you are satisfied."

The water streamed out of the rock and the people drank it up. The Lord then told Moses and Aaron that they had not made their people truly believe in His glory, and thus the two of them would not live long enough to lead the people into the Promised Land.

Aaron Dies

THE CHILDREN OF ISRAEL journeyed from Kadesh and came to Mount Hor. There the Lord told Moses that Aaron's time had come, and that he should take his brother and his brother's son Eleazar up to the mountain.

High above the camp, Aaron gave over his priestly garments to his son and blessed him. He was content, and not afraid to die. Moses and he had known many adventures together and had fulfilled God's wish to free the Chosen People.

Bidding his brother and his son farewell, Aaron closed his eyes. Now Eleazar was High Priest. The people mourned Aaron for thirty days.

The Serpent of Brass

YEAR AFTER YEAR, the Israelites wandered in the desert, passing through many small countries and towns. Whenever they had to make such a journey, they always asked permission of the local king, promising that they would be careful and peaceful as they traveled.

Sometimes they were given permission. More often they were denied it, because many of the kings were afraid of a surprise attack.

So it was that Moses often had to lead the people through rugged mountain passes and over hot, dry land. Of course, the complaining began all over again as the water became scarce and the sun burned fiercely in the heavens.

"We should never have left Egypt," the people cried. "Now we are stranded in the desert."

It was the same old complaint, and God was angered again. This time, as a punishment, He sent many poisonous snakes into the camp of the Israelites, and hundreds of people were bitten and died.

Suddenly there were fear and repentance among the Hebrews.

"Save us from these snakes," they cried to Moses, "and we will never complain again."

So Moses prayed to God and received instructions to fashion a serpent out of brass and to place it on a pole. Anyone bitten by a real snake was told to look upon the serpent and the danger would vanish.

And so it was done, and many thousands were saved by beholding the serpent of brass.

Once again, the children of Israel moved onward. They came to the country of the Amorites, and asked permission to pass through the land. But the king refused, and sent out an army to attack them.

The Israelites did not complain. Since the danger of the snakes, they seemed to have learned their lesson. When they needed water, they prayed for it like people who believed in God; and water came up from the ground. Now, inspired by faith, they prepared to battle the Amorites.

God gave them victory, and their enemies surrendered. They were attacked again when they approached the kingdom of Bashan. With God on their side, they conquered.

Now Canaan was again in sight. Forty long years had passed. All the complainers and cowards were dead. Only the beautiful Jordan River and the Kingdom of Moab separated Israel from its goal.

ONE DAY, the king of Moab looked from a hilltop. Below him, on the desert plains, he could see thousands and thousands of Israelites pitching their tents and making camp. Moab was very close to Canaan. It lay southeast of the Jordan River, and was the last great obstacle between the Hebrews and the Holy Land.

When Balak, the king of Moab, heard what Israel had done to the Amorites, he was afraid.

Balaam's Ass

There was a magician in nearby Midian named Balaam. It was said that this man had the power to destroy anything merely by cursing it. When he said "Be accursed," his enemies crumbled. When he said "Be well and prosper," his friends were well. The king of Moab called several of his princes and sent them to Balaam with a message.

"The Israelites have come from Egypt to make war on me," said the king in his message, "I have heard that they are a powerful people. You must help me with your magic and I will pay you well."

The next day, the princes arrived at Balaam's home with the message and a gift of gold from the king. Balaam heard Balak's plea for help and told the princes, "Stay here tonight. I will speak with the Lord and I will have an answer for you in the morning."

During the night, the Lord came to Balaam and asked, "Who are these men in your house?"

Balaam answered, "Balak the king of Moab sent them here to ask me to come and curse the Israelites who swarm upon his land."

God then said to Balaam, "You shall not go with these men. You shall not curse the Israelites, for I have blessed them."

In the morning, Balaam told the princes of Moab what the Lord had said. They went back to Moab to report to their king.

Balak sent ever greater princes to Balaam, offering him anything he desired if he would curse the Israelites. "If Balak would give me his house full of silver and gold, I cannot go beyond the word of the Lord," said Balaam.

Once again, he requested his guests to stay overnight. While the princes slept, the Lord came to Balaam and told him to go with these men in the morning, but to say only what the Lord told him to say.

In the morning Balaam saddled his ass. He wasn't sure just what would happen to him. But the princes of Moab were there, and he had taken their money, so he pretended to be very self-assured.

"I shall curse the Hebrews," he said to the princes. "Come, we shall go near their camp!"

And he mounted his ass and rode down the path.

Suddenly, the beast stopped in his tracks. There on the path was

OPPOSITE: Plate 32. THE ANGEL AND BALAAM, by Rembrandt (Dutch, 1606–1669), Musée Cognacq-Jay, Paris.

an angel of God with a sword in his hand. But Balaam didn't see the angel and he was annoyed.

"Get moving," he said and hit the ass with his stick. The little animal moved on. But again the angel appeared, and the poor beast was frightened and ran into a wall. Balaam's foot was bruised and he was so angry that he struck the ass a terrible blow on the neck.

The animal moved on. Once again the angel barred the path, and, this time, the beast fell to its knees, causing Balaam to topple to the ground.

So fierce was the magician's anger that he struck the ass brutally across the eyes. But, then, a miracle happened, and the angel spoke through the animal's mouth.

"Why are you beating me?" cried the beast. "What have I ever done to you?"

Balaam did not seem surprised by this miracle, and he shouted:

"I would kill you if I had a sword."

This time the angel showed himself to Balaam, and Balaam fell on his knees in fear and trembling.

"Don't hurt me," he said. "I will go home and lock myself in. I will give the money back to the king of Moab."

"No," said the angel, "you shall go on and do as you have promised. But God will use your voice as I have used the voice of this poor beast."

Trembling, Balaam went to the king and told him that he was ready to curse the Hebrews. "Good," said the king, and they both went off to a mountain overlooking the Israelites' camp.

There they built seven altars and sacrificed seven sheep to the idol god of Moab. Then Balaam stepped forward to make his curse.

"Blessed are the People of Israel," he said in spite of himself. "They will be great and prosper."

The king was shocked.

"What kind of curse is that?" he cried.

Balaam fell to his knees.

"I am helpless," he said. "I can only say what God commands."

"Is this what I'm paying you for?" the angry king exclaimed. "Come, we will try again."

Once again they built altars and made sacrifices, and Balaam stepped forward and lifted his voice:

"How goodly are thy tents, O Jacob, thy tabernacles, O Israel! . . . Blessed be every one that blesseth Thee, and cursed be every one that curseth Thee."

Balak was furious with Balaam for uttering these words. He smote his hands together and said to Balaam, "I called you to curse my enemies and all you do is continue to bless them instead. I would have given you great honors, but now I ask you to leave here immediately and go back to your home in Midian."

Before leaving, Balaam repeated that he had only said what the Lord had commanded him to say, and that he would go back to his people. Balaam then prophesied a great future for Israel, saying:

"There shall come a Star out of Jacob, and a Sceptre shall rise out of Israel, and shall smite the corners of Moab, and destroy all the children of Seth. . . . Out of Jacob shall come he that shall have dominion, and shall destroy him that remaineth of the city."

The children of Israel dwelt in the vicinity of the Moabites and Midianites for some time. They mixed with these people and many of the Israelites became corrupted by worshipping the local gods. The Lord would have wiped out all the Israelites by a plague, but he was stayed from doing this by an action of Phinehas, the son of Eleazar, the son of Aaron. The Lord then directed Moses to send the faithful out to do battle with the Midianites. The Israelites were triumphant, and among those slain was Balaam.

The Death of Moses

MANY PREPARATIONS were made before the people entered Canaan. For one thing, Moses knew that there would be fighting and war. The Canaanites were selfish, and would not welcome the Hebrew tribes, so the soldiers readied their weapons and shields.

But there were the usual duties to handle, as well. While the people were gathering their belongings, the leaders of the tribes of Reuben and Gad came to Moses and said:

"We have found this kingdom of the Amorites a good place to live, and we do not wish to enter Canaan."

Though it was the privilege of a tribe to remain behind, Moses warned:

"The others will think that you are cowards, and do not want to share the dangers of battle."

"That is not true," the tribesmen said. "We shall send our soldiers into battle, but leave our women and children behind for our return."

This was agreed to. Part of the tribe of Manasseh also requested permission to stay on the far side of the Jordan.

Fortunately, most of the people wanted to enter Canaan. This was their destiny, as God had promised. One of the most courageous and faithful of these men was Joshua, who had gone to Canaan as a spy some forty years before.

Moses knew that Joshua would be the best man to lead the people after he was dead. So he allowed Joshua more and more responsibility, and declared that the general was his successor and the choice of God.

Having done so, Moses was ready to depart. He assembled a great multitude before him and opened a large book filled with the history of the Hebrews and the laws of God.

"Happy art thou, O Israel!" he exclaimed. "Who is like unto thee, O people saved by the Lord, Who is the shield of thy help and Who is the sword of thy excellency! Thine enemies shall be found liars unto thee; and thou shalt tread upon their high places."

Then Moses spent many hours telling the people what to expect in Canaan and warning them against idolatry and wickedness. He also reminded them of the Golden Rule, and urged them always to be kind to the poor and hungry.

Above all, he recited the words that were to be the basis of the Hebrew religion:

"Hear, O Israel," he said. "Our God is the one and only God of all the universe."

Then Moses placed his hands on Joshua's shoulders to show that he was the new leader of Israel, and quietly, without showing any emotion, Moses left the camp and climbed up Mount Nebo overlooking the Jordan.

Higher and higher he climbed, until he was out of sight. When he came to the peak of the mountain, God Himself descended to his side and embraced him, so that he might look out over the river into the land of Canaan. By the Lord's own command, this was as much of the Promised Land as Moses was ever to see.

Moses was a hundred and twenty years old when he died. And the children of Israel wept for their great leader and they mourned his loss for thirty days.

"And there arose not a prophet since in Israel like unto Moses, whom the Lord knew face to face."

THE BOOKS OF JOSHUA AND THE JUDGES

The Stories of Israel's Leaders: Joshua, Who Conquered Jericho; Deborah the Woman Warrior; Gideon, Who Fought the Midianites; Jephthah, Who Made a Fatal Promise; and Samson, the World's Strongest Man.

Over the Jordan into Jericho

JOSHUA WAS NOW in full command. From God, he learned that it was time to lead the people across the Jordan into Canaan. If the Canaanites welcomed the Hebrews, then all were to live in peace. If they tried to prevent the Hebrews from entering the land, then Joshua was to send his troops against them. The Canaanites were idol worshipers, and God had doomed them to defeat.

It was springtime, and the Jordan River was swollen. Yet Joshua had such faith in God that, like Moses before him, he led the people to the water's edge and prepared to cross.

Everyone was excited, and asked:

"What is it like in Canaan? Is it a good place to live? Will the people welcome us?"

These questions were of concern to Joshua as well, and remembering the days long ago when he had been a spy for Moses, he decided to send out two spies of his own to survey the town of Jericho.

This city was surrounded by a very high wall with one gate through which visitors could pass. This gate was closed at sundown. Even so, the two spies managed to slip past the guards and entered the city. Unfortunately, they were recognized at once, and someone ran to fetch the guards. Seeing this, the spies dashed into a house built right alongside the city wall.

This was the house of a woman named Rahab. She recognized the spies as Hebrews, but did not seem afraid, and quietly beckoned them to follow her. Up they went to the roof of Rahab's house. There the woman told them to be very still, for, even at this moment, the guards were at her door.

"We have heard that there are two foreigners hiding in your house," said the soldiers to Rahab. "They are spies. You must surrender them."

"You are mistaken," the woman said. "Those men were here, but they have already left. You can still catch them if you hurry."

But the soldiers did not believe her, and began searching the house. Rahab had known that this would happen; that is why she had hidden the spies on the roof and covered them with flax.

When the soldiers could not find what they wanted, they left the house to search the streets. Rahab rushed to the spies on the roof.

"You can escape by climbing out of my window," she said. "You see, my house is directly beside the city wall. When you land on your feet below, you will be outside Jericho, and can return to your camp."

The spies were pleased, and went to the window. But, as they were about to leave, they turned and said:

"Why did you save us, you who are a Canaanite woman?"

Rahab answered:

"I know who you are. You are men of Israel. Our whole country has heard of your power and glory, and everyone is afraid. They worship their idols and ignore the one true God.

"But I believe that God is with you," she continued, "and that, some day, this whole land will be yours."

The spies promised Rahab that she would be spared when the Israelites marched into Jericho, and advised her to tie a red scarf to her window so that they would take notice. Then they hastened down the side of the house to safety.

For three days, the spies hid in the mountains. On the fourth day, they made a dash to the Israelites' camp across the Jordan River.

JOSHUA LISTENED EAGERLY as the spies reported. For one thing, they said, the walls of Jericho were weak and crumbling. Furthermore, the people there were so cowardly that a major invasion would be unnecessary. Hearing these reports, Joshua was determined to cross the Jordan and enter the fortress city.

But the Jordan was at flood, and its waters raced downstream at a furious pace. Joshua had faith in God.

"Bring the Holy Ark to the edge of the waters," he told the priests, "and God will deliver us as He has done before."

And so the priests carried the sacred Ark to the river's edge. As they stepped into the water, the flowing river suddenly stopped in its course, and all the water piled up like a wall to allow the Israelites safe passage on dry land.

The miracle of the Red Sea had happened again!

The Walls of Jericho

This time, Joshua called a leader from each tribe to witness the power of God. There were now so many people in the camp that not all of them could see the miracle.

Joshua then told each of these men to fetch a stone from the river bed and to carry that stone into Canaan. Once there, they were to build an altar that would remind Israel and all the world of God's great power.

Then the mighty Israelites crossed the Jordan, over 600,000 strong, and they entered the land of Canaan as God had promised Abraham, Isaac, and Jacob.

The first day, the Hebrews camped in a place called Gilgal, an oasis outside the walls of Jericho. Here, fruit and corn grew in abundance. No longer did the people need manna; and the manna ceased to fall. The sweet green land of Canaan was flowing with "milk and honey," as God had promised.

Against the evening sky the fortress walls of Jericho loomed in silence. The people cowered behind them, waiting for an attack. They had witnessed the miraculous crossing of the Jordan. In fear, they turned to their gods and idols, but none had any power compared to God.

Joshua was restless. He knew that a great battle lay before him. Yet he was unsure, for the walls of Jericho seemed mighty, indeed. As he wandered in the camp, he met a powerful-looking man clad in armor. Not recognizing him, he said:

"Are you a friend of Israel or an enemy?"

And the man revealed himself as an angel of God who had come to instruct Joshua before the battle.

"Take your army and your priests," said the angel. "Go before the walls of Jericho once every day for six days and march, march around the walls. The priests will carry the Holy Ark and the soldiers will blow their trumpets.

"On the seventh day," the angel continued, "send up a shout among your people, and the walls will come tumbling down."

Joshua knelt before the angel and received his blessing. Then he returned to camp and prepared his men for the conquest of Jericho.

For six days, the army marched around the walls with the priests and the Ark. The blare of trumpets filled the countryside, and the tread of marching feet caused the earth to tremble.

Inside the city, the people were amazed and frightened. They had never seen an army like this one.

On the seventh day, the mighty army massed before the walls and stamped and pounded with their feet and blew upon their trumpets, hour upon hour, until the people of Jericho were deafened by the noise. Then Joshua rode into the midst of his men and called to them at the top of his voice:

"Send up a mighty shout, you Children of Israel—all at once, together!"

And the walls came tumbling down!

Indeed, not one stone was left standing of the mighty fortress, and all the people in the city scurried away as the Hebrews advanced with their torches and swords. By evening, the entire city was burned and destroyed. All the gold and silver and precious jewels were taken by the Hebrews and placed in the Tabernacle as tribute to God.

Only one house in Jericho was spared. On its window was tied a scarlet scarf, for it was the house of Rahab, the woman who had saved the spies.

JOSHUA'S FAME SPREAD throughout the country. Everyone feared the Israelites and the God who inspired them. Because of this, many cities surrendered or were beaten by Joshua's troops.

One day some of Joshua's spies returned from the city of Ai and reported good news. Ai was a very weak city, they said, with few people, and it would take only a short time to conquer. Joshua sent his army marching toward Ai.

A few hours later, the Israelites were amazed to see the soldiers returning in defeat, carrying their dead and with their spears and lances broken.

"What happened?" cried Joshua. "Why have we been defeated in this easy battle?"

The answer came from God.

"One of your people is a thief," said the Lord. "He has stolen gold and precious things from the treasures taken at Jericho. I can not help the Israelites when there is sin among them."

Hearing this, Joshua ordered a thorough search of the camp. It was soon discovered that a man named Achan had stolen gold and precious garments from the city of Jericho. Achan confessed, and the stolen property was destroyed. Joshua had to punish Achan very severely, and he was put to death as an example to all others in the camp.

Now, freed from sin, the soldiers would be victorious. They marched again into Ai and, this time, they conquered the idol worshipers who lived there. God allowed the soldiers to take possession of the cattle and treasures they found before burning the city.

The Battles of Canaan

Plate 34. THE FALL OF JERICHO, by Jean Fouquet
(French, about 1416–1480), Bibliothèque Nationale, Paris.

To celebrate their victories, Joshua and the Israelites gathered in the valley of Gerizim. God instructed the people to build altars of stone inscribed with the words of the Law, so that all might read the Commandments.

Then the tribes formed a giant circle around these altars, and, as Joshua recited the word of God, all the people cried "Amen," which means, "so be it." Thus did they give their thanks to the Lord.

IN THE KINGDOM of Gibeon, the people were afraid of Israel. Some rich men of the city had a plan. They dressed themselves in ragged clothing and put on torn sandals and tattered coats. Then they rode into the camp of Israel on broken-down donkeys, pretending that they had come from far away, beyond Canaan.

When Joshua saw these beggars he asked:

"Where do you come from?"

And they said:

"We come from a distant country; you can see how far we've traveled by our ragged clothes and shoes. Let us be your allies, since we do not wish to be your enemies."

Joshua was sympathetic, and promised to protect what he thought to be a distant outpost.

A few days later, the Israelites came upon the kingdom of Gibeon itself. There it was learned that the three supposed beggars were actually rich men who had tricked Joshua into making a pact that bound him to protect their country. Joshua's advisors were angry at this trick, and decided to punish the Gibeonites.

"It is true that we promised to protect them," the advisors argued, "but it doesn't mean that we must be nice to them. They tricked us, so we shall make them our slaves."

The Gibeonites accepted this fate, reasoning that it was better to be alive as slaves than dead as enemies of Israel.

But other kings in Canaan were preparing for war. The king of Jerusalem, for example, decided to attack the Gibeonites and thus force Israel into battle, since Israel was a sworn ally of Gibeon.

FOUR OTHER KINGS joined the king of Jerusalem for the war. When the Gibeonites saw the advancing armies, they sent messengers to Joshua.

Beggars from Gibeon

The Sun Stands Still

121

"Come, you must protect us as you promised," they said, "for, remember, we are your slaves and your allies."

Joshua knew that he could not break his oath to protect the Gibeonites, and he called out his armies. Yet he was unsure. His men were strong and well-trained, but now they faced five separate armies of five separate kings.

Joshua prayed to God, and God replied, "I shall protect you. Your enemies will not win, I promise."

After a long march, the Israelites came upon their enemies and the battle began. Though outnumbered, the Israelites fought well and hard. Soon the armies of the five kings began to break up and run in all directions. As they ran, a hailstorm fell on the field and many were killed. But they had one advantage—night was falling.

"To the woods, to the woods," shouted the Canaanites. "We will hide in the darkness."

Joshua knew that darkness was just what the enemy needed to escape, so he rode to the height of a hill and in a mighty voice he cried:

"Sun, stand still above Gibeon; and, Moon, stay above the valley of Ajalon!"—and the sun stopped in the heavens, as he had commanded, and the battle raged within the full light of day.

Only when the Israelites had completely destroyed their enemies did the sun continue in its normal course and sink behind the distant hills.

The Israelites Occupy Canaan

MUCH OF THE LAND of Canaan now belonged to Israel, as God had promised. Altogether, Joshua defeated thirty-one kings of the small cities of Canaan. Now he was old and he wished to rest. So he camped with the Israelites at Gilgal.

In order to make sure that God's commandments were fulfilled, Joshua divided the conquered land among the tribes of Israel. Originally, there had been twelve, but Reuben and Gad had remained behind before the crossing of the Jordan. Part of another tribe was with them. This left nine-and-a-half tribes to people the land of Israel. God wished them to do so because the Canaanites were benighted idol worshipers. Only the Israelites believed in the one true God. It was, therefore, their destiny to conquer.

Many Canaanites, however, still remained in the land because the Hebrews were tired of fighting. Instead of going on, they brought the Tabernacle to a place called Shiloh, where they celebrated Passover and other joyous feasts.

Joshua was unhappy because of this laxity, and when he knew his time had come, he called the leaders of the tribes together and said:

"Our people must conquer all of Canaan as God commands. It is wrong for us to leave any of the idol worshipers in this country. They will poison our minds.

"Drive them out," he said. "Do not make friends with them! Keep your sons from marrying their women. Do all these things and God will be pleased.

"For, remember," Joshua continued, "the Lord our God has been most generous and merciful to Israel. He promised Abraham this beautiful country; he led us out of Egypt under Moses; and now we have come here; and we are happy and prosperous. Therefore, obey all the Lord's commandments forever, and we shall survive."

These were Joshua's final words to the People of Israel.

AFTER THE DEATH of Joshua the tribes of Israel settled their portion of the land and lived in the ways of the Lord until the elders who had accompanied Joshua were themselves dead. Then, the new generation of Israelites did evil in the sight of the Lord. Many married Canaanites, Hittites, Amorites, and others who worshipped false gods.

The anger of the Lord was hot against Israel, and he caused them to be conquered by the kings of Mesopotamia. After eight years of living under the domination of the Mesopotamians, the anguished Israelites called on the Lord for help. He heard their pleas and decided they had suffered enough. Therefore, the Lord chose a good man, Othniel, to be their leader. His spirit came upon Othniel, who led the forces of Israel to victory over the Mesopotamians.

For the next forty years, Othniel was judge over Israel, and the people knew peace and remembered the Lord their God.

When Othniel died, the people turned back to sin and idol worshiping. As a punishment, God sent the armies of Moab into Israel, and soon Eglon, the fat Moabite king, ruled all the land.

This evil king demanded money, jewels, and food from the Israelites, and he treated them like slaves.

"We are being punished for our idolatry," cried the people. "Dear God, forgive us and we will repent."

God was merciful. He inspired a brave man named Ehud to rise up and lead the Hebrews to freedom.

To do this, Ehud had a plan. He realized that the Moabites would be helpless without their king, so he determined to kill Eglon. One day,

The First Judges

Plate 35. JOSHUA STOPS THE SUN, by Giovanni Battista Tiepolo
(Italian, 1696–1770), Museum of Poldi-Pezzoli, Milan.

Ehud arrived at the king's palace bearing gifts from the people of
Israel. He told the king that he had a secret message for him. Eglon
dismissed his servants from his parlor so that none but he could hear
Ehud's message.

When Eglon arose from his throne and came close to Ehud to hear
the message, Ehud took a dagger, which he had hidden under his clothing, and plunged it deep into the fat belly of the king.

Then Ehud locked the doors of the parlor and escaped. It was many hours before the soldiers found their murdered king. They were in such a panic that it was easy for Ehud's army to defeat them. Once again, Israel was free.

But the good times did not last. A few years later, the people began worshiping the forbidden idols. They had no leader, and it seemed as though none could be found throughout the tribes of Israel.

BUT THERE WAS one person who lived near Shiloh who loved God and was determined to save the people. This person was not a strong, brave man, but, rather, a woman named Deborah. No one in all Israel

A
Woman
Takes
Command

was so good and wise as she. People often traveled many miles to her house for advice, and it was eventually decided, by the elders of the tribes, that she should be the judge over Israel.

The Lord told Deborah to prepare the Israelites for war. So she called upon Barak, a captain in the army, and asked him to be leader of the troops.

"We must fight our enemy, Sisera," she said. "That is God's command. We must find his armies at the river Kishon and conquer him. Will you lead our forces?"

Barak agreed to do so on one condition—that Deborah join him in the battle—for he knew that she was a brave woman inspired by God.

"I will go," she said. "But neither of us shall win the honors for our victory, for it is a foreign woman who will be the hero of this war."

The next day, the armies of Israel marched toward the river Kishon, which was a stronghold for Sisera's mighty army. At a command from Deborah, the Israelites advanced with such force that Sisera was frightened and ran from the field. He was the only survivor.

He ran until he found himself in a small village that he thought friendly to him. He entered a tent hoping to hide. Inside the tent a woman was preparing her meal.

"What do you want?" she said.

He answered, "I am Sisera, leader of the armies against Israel. You must hide me, for I know that your city is friendly to my cause."

But Sisera was wrong, for this was the house of Jael, a woman who believed in the one true God.

"I will help you," said Jael. "You may rest in my tent while I keep watch outside."

Sisera was pleased. He asked for some refreshment and Jael gave him warm milk to drink. Tired and feeling safe, the evil general went to sleep.

Then Jael quietly crept back into the tent and, with a large nail, used for a tent-pin, she killed the wicked Sisera who had done such harm to Israel. This, then, was the heroine of whom Deborah had prophesied.

Freed from Sisera, the Israelites returned to their homes in triumph, and sang their praises to God and Deborah.

The Story of Gideon

FOR FORTY YEARS, the Israelites lived in peace and worshiped God. They prospered and were happy. Then they began to worship idols again; and the Lord became angry, and punished them. He sent hordes of Midianites, Amalekites, and eastern tribesmen into the land of Israel. The invaders dominated the land for seven years.

Every day, the power of the Israelites grew less, and the Midianites took over more and more. Before long, Midianite sheep were grazing on Israel's soil and Midianite farmers were cutting the Israelites' wheat. Finally, the Midianites completely overran the country. They drank the water and plowed the earth as though they owned it. Because of this, the Israelites had nothing to eat; and they were too helpless to protest. Hungry and ashamed, they retreated to the mountains and caves, leaving the good land to their enemies.

Poor, starving, sunk in misery, the Israelites finally called upon God to help them. And God did. He sent an angel to one man who refused to surrender his pride and dignity, a farmer named Gideon. Instead of handing over his wheat to the Midianites, Gideon hid it for his own people.

The angel came to Gideon's farm and sat under an oak tree.

"Greetings from the Lord," said the angel. Gideon, surprised, looked up from threshing his wheat.

"You mustn't be afraid," the angel went on. "You are a man of strength and courage. I have come with this message: God is with you."

Gideon was amazed.

"If God is with the Israelites," he said, "why has all this happened to us? Where are His miracles? Why has He put us in the hands of the Midianites?"

The angel smiled, and repeated God's commandment:

"You, Gideon, will save your people. Go! Destroy the Midianites! God is with you, and you must trust in Him."

But words were not enough for Gideon; he wanted real proof of God's favor. The angel agreed, and asked for food. When Gideon brought meat and bread, the angel told him to place the meal on a rock. Then the angel touched the food with his staff, and it all burst into sudden flame. In the same instant, the angel vanished into thin air. Ashamed that he had doubted God, Gideon built an altar on the spot where the angel had stood.

That night, the Lord spoke to Gideon.

"In this land, the Israelites worship a false idol, Baal," said God. "Go to your father's garden tonight, and tear down the idol of Baal."

While it was still dark, Gideon and ten servants went into the grove of trees where the ugly idol of Baal was standing. It didn't take long to topple it over and break it into pieces. When that was done, Gideon built an altar to the true God, and sacrificed an ox as a sin offering.

Plate 36. GIDEON SMASHES THE IDOLS OF BAAL,
Gobelin Tapestry,
(France, 16th century), Kunsthistorisches Museum, Vienna.

The next morning, several persons came to worship Baal. All they found was the altar to the Lord.

"Who did this?" they shouted, and someone said, "Gideon, the son of Joash."

The people were furious and ran to Joash.

"You must punish your son for destroying our god," they cried. But Joash was very wise.

"If Baal is truly a god," he said, "let him punish my son himself. A god would never have allowed anyone to destroy his altar."

All were silent, for they realized Joash was right.

Now Gideon knew that he was on the side of God. He sent messengers throughout the land to recruit an army for Israel. The people were excited, and rallied to the cause. But, as this went on, Gideon began to wonder again whether he really was strong enough to carry out God's assignment.

"Forgive me, Lord," he said, "but, once again, I need proof of Your faith in me. Therefore, I humbly ask You for a sign. Here is my plan. I shall take the wool of a lamb and leave it on the grass all night. If the morning dew falls on this fleece but not on the grass, then I shall know that You are with me, and I will do Your bidding." And Gideon took the fleece of a lamb and left it on the grass.

In the morning, he found that the dew had indeed soaked the fleece but had not fallen on the grass, which was dry.

"I am still not sure," said Gideon. "Let me have but one more proof, dear Lord. I shall take another fleece and leave it on the grass all night. If it remains dry and the grass becomes wet, then I shall know that You are with me."

The next morning, Gideon found that the wool was dry and the grass was wet.

"Thank you, Lord!" he exclaimed. "Now I am ready to do Your bidding."

Over thirty thousand Israelites joined Gideon on Mount Gilboa and prepared to attack the Midianite camp below. Gideon was pleased with his large army, and felt certain that he would be victorious. Then he heard a strange commandment from God:

"There are too many troops," God said. "When the Midianites are defeated, the Israelites will think that they won because they were so strong. They must know that I alone bring victory or defeat. Dismiss all those men who are afraid."

So Gideon proclaimed that all those men who were the least bit afraid were to leave the camp and return to their homes. Two out of every three admitted to such fears; thus, when they had departed, only ten thousand soldiers remained. This was still too large an army for God's purpose. He ordered Gideon to lead his troops to the river to drink.

"All those who drop their weapons and fall on their faces to drink shall be dismissed," said the Lord. "Only those shall go into battle who hold onto their weapons with one hand and lap their water like dogs out of the other."

*Gideon
and the
Fleece*

*Gideon
the
Avenger*

As it turned out, exactly three hundred men lapped their water like dogs. These were to be Gideon's army.

That night, the Lord said to Gideon:

"Do not be afraid because you have only three hundred men. Take your servant and go into the Midianite camp when it is dark. Listen to what the soldiers there are saying, and you will be encouraged."

So Gideon and his servant crept alongside the enemy tents, taking care not to be discovered. By the light of the fires, they could see Midianites, Amalekites, and eastern tribesmen stretching away into the distance. There seemed to be as many camels as there are grains of sand on the seashore. Gideon's confidence began to be shaken. Then he heard two men talking in a nearby tent.

"I had a dream," said one, "in which I saw a loaf of barley bread tumbling down into our camp. It overturned all our tents."

"That means that Gideon will defeat us," said the other. "He will attack us, and he will win, for God is with him."

Gideon was truly inspired when he heard those words, and rushed back to his army to launch his attack.

With only three hundred men, Gideon had to be extremely cautious. He divided his army into three groups of one hundred men each. All the men carried was a trumpet in one hand and, in the other, a pitcher with a lit torch inside. He told each group to blow upon its trumpets and smash its pitchers when he gave the signal. The men agreed.

Then each group took a position above the camp where the Midianites were sleeping. Gideon and his hundred men crept into the camp. At the stroke of midnight, Gideon's trumpet was heard throughout the countryside. This was the signal! An instant later, three hundred trumpets blew! three hundred pitchers crashed! three hundred lights flamed out!

"The sword of the Lord and of Gideon!" shouted the Hebrew troops!

The sleeping Midianites awoke in fright. They milled around, not knowing where the attack was coming from. In every direction they saw the fires of Gideon's army. Fearful and confused, they ran from their tents. Many fell on their own swords and died. Others broke their arms and legs in the mad scramble to escape. Still others began fighting one another. By the time the morning sun arose, the Midianite army was destroyed and running in all directions.

The people of Israel were jubilant. They wished to reward Gideon and his entire family.

"Become our king," they said.

Gideon did not wish to be king. He loved God above all, and had no taste for personal glory. Until he was an old man, he ruled as a judge of Israel.

WHEN GIDEON DIED, his son Abimelech said to himself:

"The people wanted to make my father king, but he refused. If they ask me, I will not refuse."

He began to gather support, so that he might rule over Israel. Above all, he wanted power, glory, and wealth.

Before long, Abimelech was steeped in crime, since power often turns men against God. He robbed the Temple for money. He hired murderers to do away with his enemies, and he even killed his brothers. Some of the tribes were so afraid of Abimelech that they invited him to become their king. He was crowned in the city of Shechem.

One of Gideon's sons had escaped the evil tyrant. His name was Jotham. He went about the countryside trying to make the people understand just how evil Abimelech really was.

"He is like a tree of thorns," said Jotham, "he will hurt himself and everyone else."

True to these words, Abimelech soon brought war and destruction upon the land. Eventually his enemies killed him, but only after many people had died. The Israelites finally realized that they were better off with leaders like Gideon, and they gave up the idea of having a king. For many years thereafter, judges ruled in the land.

IN THE CITY of Gilead, there lived a brave man named Jephthah. His mother was unpopular in the village, and so Jephthah was driven from his home when he was very young. Nevertheless, he kept faith in God.

Evil days were once again upon Israel, for the people had returned to idolatry. Thus, wars continued, year after year, and the food supply became very scarce.

Many people knew that they were being punished by God, and they prayed for deliverance. But God was truly angered with the Israelites. Over and over, He had forgiven them, and yet they continued to worship idols.

"I will not deliver the people any more," said the Lord.

As the hardships continued, the people became repentant. They tore down their idols and cleansed their souls. God was appeased. He inspired the elders to seek a leader who would defeat the enemies of Israel.

"We will go to Jephthah," the elders said. "He is brave and righteous, and a good soldier as well."

When Jephthah heard the elders' plan, he was at first reluctant, remembering how the people had forced him to leave his home. But the elders begged him and promised that he would become judge over Israel if he conquered their enemies, the Ammonites. Finally, the good soldier agreed.

The king of the Ammonites sent a message to the Israelite camp.

"Surrender!" he said, "This land is really ours, because your people took it from us after they fled from Egypt."

Bravely Jephthah replied:

"God promised this land to Israel long ago when we were slaves in Egypt. We took it in the name of the Lord from other people than the Ammonites. We will never surrender what is rightfully ours."

And so the battle raged, and neither side came any closer to victory. Jephthah could no longer bear the strain. One day, he fell on his knees and made a fatal promise to God.

"Let us win this war," he cried, "and I will sacrifice the first thing that greets me when I return to my home."

Soon after, the enemy was defeated and the Israelites won the war. The victorious Jephthah went home in triumph. As he approached his house he remembered his promise to God. Fearfully, he started to turn away, when suddenly, the front door of his house swung open, and there stood Jephthah's daughter—his only child!

"Stay back," he cried, hiding his face. But it was too late. The girl came joyously running from the house into her father's arms, dancing and rejoicing in his victory.

Jephthah felt obliged to fulfill the oath that he had sworn. With tears in his eyes, he told his daughter that she must die as a sacrifice to God. The young girl understood, and asked for a little time to say good-by to her relatives and friends.

"What you have promised the Lord," she told her father, "you must do. Only let me live two short months. I will go to the mountains with my friends and prepare myself. Then shall I return."

On a dark morning, the sacrifice was done. God surely did not wish such a terrible offering, but Jephthah was a very strict man, and he felt that he could not make a promise to God and then break it.

For six years he ruled Israel as judge—living alone, sadly mourning his daughter.

And it became a custom that the daughters of Israel spent four days each year in lamenting the daughter of Jephthah.

LIKE THE CHANGING TIDES, the Children of Israel moved from idol worship to the worship of God, and then back again. One year they sinned; the next year they repented. It seemed an endless story of good and evil.

Perhaps one of the reasons for this weakness was the presence of many idol worshipers in Canaan. The Philistines, for instance, were an unfriendly people occupying the western coast of Canaan. They prayed to a giant god named Dagon, who had the head of a man and the body of a fish. Many foolish people believed that this ugly statue was the one true God.

The Israelites also fell on their knees before Dagon, making themselves easy prey for their enemies. Before long, the Philistines had conquered Israel and ruled it with an iron hand.

But there are always good people who love God, such as Manoah and his wife, who lived quietly and righteously on their farm. They had only one hardship to face: they were childless. Every day, Manoah's wife prayed for a son.

One day, while she was working in the fields, an angel came to her and promised that a baby boy would soon be born. He added, "This child will deliver his people Israel from the Philistines. It is so decreed by God. However, there are two things that this boy must never do."

"What are they?" asked the woman.

"First," the angel replied, "he must never cut his hair, for long hair is a sign of godliness. Secondly, he must never drink wine or other strong drink. If he obeys, he will be the strongest man who ever lived."

Manoah's wife was overjoyed, and ran to tell her husband. Later, while the two were working in the fields, the angel came again, and, when Manoah offered a sacrifice to God, the angel carried it to Heaven amid the flames. Manoah was overcome with gratitude, and promised to raise his son as the Lord commanded. In due time, the boy was born. His name was Samson and he was a Nazarite—or one who leaves his hair uncut in obedience to God.

As Samson grew up, he became stronger and stronger, while his hair grew very long. By the time he was twenty, he was as strong and handsome as any man in history. One day he went to his father and said:

"I have seen a very pretty girl in the city of Timnah, and I want to marry her."

The Birth of Samson

"But Timnah is a Philistine village," replied the father. "Why can't you find a girl from our own people?"

"Get her for me," said Samson to his father, "for she pleases me well."

"Very well," the father answered. "We will arrange it."

His father and mother did not know that the Lord had brought about Samson's choice. The family started out for Timnah and on the way, while passing through a vineyard, a lion suddenly appeared and roared at Samson. The spirit of the Lord came on Samson and he tore the lion apart and went on his way. His parents did not see what had happened.

The Wedding Riddle

IN TIMNAH, arrangements were made for the couple to be wed. Samson was very happy and journeyed home to prepare for the wedding feast. On the way, he saw the dead lion that he had killed a few days earlier. A swarm of bees had made a hive in the body of the lion, and they were producing lots of honey. Samson grabbed up the honeycombs and ate as he went on his way.

Later, at his wedding feast, he thought he would have some fun.

"I have a riddle," he said to his thirty guests. "If you can guess the answer before the seven days of feasting are over, I will give each of you a brand-new coat. If you can't, you must each give me the same." The guests accepted the challenge.

"Listen," Samson said. "Out of the eater came forth food, and out of the strong came forth something sweet. What is it?"

Everyone was puzzled, indeed. They did not know that Samson was referring to the lion he had killed, and the honey he had eaten.

For seven days, the guests tried to solve the riddle. Finally, they decided to speak to Samson's new wife.

"He loves you," they said. "Find out the answer before tomorrow, or we will burn down your house."

The girl was terrified, and she went to Samson, crying and begging him for the answer. At first, he refused, but, finally, being weak to the charms of a woman, he told her the story of the lion.

The next day, the guests assembled at dinner, and when Samson asked them if they had found the answer, they replied:

"What is sweeter than honey?

and what is stronger than a lion?"

Samson knew that his wife had tricked him. He was so angry that he ran out into the streets, grabbed thirty Philistines, and tore the coats off their backs. Then he threw these coats at the feet of his guests as payment for losing the riddle contest. Once he had done this, he ran back to his father's house.

Meanwhile Samson's wife, believing he had forsaken her, hastily married someone else. This was the way among the Philistines.

Samson's Revenge

AFTER A FEW WEEKS, Samson regretted having run away from his wife, so he decided to return to the Philistines and apologize. He arrived at the home of his father-in-law.

"What do you want?" the old man said.

"My wife," Samson replied.

"Ha!" laughed the father, "you left your wife and she has married another. Why not take her younger sister, instead?"

Samson was furious. He rushed out into the wheat fields and grabbed three hundred little foxes. Then he tied them all together, each with a burning torch on its tail. The terrified foxes ran screaming into the fields, burning up everything in sight. When the Philistines came upon their fields in the morning, all they found were ashes. It soon was discovered that Samson had set the fires. The angry farmers ran to Samson's wife, and, in a rage, they killed her and her father.

When Samson heard of this, he became furious, as before.

"My wife deserted me," he said, "but she was still my wife; and I want revenge!"

And vengeance he had. With his own bare hands, he killed hundreds of Philistine soldiers. The people were afraid, indeed. They followed Samson to a place high on a mountain where he was hiding with the tribe of Judah.

"Surrender Samson to us," cried the Philistines, "or we will surely attack you."

The tribe of Judah was worried. They begged Samson to surrender and he finally said:

"You may bind me and lead me to the Philistines. But do not try to kill me, or I will break my bonds."

The people of Judah promised, and tied Samson with strong ropes. Then they delivered him to the Philistines. As soon as Samson was among his enemies he burst his bonds, and, picking up the jawbone of a dead ass, he slew over a thousand soldiers. This was truly a miracle of God.

More than ever, the Philistines were determined to capture this Hebrew warrior. They followed him to the city of Gaza, where he was spending the night.

"Close the gates of the city," they whispered to the guards. "Then Samson won't be able to leave and we may slay him."

But Samson couldn't be stopped. When he heard of the plot, he simply walked up to the gates, which were made of bronze, and ripped them from the walls. Then, with the gates on his back like a knapsack, he walked to his own home town.

The Philistines were amazed and terrified by the strength of this great man.

"We must learn his secret!" they exclaimed.

FOR MANY YEARS, Samson was judge over Israel. The Philistines feared him because of his power and his mighty temper. Whenever they could, they tried to learn the secret of his strength, but always in vain.

In the valley of Sorek, there lived a Philistine woman named Delilah. She was very beautiful, and worshiped Dagon, the fish god. One day, Samson saw her, and he immediately fell in love with her and visited her in her house in the valley of Sorek.

The Philistines' leaders learned about this, and believed that Delilah could help them discover Samson's secret. So they went to her with money and jewels, and urged her to betray the man she loved.

"I will do it for my people," she replied.

A few days later, Samson came to Delilah's house. While they were at supper she asked:

"Samson, what is the secret of your great strength?"

He was amused by this question, and decided to have some fun.

"If you tie me with seven moist strips of leather, I shall be helpless," he said.

Eager to see if this were true, Delilah bound Samson with leather. Then she called the Philistine soldiers triumphantly. But, when they entered the house, Samson snapped the bands as though they were threads. Delilah pretended to be amused and said:

"I knew you were fooling."

Later she asked him again:

"What is the secret of your strength?"

Samson enjoyed the game and replied:

"If you tie me with brand-new ropes, I shall be helpless as a child."

That night, Delilah tied Samson with new ropes while he was sleeping. Then, pretending to be afraid, she cried:

"Samson! the Philistines are coming!"

Samson jumped up and snapped the ropes as though they were cobwebs.

Again and again, Delilah asked for the secret of his strength, and

Samson and Delilah

Samson always made up a foolish answer. Again and again, the Philistines tried to capture him, and he always escaped. Delilah, meanwhile, pretended that she was simply playing a game.

But the Philistines were impatient, and they threatened to punish Delilah if she didn't succeed. Finally, one night when she was dining with Samson, she said:

"I used to be in love with you, but since you won't tell me your secret, I wish you to leave my house and never return."

Samson was upset. He tried to reason with the beautiful Delilah, but she refused over and over to show him any affection.

"All right," he exclaimed, "I will tell you my secret.

"I am a Nazarite," he said. "That means I have never cut my hair.

Plate 38. SAMSON AND DELILAH, by Sir Anthony Van Dyck (Flemish, 1599–1641), Dulwich Gallery, London.

If my hair were shorn, I should be as helpless as any other man."

Delilah believed this, and signaled the Philistines to be ready. Then, when Samson went to sleep, she had a servant cut off all his hair down to the scalp.

"He's helpless!" she cried to the Philistines, and they rushed in upon him. True to her claim, Samson could not defend himself, and was indeed as helpless as a newborn child. The cruel Philistines struck out his eyes with their swords, and then triumphantly dragged their prisoner through the city streets, crying, "At last, the mighty Samson has fallen!"

Samson Dies

BLINDED, HELPLESS, and ashamed, the great Samson was thrust into prison, where he was chained and made to turn a millstone that ground the grain. The Israelites were in mourning for their mighty leader, for now their enemies were descending upon them.

Many weeks went by, and Samson's hair grew out. He felt his strength return, but said nothing.

Meanwhile, the festival of Dagon was approaching. The priests of Dagon decided to put Samson on display at the festival. Thousands of people journeyed from miles around to see this sight.

During the height of the festival the people became merry, as did the priests and princes of the Philistines. They commanded a little boy to lead Samson into the temple, to show how truly helpless he had become.

Samson knew that the temple was crowded with his enemies. He asked the boy to lead him into the center between the two great pillars that held up the roof. Then he warned the child to flee.

Wrapping his arms around each pillar Samson lifted his voice:

"I have sinned, dear Lord," he cried, "but I repent. Make me strong enough for this final task, and I will gladly die among my enemies."

His enemies, led by the victorious priests, jeered him and danced around him. The greater their scorn, the more he prayed. Then he felt a giant's strength flowing through his arms. With a mighty thrust, he pulled the pillars out from under the roof, and the entire heathen temple crashed to the ground!

That day, thousands of Philistines died, more than Samson ever slew in life. Samson, once the mightiest of men, also lay dead among his enemies. Later, when the confusion had cleared, Samson's family carried him home and buried him in a quiet place.

THE BOOK OF RUTH

A Story of Love and Faithfulness.

Ruth and Naomi

ONCE THERE WAS a terrible famine in the land of Judah, and many men left the country and traveled to Moab, where there was food. One such man was Elimelech, who took his wife, Naomi, and his two small sons, and settled in the Moabite kingdom.

Though Moab was a land of idol worshipers, Elimelech raised his sons in the belief of the one true God. After his death, the boys married Moabite women, Ruth and Orpah, whom they taught the love of God. Ruth and Orpah gratefully accepted the new religion.

Unfortunately, the two young men were killed, leaving Naomi alone in a foreign land. She decided to return home to Bethlehem, in Judah.

"You must stay with your people," she told her daughters-in-law, "and I shall go back to mine."

But the two girls felt sorry for Naomi, and walked with her down the road. They wanted to go with her to Judah.

"You will be lonely there," she told them, "just as I am lonely here. Remain in Moab and find yourselves new husbands who will care for you."

Orpah sadly agreed, and kissed her mother-in-law good-by. But Ruth would not return, saying:

"Entreat me not to leave thee, or to return from following after thee: for whither thou goest, I will go; and where thou lodgest, I will lodge; thy people shall be my people, and thy God my God: Where thou diest, will I die, and there will I be buried: the Lord do so to me, and more also, if aught but death part thee and me."

Naomi was deeply touched. She placed her arm around Ruth, and they both walked all the way to Bethlehem.

Ruth Meets Boaz

WHEN THEY ARRIVED at the city, many of Naomi's friends recognized her at once. They were delighted to see her again, and called her by name.

"Naomi, welcome home," they said.

"Do not call me Naomi any more," the bereft woman replied. " 'Naomi' means 'pleasant.' Call me 'Mara,' instead, for that is the word for bitterness." But Ruth tried to keep her mother-in-law from being sad.

"I will go into the fields and gather the leftovers of the grain," she said. "Then we shall be able to eat."

Naomi agreed, for it was the custom, as Moses had commanded, for prosperous farmers to leave part of their grain in the fields for the poor to gather. Gathering these leftovers was known as gleaning; and this is what Ruth set out to do.

She came upon the fields of a rich man named Boaz, who was of the family of Elimelech. He saw Ruth gleaning in the fields, and asked who she was. A servant told him her name and how she had returned with Naomi.

"Let her glean the fields as much as she wishes," he told his servants, "and be kind to her."

For several days, Ruth returned to the fields and gathered the leftovers in her apron. Since she was a stranger, she spoke to no one and seemed very lonely indeed. Boaz felt sorry for her. He approached her and said:

"You must be thirsty. Feel free to drink some of my water."

Ruth smiled with thanks.

"You are kind to a stranger," she said.

"I have heard of your devotion to your mother-in-law," answered Boaz, "and I respect you for that."

Then Boaz invited Ruth to have some lunch, and he instructed his servants to leave extra grain for her to gather. In this way, she was able to glean more than a bushel of barley. Excitedly, Ruth returned to Naomi and said,

"I have gleaned in the fields of a man named Boaz, and I have brought you much wheat, and even some food that he was kind enough to offer me."

Naomi was delighted, for Boaz was her late husband's cousin. Though he was older than Ruth, Naomi thought that he would be an excellent husband.

When the harvest was over, Boaz gave a celebration. Naomi urged Ruth to attend, and told her to put on her best dress and sandals.

All through the celebration, Ruth sat quietly to the side. Many young men asked her to dance. But she politely refused, and remained behind when the others had gone.

Meanwhile, tired from the celebration, Boaz stretched out on a pile of hay and fell asleep. He did not see Ruth sitting quietly in the shadows. After an hour or two, he awoke, feeling a draught. There was Ruth kneeling at the foot of his bed.

Plate 39. RUTH AND BOAZ, by Nicolas Poussin
(French, 1594–1665), The Louvre Museum, Paris.

"Why did you not go home with one of the young men?" he asked in surprise. Ruth bowed her head and did not answer. Then Boaz guessed that Ruth loved him, and his heart leaped with joy.

One problem arose. According to custom, a widow could only re-marry someone of her late husband's family. Boaz fitted this description, but there was another man in the city even more closely related. This man had first claim on Ruth.

"Tomorrow," Boaz said, "I shall go into the main square and make my wishes known. If this other man permits, you and I shall be wed."

Ruth went home to Naomi, and waited anxiously to hear the an-swer. At noon, they saw Boaz returning to the house. He had wonderful news: the other man did not wish to marry Ruth, and Boaz was now free to do so.

In due time, they were wed, and Boaz took Ruth and Naomi to his farm. There they lived in perfect happiness, and soon a son named Obed was born. Many years later, the descendants of this happy mar-riage were to provide Israel with its greatest kings.

THE FIRST BOOK OF SAMUEL

(also known as the First Book of Kings)

The Story of Samuel, Who Became the Priest of God; of Saul, the First King of Israel; of Jonathan, His Son; of David the Minstrel, Who Became a King; of War between David and Saul; of the Death of Saul and Jonathan.

HANNAH, THE WIFE OF ELKANAH, lived near Shiloh, where the Holy Tabernacle was located. Every year, husband and wife went to offer sacrifices to God, for they were people who observed His Commandments. But they had no children, and this made them unhappy. Thus, whenever Hannah came before the altar of God, she would kneel and silently pray for a son.

One day, the High Priest Eli saw Hannah kneeling in the Tabernacle and muttering to herself in prayer.

"This woman must be ill," he thought, and he approached her and offered help.

"I am not ill," the woman replied. "I am sad because I have no son, and I have prayed very hard for God's blessing."

Eli was very sympathetic, and told Hannah that she would someday have a child, as she wished.

"Oh, how wonderful!" she said. "If a son is born to me, I will dedicate him to the service of God, and he will live in the Temple all his days."

In a year, a boy was born to Hannah and Elkanah, and his name was "Samuel," which means "heard of God." In time, when the child was old enough, Hannah took him to the Temple, as she had promised. Then he was put in Eli's care to serve the Lord.

Samuel was an obedient and intelligent boy. He spent his days helping Eli and praying to God. Every year, his mother visited with new clothing for him, and they rejoiced at God's blessings.

But, in all this, Eli's heart was heavy, for his own sons were wicked

*The
Birth
of
Samuel*

men. God was angry because they also served in the Temple. Because of His anger, the Lord decreed that one day a new man would become High Priest when Eli and his sons had died.

This man was to be Samuel, and one night, when Samuel was asleep, God revealed His purpose.

"Samuel, Samuel!" called the Lord. "Awake!"

Samuel arose and walked to Eli's room, for he thought the priest had called him.

"I am at your service," said Samuel to Eli.

But Eli was confused.

"You are mistaken," he said. "I did not call. Go back to sleep."

So Samuel went back to his bed. A few minutes later, he heard the voice again, and rose and went to Eli.

"Did you call me?" he asked.

Eli answered again:

"No, my son. Go back to bed."

A third time Samuel heard his name spoken softly through the long dark halls of the Temple, and he arose and went to Eli.

Now the old priest realized Who was calling.

"When you hear your name again," Eli said, "you must answer, 'Speak, Lord, for I hear.' Now, go back to bed."

Samuel did as he was told, and, when he heard his name again, he answered, in a reverent voice, "Speak, Lord, for I hear."

And God did speak to him.

"You, Samuel," said the Lord, "will be a leader of your people after Eli. His sons are not fit to serve in My Temple. They will die, and Eli will also be punished, for he did not try to correct them. That is My decree."

Samuel was inspired, and he lay back quietly on his bed thinking of what the Lord had said.

In the morning, he went about his duties as before. Eli came up to him.

"I know that the Lord has spoken to you," said the priest. "You must tell me what He said, even though you think it will hurt me."

OPPOSITE: Plate 40. SAMUEL AND HANNAH, by Rembrandt (Dutch, 1606–1669), Private Collection, London.

It was true, Samuel was afraid to tell Eli what the Lord had said, for he loved the old priest and did not want to hurt him. But Eli insisted, and Samuel sadly said:

"The Lord will punish your sons and He will punish you. Someday I am to lead the people, but, until that time, I am still your faithful servant."

Eli was courageous.

"The Lord does what is best," he said. "Let us go about our work in the Temple."

And so, for many years, Samuel served in the Temple; and the people knew that God had chosen him to be a prophet, a leader of their religion.

The Holy Ark Is Captured

WHILE SAMUEL WAS a young man, many wars were fought with the Philistines. God did not help the Israelites, because they had turned to idolatry. Many soldiers were killed, therefore, and many cities plundered. Because of their defeats and hardships, the people gathered together and tried to think up a plan that would turn back their enemies.

The elders of Israel had an idea.

"When Joshua fought the battle of Jericho," they said, "he took the Holy Ark with him, and the walls came tumbling down. Let us take the Ark from the Temple and also bring it into battle."

The generals thought that this idea was excellent. They had forgotten that only God could protect the people and that only God could command the whereabouts of the Holy Ark.

So they carried the Ark into the battlefield, and when the common soldiers saw it they shouted for joy. The Philistines, nearby, heard this shout and they were alarmed.

"The Hebrews have brought their sacred Ark into the battle," they said. "We shall surely be defeated."

But among the Philistines there were brave men determined to fight to the death, Ark or no Ark. To their surprise, they won the battle, killing many hundreds of Israelites. The sons of Eli were slain, and the Philistines captured the sacred Ark.

Meanwhile, Eli the priest sat by the side of a road, awaiting news. He saw a Hebrew messenger running toward him.

"We are defeated!" cried the soldier. "Your sons are slain and the Holy Ark has been taken!"

When Eli heard this, he was stricken and fell dead. Now gloom and despair spread over Israel.

THE PHILISTINES were triumphant. They carried the golden Ark of the Hebrews into their idolatrous temple and placed it next to a statue of Dagon. They laughed and rejoiced at their wonderful victory.

But, the next morning, a strange thing happened. When the worshipers entered the Philistine temple, they found the god Dagon lying face down on the floor before the Ark.

"Some evil person must have done this," they said, and they replaced the statue.

On the next day, however, the statue of Dagon suddenly fell to the floor and broke into hundreds of pieces as though struck down by invisible hands. Now the people were afraid. Soon they learned that many Philistines were falling ill and dying in the city.

"It is the wrath of the Hebrew God," said the Philistines. "We must get rid of this Ark."

So they secretly carried the precious treasure to another city and left it there. Before long the people of that town also became ill and suffered. They, in turn, took the Ark to still another place; and the same ill effects occurred.

"We must get rid of this Ark altogether," said the wise men of the Philistines. "Here is the plan.

"We will place the Ark on a wagon drawn by two healthy cows. These cows will be free to wander as they please. If they remain in our country we shall know that the Ark is harmless, and that all our trouble has just happened by chance. But if the cows go directly to Israel we shall know the power of the Hebrew God, and we shall be relieved."

And so it was that two cows were yoked to the cart and set off down the road. Without stopping a minute, the cows headed straight for Israel, pulling the Ark behind them.

They arrived at a city called Bethshemesh and walked right into the midst of a field of corn. There several farmers were working. They were amazed to see their Ark returned and rushed upon it. Some of them even opened the sacred lid—an act forbidden by God. These men soon died as a punishment.

Seeing this, the people of Bethshemesh were alarmed, and they asked that the Ark be taken to another city. This was done by the Levites, who were responsible for all sacred objects. For many years, a Levite man named Abinadab kept the holy treasure and cared for it.

THOUGH THE ARK was safe in Israel, the Philistines still held the upper hand. As usual, they caused great suffering and hardship.

Samuel the Prophet

"Who is there in all this land to help us?" the Hebrews asked.

And then they remembered Samuel, a man who was both righteous and wise, and they turned to him for guidance.

"First you must rid your homes of idols," said Samuel, "and you must serve only the one true God. Then you will be relieved."

The people trusted Samuel, for he spoke with true conviction; and they immediately set about to cleanse their homes and smash their false idols and gods.

After this, Samuel called for a general meeting of all the faithful to be held in the city of Mizpeh. Thousands journeyed there to hear the wise prophet.

The Philistine army was camped nearby. When they saw the great number of Hebrews filing into Mizpeh they thought that a battle was being launched. So they armed themselves and marched into the city.

The Israelites were terrified. Here they were, unarmed, at the mercy of their enemies. Fearfully they turned to Samuel for help.

"Only God can help," he replied. "Pray and we shall be saved."

The Philistines came marching down the hill while the Israelites trembled and prayed on their knees. Suddenly there was an enormous clap of thunder in the sky, followed by a terrible rainstorm. The storm crashed down upon the countryside and completely scattered the Philistine troops. Then the Hebrews picked up the fallen weapons and chased their enemies far beyond the border.

From that day forth, the Philistines stayed in their own country and the Hebrews were free. Everyone praised Samuel, and paid him such homage as befitted a king.

The Beginning of the Kingdom

A KING! All the nations had a king, save Israel. True, the prophet Samuel was a wise man and an able leader, dedicated to God and his people, but he lived in an ordinary house and wore no crown. Besides, his sons, whom he had established as judges over the people, were not honorable men. They often took bribes, and pretended to forgive sins in the name of God. The people did not want to be ruled by these men after Samuel died. So it was that the elders of the nation came before Samuel, and said:

"Give us a king to rule over us, as in all other countries, and then we will know that we are equal to all other men."

Samuel was worried and displeased. He thought that the people did not appreciate what he had done for them. He said nothing, but he turned to God and quietly awaited His message.

"The people have rejected Me," said the Lord, "not you. Do not be discouraged. Speak freely. Tell them what you think, and, if they persist, let them have their king."

Then Samuel went before the people, and spoke these words:

"You want a king. But will a king be kind to you? He will take your sons to guard his palace. He will take your daughters to prepare his food. He will live off your money and wear fine garments that you make for him. Whatever is best in the land he will want for himself, and you will have to pay for it. One day you will bemoan having set this king above you. It will be too late, then. God will neither heed you nor relieve you."

The people listened solemnly, but still they insisted upon a king. Samuel threw up his hands and said:

"Go then. God will give you what you wish."

THOUGH SAMUEL did not favor the idea of a king, he nevertheless obeyed the Lord and began his search for a man worthy of Israel's crown. He prayed for guidance, and God replied:

"Stay near your house. Tomorrow, at this time, I shall send a man to you as though by accident. He will be brave, strong, and taller than any other man in the land. He will be the king." Samuel waited to do the Lord's bidding.

At the same time, in a nearby tribe, a farmer named Kish discovered that many of his asses had strayed from the pasture, and were missing. Immediately he called his son Saul to take a servant and find the missing animals.

Saul and his servant left at dawn and journeyed over the hills and into the valleys. But they could not find the asses.

"Let us return," said Saul after many hours, "for my father will worry that we also are lost."

"Those asses are valuable," the servant said. "We should do our best to find them. Why not ask the wise prophet Samuel? He lives not far from here."

Saul agreed, but he felt embarrassed to visit such an important man without a present.

"I have a silver coin," the servant said. "It will serve as a token of respect." It was destined that Saul meet Samuel that day.

So the two young men journeyed to Ramah, which was Samuel's home. They noticed preparations being made for a feast in the city and, in the excitement, they had trouble finding Samuel.

A
King
Is
Anointed

But the old priest recognized Saul at once, for here was the brave young man, the tallest in the land, whom God had chosen as the first king of Israel.

"Welcome, son of Kish," said Samuel. "I am the man you are seeking. You must come and feast with me, for we have expected you."

Saul was astonished. He tried to speak, but Samuel continued, for he knew what Saul was thinking.

"You needn't worry about your father's asses. They have been found and are safe on his farm."

What a remarkable prophet, Saul thought to himself, and how kind to invite him to a feast.

"You treat me like a king," said Saul in his innocence. Then Samuel leaned over to him with a grave expression.

"All of Israel delights in you, my son," he said. "That is the Lord's desire."

Such words were confusing to Saul. After dinner, he asked to retire, so that he might cope with these strange events in the morning.

When the morning dawned, Samuel roused the sleeping Saul, and walked with him down the road toward the land of Benjamin.

"Send your servant on ahead," said Samuel, "for I must fulfill God's secret commandment."

Saul obeyed, and, when the two were alone, Samuel withdrew a small cup of oil from his robe, and put oil on Saul's forehead. Then he kissed him on the cheek, thus completing the sacred act of anointment, and he said:

"By the will of God, you are to be king of Israel and rescue your people. The Spirit of God will now be with you. For seven days, meditate and prepare yourself. Then we shall meet in Mizpeh, where you will be crowned."

Saul was still astonished, and begged the old prophet for proof of his words.

"When you return home," Samuel continued, "three things will happen. First, farmers will come to tell you that your father's mules have been found. Then three bakers will present you with loaves of bread. Finally, some musicians and holy men will come down the road, singing and celebrating your return. Go, now, and prepare for greatness."

Saul went home, and to his amazement, Samuel's three predictions all came true. So great was the tall man's astonishment that he said nothing to his father about his anointment. When asked where he had been, he simply said:

"I went to find the asses and I saw the prophet Samuel."

AT THE APPOINTED TIME, Saul met Samuel in Mizpeh. A huge throng had come to witness the coronation.

"Here is your new king," the High Priest announced in a loud voice. "Here is the man whom you want in the place of God. Come forward, O King, and receive the crown."

At first, no one moved, for Saul was shy and hid among the crowd. But he was so tall that Samuel could easily see him above the shoulders of other men.

"Come forward," he called, "so that we may see you!"

Finally, Saul, still reluctant, obeyed Samuel and walked to the front of the congregation.

"God save the King!" shouted the people as Samuel placed the crown on Saul's head.

Naturally, some men did not approve of the new king. They thought him too simple and rough. Indeed, soon after the coronation, Saul humbly returned to his farm and his plow, as before. But his bravery and wisdom were soon to be tested.

In the city of Jabesh the people lived in fear, for the Ammonites were always threatening their homes and families. One day, Nahash, the Ammonite king, proposed a wicked plan:

"I will leave you alone," he told the people of Jabesh, "if you will surrender and allow my soldiers to strike every man blind in one eye. In this way, I shall be assured of your submission."

The men of Jabesh were horrified. They secretly sent messengers all over the land seeking help. Saul heard their entreaty, and was enraged by the Ammonite king's proposal. Filled with the Spirit of God, he assembled an army and rushed to Jabesh. Nahash, meanwhile, was preparing to carry out his threat, and his armies were assembled.

"No one will ever help the people of Jabesh," he laughed.

But suddenly, over the hills surrounding the city, came the armies of Saul. They scattered the Ammonites and killed their leaders. The town of Jabesh was saved! Everyone praised and glorified the victorious king. People said, "Let us kill those who did not approve of our new king." But Saul had become a man of justice in his triumph.

"No one will die today," he said, "for the Lord has saved us from our enemies."

SAMUEL WAS NOW very old. He had given Israel a king, in accordance with God's command. Not wishing to interfere in the new government, he decided to retire to his home and only give counsel when it

Jonathan
the
Son of
Saul

was needed. Before leaving, he warned the people in a stern voice:

"Every time you turn away from God, you will be punished, each of you, from the lowliest shepherd to the king himself. Remember what I have said."

Saul ruled well, and was respected and even feared. He assembled a large army to fight the Philistines, who still threatened Israel. One part of the army Saul commanded himself; the other and smaller part was led by Jonathan, his son.

Jonathan was a brave and handsome young man. He felt that he had to prove himself before the people, so he led his army against a Philistine fortress in a surprise attack. The Philistines fled in disorder, after little resistance, but they swore to return in greater strength.

They lived up to their threat. Soon after, thousands of Philistines marched into the land. They captured a Hebrew arsenal and destroyed the spears and swords that Saul's soldiers needed. Only Jonathan and Saul were left with any weapons.

But the king would not despair. In order to prepare for the Philistine attack, he called all his men to the city of Gilgal. They came, but fearfully. Samuel also heard of the trouble and sent word that he too would come to Gilgal to offer the proper sacrifices to God.

Saul waited seven days for Samuel. Meanwhile, the soldiers grew restless, as news spread of the Philistine invasion. Some of them fled like cowards; others hid in caves like mice. Saul became angry and impatient.

"Why doesn't Samuel come?" he cried. "We need to make our sacrifices!"

Days went by, and Samuel still did not come. Finally, the king decided that he would offer the sacrifices himself. He prepared the altar and went through all the rituals that only priests were allowed to perform.

At that moment Samuel came upon him. He was furious.

"You have committed a great sin," he said to Saul, "by taking it upon yourself to offer holy sacrifice. Because of this, you shall not rule long in Israel, nor shall your son follow you on the throne."

Saul tried to excuse himself, and argued in a loud voice. But Samuel would not listen. Disgusted and upset, he returned to his home without advising the king. Thus, Saul was left with only six hundred men and much shame before God.

Jonathan felt responsible for the proper conduct of the war. Determined to place himself at God's mercy, he summoned one servant and said:

"You and I shall go into the Philistine camp. If they dare us to attack, we shall know God is with us. If they chase after us, we shall know that we must flee. Are you ready?"

The servant replied that he would go; and the two young men climbed the hill into the Philistine stronghold.

When the enemies saw the two Israelites, they laughed and joked.

"See, the Hebrews are coming out of their holes," they said. Then they dared them to attack.

This was just what Jonathan wanted to hear! With a mighty shout, he and the servant rushed upon the Philistines and killed twenty men before the enemy knew what had happened. At the same moment, the earth trembled and quaked. The remaining Philistines were so afraid that they ran in all directions.

Saul heard the commotion. He realized at once that Jonathan had launched an attack, and he was determined to join in the battle. Commanding his six hundred men to follow, he rushed up the side of the hill. Many other Israelites, who had hidden in caves, forgot their fears and joined in.

Now once again, Saul became mindful of God. In the midst of the battle, he sent an order throughout the camp:

"In respect to the Lord for our victory," he said, "no man may eat before sundown. Anyone doing so will be put to death."

But Jonathan did not hear this command, and when he had done his duty, he rested in a forest near a beehive filled with delicious honey. Jonathan was hungry and scooped some of the sweet fluid into his mouth.

Saul learned about this breach. Believing that his command to abstain from food was sacred and allowed no exception—not even for the king's son—Saul commanded that Jonathan be executed for breaking the fast.

"We cannot do that!" the soldiers gasped. "He is a hero! He led us to victory!'"

So loudly did they protest that Saul dared not lift a hand against his son, and Jonathan was saved from his father.

PERHAPS BEING KING was too much for Saul. Usually, he ruled well and wisely. At times, he was impatient and cruel. Above all, he regarded his success as his own doing, and he paid little homage to God.

One day, Samuel came to see Saul in Gilgal and told him that God wished to destroy the Amalekites, idol worshipers and wicked men.

"Now, utterly destroy them," said Samuel, "and leave no one alive,

*The
Disobedience
of Saul*

neither their people, their cattle, and especially not their king."

Saul agreed, and set off for war. After many days, the Israelites, were victorious. Flushed with pride and full of glory, Saul ordered the captured Amalekite king to be led back to Israel in chains. He also selected the best cattle and sheep as booty for the triumphant troops. He did all this in spite of God's commandment.

Then the Lord spoke to Samuel.

"Saul is disobedient," He said. "No longer will I favor him."

When Samuel heard this, he wept, for he had great affection for Saul. Yet he also knew his duty, and, wearily, he walked toward the tent of the disobedient king.

Saul was alarmed when he saw Samuel approaching, for he thought he had fulfilled God's commandments.

"Awake!" the prophet cried. "You have sinned! You have disobeyed the Lord!"

Saul protested, and declared himself innocent of any crime.

"Innocent!" Samuel exclaimed. "You were told not to take any prizes of war, and yet I can hear the bleating of the sheep and the lowing of the cattle that you have stolen from the enemy."

Saul fell to his knees. He tried to make excuses, but in vain. Finally, admitting his guilt, he cried:

"Let me offer a sacrifice to God, so that He will forgive me."

But Samuel was stern.

"You cannot wipe out a sin so easily," he thundered. "The Lord is through with you!"

Saul was trembling. He reached out and grabbed the prophet's cloak in his powerful hands. "Do not go!" he pleaded. But, as he spoke, the garment tore in two.

There was a moment of silence. Samuel turned back to Saul.

"As you have torn my cloak," he said, "so will God tear from you the throne of Israel, and give it to a better man."

Saul begged Samuel to help him atone for his sins by worshiping the Lord with him before the assembled people. Samuel agreed, and, when this had been done, he asked that Agag, the king of the Amalekites, be brought before him. Agag appeared penitent and said, "Surely, the bitterness of death is past." But Samuel took a sword and said, "As your sword has made women childless, so shall your mother be childless among women." And Samuel cut Agag down with the sword before the Lord in Gilgal.

Then the old man left Saul at Gilgal and returned to Ramah, and wept. Never again was he to see the tall, sturdy farmer whom he had crowned king of Israel.

IT NOW BECAME Samuel's task to find another man who might some day serve God as king of Israel. Though his heart was heavy for Saul, the old prophet knew his duty, and prayed for guidance.

The Lord replied:

"I have chosen a man to succeed King Saul. You must go find him in Bethlehem, and anoint him with oil."

But Samuel was fearful. He knew that Saul was easily angered and might kill anyone who tried to deprive him of the throne. God, however, had a plan to protect the prophet.

"Go to Bethlehem and offer a sacrifice," He said. "Among the people who attend will be a man named Jesse. He will bring his sons. One of these young men is the future king."

So Samuel took the jar of sacred oil and proceeded to Bethlehem to offer a sacrifice in the public square. True to the word of God, the farmer Jesse and seven of his sons came to attend the ritual.

Samuel studied the faces of these young men, and was favorably impressed with them all. But still he heard no command from God about which should be anointed king. So he asked Jesse to have each boy pass slowly before him. This they all did, the largest to the smallest —but still God revealed no choice.

"Have you any other sons?" Samuel asked the farmer.

"Only the youngest, who is tending my sheep," Jesse replied.

"Send for him at once," the prophet exclaimed—and he thought to himself, this must be the one.

High up on the hills, a young shepherd sat strumming the strings of a small harp and sang the words of a song he was composing:

> The Lord is my shepherd. I shall not want,
> He maketh me to lie down in green pastures;
> He leadeth me beside the still waters,
> He restoreth my soul . . .

Suddenly, in the midst of his song, he saw a messenger running toward him.

"David! David!" the messenger cried. "You are wanted by your father in Bethlehem."

The young shepherd was surprised. But he arose, left his sheep in the pasture, and followed the messenger into the city.

When Samuel saw this youngest son of Jesse, his heart rejoiced. Surely this was the future king! His face was bright and ruddy. His gaze was strong and clear. His whole bearing was filled with the majesty of God.

"Arise and anoint him," said the Lord. "This shepherd named David shall be king of Israel."

Thus it was, and Samuel poured the precious oil on David's head while Jesse and David's brothers watched in awe. Now David was the anointed future king of Israel. Samuel said:

"With the anointing, the Spirit of the Lord has entered David. Some day, he will be the acknowledged king of Israel. For the time being, however, he must tend his sheep and play his harp as God wills. Indeed, his life is in the hands of the Lord."

David the Singer of Psalms

DAVID WENT BACK to the hills and tended his sheep, as Samuel had instructed. He also continued to compose his lovely songs, or psalms, as they were called.

One day he was wending his way through the streets near Saul's palace. As he walked, he sang:

> The earth is the Lord's and the fullness thereof;
>> the world and they that dwell therein.
> For he hath founded it upon the seas,
>> and established it upon the floods . . .
> Lift up your heads, O ye gates;
>> even lift them up, ye everlasting doors;
>> and the King of glory shall come in.
> Who is this King of glory?
>> The Lord of hosts,
>> he is the King of glory.

In the palace, the king lay ill with a fever, and with a great torment in his heart. The Spirit of the Lord had left him when David was anointed, but he did not know that. All day long, he tossed and turned beneath his covers, and it seemed to many that he had lost his mind. But the moment he heard the sound of the harp and David's sweet voice drifting through the window from the street below, he was soothed and calm again. Seeing this, his doctors sent for the young shepherd so that he might continue to play his soothing music.

In the palace, David was immediately at home, for his good looks and charm caused everyone to love him. Even the unhappy king was calm when he heard David's gentle harp, and he became deeply attached to the man who was destined to take his throne.

For many months, David stayed in the palace. Every night and every noon, he sang his songs to Saul—and Saul was at peace.

Plate 41. THE ANOINTING OF DAVID, by Paolo Veronese
(Italian, about 1528–1588), Kunsthistorisches Museum, Vienna.

FOR SOME TIME, the Philistines camped near the borders of Israel, and the Hebrew armies kept guard on the hills near the city of Saul. The king was better, it seemed, and there was talk of another battle with the Philistines.

David, meanwhile, had been sent home to help with the sheep, for his brothers wished to join the army and had left the farm. In Bethlehem, the young musician missed the excitement of the palace, and he was concerned about the Philistines.

One day, his father summoned him and said,

"Go to the battlefield. Your brothers are soldiers there and they need food. You will take some corn and bread to them, and see if they are well."

This was good news for David. He took his staff, armed himself with his leather sling, and eagerly set off.

The armies were assembled, and faced each other across a valley, but there was no war. It seemed as though each was waiting for the other to throw the first spear. For weeks, Saul and his generals watched from their fortress and the Philistines watched from theirs.

Then, one hot afternoon, the Israelites saw an enormous man, clad in armor, coming from the Philistine camp. He was twice the size of any other man in the world. He had a great red beard and fiery eyes. His body was like a mountain, and the spear he carried was like a tree. This was the giant Goliath, who was in the service of the Philistine army. Goliath stepped forward to make a boastful speech to his enemies:

"I am stronger than any man in the world," he announced. "I dare anyone to do battle with me alone. If there be such a man among you —which I doubt—and if he can manage to kill me—which I defy him to do—then all the Philistines will surrender.

"But if I kill him—which I will," he continued, "you, the Hebrews, will be our slaves."

Then he roared a hideous laugh.

King Saul and his men made no reply. In fact, some of them ran away in fear. Goliath, however, was not afraid. Every day he stepped forth in the sunlight and made his boastful challenge; and every day he received the same reply—silence.

During one of Goliath's boastful speeches, David came into the Israelite camp to see his brothers.

"Who is that?" the shepherd boy asked.

And his brothers replied,

"That man is a terrible giant, and we are all afraid of him."

"Not I!" David exclaimed. "Let me go before Saul. He knows me. I will accept the Philistine challenge."

The brothers laughed; and then they became angry because David would not listen to them. In spite of their anger, David insisted on seeing the king.

Saul recognized the musician at once and was pleased to see him. But when David announced his intention to fight Goliath, the king became doubtful.

"You are only a boy," said Saul, "and Goliath is an old hardened soldier. Forget this nonsense, and go home."

But David would not hear of this.

"O King," he said. "Many times I have fought with lions and bears who attacked my sheep. And I have always subdued them. This great hulk of a man is no worse. Besides, the Lord is with me and I cannot fail."

Saul was impressed. He promised David the hand of his daughter in marriage if he indeed subdued this giant.

158

Then he buckled his own armor on the boy, and handed him his own sword. David walked a few steps under the weight of the heavy armor, and swung the sword through the air. Then he took the armor off, and handed Saul back his sword.

"I am not used to armor," David said, "and I have never fought with a sword. My trusty sling and my faith in God are my entire strength. With these, I shall go to face the giant."

Then David selected some hard, round stones from the bed of a nearby brook, put them in his shepherd's bag, and, picking up his staff and sling, went to meet the giant.

Saul watched as the youthful shepherd scrambled down the hill to the place where Goliath appeared every day. Soon the giant's ominous shadow was seen, and then the giant himself emerged, in all his fearsome strength.

"What's this?" he roared, seeing David. "A little boy against me? A boy with a stick? What do you think I am, a dog? I'll tear you to pieces and leave them here for the birds and the beasts!"

David looked at the Philistine with a clear, steady gaze, and said:

"You come to me with a sword, and with a spear, and with a shield. But I come to you in the name of the Lord of hosts, the God of the armies of Israel, whom you have defied."

Goliath laughed and came running toward David, who bravely stepped forward to meet him. Taking a stone from his bag, David fitted it into his sling. Then he whirled the sling around and around above his head.

"This day will the Lord deliver you into my hands!" he cried to the giant—and, with that, he let loose one end of the sling. The stone flew with tremendous force directly into Goliath's forehead.

Crash! The great giant fell like a toppled tree, and his great hulk lay still at David's feet.

Triumphantly, the shepherd jumped upon Goliath's chest, and, with the giant's own sword, severed Goliath's head and held it aloft by its hair. When the Philistines saw this fearsome spectacle, they ran in terror with Saul's army, quick on their heels, driving them far beyond Israel's borders.

THE GIANT-KILLER! Great hero of the day! Many such praises were heaped upon David when he returned in triumph with Goliath's head. King Saul was delighted, and had the shepherd boy brought to the palace.

David in the Palace

Plate 42.
THE YOUTHFUL DAVID
(WITH GOLIATH'S HEAD),
by Andrea del Castagno
(Italian, 1423–1457),
The National Gallery of Art,
Washington, D.C.

"You are a true warrior," said the king. "I shall make you a captain of my armies."

The soldiers cheered when they heard this news, for they had grown to respect this handsome young man from Bethlehem. Jonathan, the king's son, was especially taken with David. One day, he approached him in the palace gardens.

"I have watched you and admired you," said the prince, "and I wish to be your friend. Please take this present as a token of my respect." And he handed David a beautiful robe and a belt. David was very happy, for he knew Jonathan to be a fine young man who honored God. The two were to remain the closest of friends all their lives.

But Saul the king was brooding again. Slowly, he began to grow jealous of the popular young David. He thought to himself: even my own son is bewitched by him. Every day, his suspicions grew worse.

Finally, he feared losing his mind. "I must forget these problems," he said. "I will hold a parade, so that the people may cheer me and gladden my heart."

When the parade was announced, all the women of the town lined the streets carrying many musical instruments which they played before the marching soldiers. Saul appeared on his regal horse, and, a few paces behind, David the captain rode on his black charger.

When the women saw Saul and David, they chanted a song:

> Saul has slain his thousands,
> and David his ten thousands.

Saul heard this and his heart grew hard and bitter. Now, he thought, even the people were making fun of him and preferring David, and he feared that David might usurp his throne.

For days he brooded, and his fever returned. His physicians, remembering how David's singing had soothed him before, sent for the young musician.

David was not aware of Saul's anger. He picked up his harp, and sat at the foot of the king's golden throne. Then he began to sing very softly. Saul had been half asleep. When he heard the music, he awoke. Seeing David, he grabbed a spear.

"I'll kill you!" he cried, and he hurled the weapon across the room, missing David by inches.

There was a pause. The king grew even more enraged. Once again, he grabbed a spear and hurled it at his imagined enemy. But the weapon merely fell to the floor. David rose from his place, quickly left the room, and said nothing.

Now Saul was intent upon ridding himself of his rival. He refused to allow David to marry his daughter, though he had promised as much during the fight with Goliath. He also sent David into many dangerous battles, hoping he would get killed, but to no avail. Then, spitefully, he demoted David from the rank of captain. Still his rival did not break under the strain. It was more than Saul could bear.

David Flees

AS THE WEEKS went by, the whole palace knew of the conflict between David and Saul. One person who was especially unhappy was Michal, the king's beautiful daughter, for she was in love with David and her father knew it. In order to rid himself of the young hero from Bethlehem, Saul promised David that he could marry Michal if he

killed a hundred Philistines. Saul was sure that David himself would be killed.

To his surprise, David returned a conquering hero, demanding his bride. Saul had to allow the marriage, as he had promised, but it only made him hate David all the more.

Finally he hit upon a terrible plan, and he called his son Jonathan.

"You are trusted by David," said the king. "He will not suspect you. Therefore, I want you to go into his room and kill him tonight."

Jonathan was horrified. He rushed to David and told him of the king's plan. David decided to hide in the nearby hills until Jonathan could reason with his father.

The next day, Saul seemed less troubled. Jonathan went to him.

"Father, I beg you," he said, "do not be enemies with David. He is your friend and your loyal servant. Why do you want to kill this hero who has done so much for you? Let him live, and we shall all be friends."

Saul listened, and finally agreed. He told Jonathan to bring David to a feast that evening.

But treachery, not love, filled the king's heart. When he was alone with David he asked him to play his harp. Then, as he had done twice before, the king hurled his spear at the young musician—and, as before, David escaped. He ran home where Michal, his bride, was waiting.

"I have bad news," she said. "My father is sending soldiers here to arrest you. You must run away into the hills."

David agreed. But it was too late. At that very moment, Saul's soldiers were demanding entrance at the door.

"Hurry, this way," Michal said. And she lowered her husband out of the window with a rope.

Then, returning hastily, she filled his bed with pillows, so that it appeared as though a man were sleeping there.

"My husband is ill," she told the soldiers as they entered. And indeed when they looked into David's bedroom, they saw what appeared to be a man, fast asleep under the covers.

They returned to the palace and told Saul that David was ill. But

OPPOSITE: Plate 43. DAVID PLAYING THE HARP BEFORE SAUL, by Rembrandt (Dutch, 1606–1669), Mauritshuis, The Hague.

the king was so furious that he ordered them to bring his enemy, bed and all, into his presence.

When this was done, Saul approached the bed. Lifting his sword in his hand, he pulled back the covers—only to find a heap of pillows.

"You did this!" he cried to Michal. "Behold, even my own daughter turns against me!"

And his hatred for David grew in his soul.

Jonathan's Signal

FOR SOME TIME, David stayed with the prophet Samuel in the town of Ramah. Saul learned of this, and sent soldiers to capture his enemy. But, every time they approached Samuel's house, they could hear him praying, and they were overcome by mercy and the Spirit of God. The king himself came to Ramah armed with his spear. But he, too, could not resist the power of prayer, and he found himself kneeling outside the house in respect to God.

David knew this was his chance to escape. In secret, he returned to the palace, where he met with Jonathan.

"I cannot understand why your father wants to kill me," David said. "I have done no wrong to him."

"He does not want to kill you," the prince replied. "In any event, I can reason with him."

But David was not convinced. He knew that Saul also distrusted Jonathan, and he feared for his friend, for he loved Jonathan as he loved himself, and Jonathan loved him.

"We will test the king," David remarked. "Tomorrow is a feast. He will expect me at his table as usual. But I will not come. You, Jonathan, must explain that I have gone to Bethlehem to be with my father.

"If the king becomes angry," David continued, "then we will know that he wants to kill me. If he agrees to my absence, I will be relieved."

Jonathan promised to test his father, and, in order to inform David of the king's reaction, he also conceived this plan:

David would hide in the fields behind a rock. To this place Jonathan would come with a servant to shoot arrows, as though he were practicing. If all was safe, he would say to his servant, "Fetch the arrows; they are over there to your right." If all was ill, Jonathan would say, "Fetch the arrows; they are beyond you, go your way." The two friends agreed, and parted.

The next day, the feast began. All the dignitaries of the court assembled at the table of the king—all except David. When Saul noticed his absence, he demanded to know why. Jonathan explained.

"David has gone to Bethlehem to visit his parents."

Saul was enraged.

"Who gave him permission?" he cried.

Jonathan took the blame. "I could see no wrong in it," he explained.

"You are a fool," shouted the king. "As long as David is alive, you will never be heir to my throne. He must die, and I demand it."

Then, suddenly, Saul grabbed his spear and hurled it at his own son, Jonathan. By the grace of God, the spear fell short of its mark, and Jonathan was spared. But now he knew that his father had been forsaken by God. He picked himself up and left the table.

The next day, Jonathan went out into the fields with his bow and arrows. Standing near the rock where David was hiding, the prince aimed and shot three arrows into the air. Then he called to his servant in a loud voice.

"Fetch the arrows; they are beyond you, go your way." This was the signal for danger, and David knew it. When the servant left the scene, David came from his hiding place and embraced his friend.

"I must flee," he said to the prince, "and we may never see each other again. But I swear eternal friendship to you, for you are closer to me than a brother."

Jonathan was deeply moved.

"Go in peace, in the name of the Lord," he said, "but swear to me that you will not forget our friendship at any time and that between your children and my children there will always be peace."

Then they embraced again, and bade each other a sad farewell.

FOR SEVERAL DAYS, David, outcast and alone, roamed the wilderness until he came upon the town of Nob. Here, Ahimelech, the high priest, tended the Holy Ark of God. When Ahimelech saw David, he recognized him at once and greeted him cheerfully. The priest did not realize that David was fleeing from Saul, or he would have been obliged to report him. Instead, wishing to be as cooperative as possible, Ahimelech gave David five loaves of showbread from the Tabernacle, so that David, and some men he said were awaiting him, might eat.

Soon trouble appeared in the form of a man named Doeg. This person was in the service of Saul, and he was notorious as a treacherous spy. When David saw him, he knew that he had to flee again.

"I need a weapon," he said to Ahimelech. "Can you provide me with one?"

The War between David and Saul

The priest nodded, and brought out a tremendous sword from the Tabernacle.

"This is the sword with which you severed Goliath's head," said the priest. "Take it. It will serve you well."

David was pleased. Taking the sword, he bade Ahimelech farewell, and departed.

Again the hero was forced to flee across the mountains. Everywhere, people were afraid to hide him. He knew now that there was no place to go where he might be safe, except the land of the Philistines. Surely, Saul would not follow him into enemy ground.

When David arrived in Philistia, the Philistines recognized him at once, and they wanted to kill him. But David was resourceful. He pretended to be out of his mind, for he knew that the Philistines would not harm a crazy man. However, after a week, they forced him to leave their kingdom.

Once more David was on the run. At a place called Adullam he found a large cave in a hill, and, with some of his friends and followers, he hid there and prayed for strength. In time, many others joined him. David's own mother and father were among the visitors.

He was, of course, happy to see his parents, but the dark, cold cave was no place for elderly people. So David arranged to take them to the kingdom of Moab, where they were welcomed. David, however, returned to the cave.

For a long time, he and his followers remained in hiding. They were waiting for the word of God. King Saul, meanwhile, sat in his palace, suspicious of everyone.

"David is hiding, and no one will tell me where," he cried. "Everyone is against me, even my own son."

But the king did have one faithful follower in the man named Doeg.

"I saw David at the Tabernacle with the High Priest," said the spy. "The priest gave him bread and a sword."

Saul was outraged. He called Ahimelech, the priest, and denounced him. The holy man was surprised.

"I did not know David was your enemy," he said. "I thought you were friends, so I gave him bread and a sword."

But Saul could not be convinced. In a terrible rage, he ordered Ahimelech and all his associates murdered on the spot. No one but the wicked Doeg dared to commit such a crime, but his sword was very quick. In one day, Doeg killed over eighty priests. Only one escaped. He ran to David in Adullam and told him of the massacre. Now David knew the great extent of Saul's wickedness.

THE FEUD BETWEEN David and Saul continued. All the people were saddened except the Philistines; they were delighted. With the king and his bravest soldier fighting each other, they thought, surely any strong army could defeat the Israelites.

So they attacked at a place called Keilah. But David was nearby, and he met the invasion head on, winning a great victory for his country. News spread of this achievement, and King Saul heard of it. Instead of being grateful to David, he was more determined than ever to capture him. So he set out for Keilah.

When David learned of Saul's approaching army, he prayed to the Lord, and the Lord instructed him to hide with his troops in the hills.

David obeyed. While he was hidden, he had a visit from his faithful friend Jonathan. They talked of old times and pledged anew the wonderful friendship between them.

Below in the valley, Saul had arrived with three thousand soldiers waiting to attack David. But God intervened. He forced the king to return to his palace, for the Philistines had launched an invasion in its vicinity. While Saul was thus busy with the war, David and his followers could regroup their forces.

A few months passed. David led his army to a place called Engedi, where there were many hillside caves.

One day, a messenger brought the news that Saul was heading in that very direction. David sent most of his troops back into the woods, and, with a few brave men, hid himself in one of the caves.

To this very place King Saul and his guards came searching for shelter. They were not aware of David's presence, so they removed their armor and prepared to rest.

Saul lay on his shield and placed his spear by his side. Then he fell asleep.

From the dark corner, David and his men watched quietly.

"Let's kill him now," whispered a young lieutenant.

But David would not let him.

"He has been anointed by God," he said, "and we must not harm him. I have a better way."

Then David approached the sleeping king and, with his sword, cut off part of Saul's robe. Signaling his men to follow, he left the cave and went down into the valley.

When morning dawned, David arranged his troops at the foot of the hill. Looking up toward the cave where Saul was asleep, he cried:

"Saul, my king and my lord!"

Saul rushed from the cave with his men, and was amazed to see his enemy, David, standing before him.

"You want to kill me," David said, "because you have listened to wicked advisors. But I wish you no harm. Last night I could have killed you easily, and my soldiers urged me to do so. But I would not touch the anointed of God."

Then, holding up the piece of Saul's own robe, David continued:

"Here is the hem of your robe, which I cut with my sword last night. If I had wanted to harm you, I could have cut your throat as easily. Now you must judge whether I am truly your enemy or your friend."

Saul didn't know what to say. He was deeply moved and yet afraid.

"I know you will be king one day," he said to David, "and, for that reason, you are my enemy. But I am grateful that you spared my life, and I promise that I will not harm you."

In the midst of this reunion between David and Saul, news came of the death of Samuel, the prophet, and all the people went to Ramah to mourn.

David Meets Abigail

DAVID KNEW that Saul would not keep his truce. He therefore ordered his men back into the wilderness to prepare for any future attacks by the king.

Soon food ran out, and the men became quarrelsome.

"Let us get some food from Nabal," they said.

Nabal was a farmer who grazed his sheep near David's camp. Though the soldiers were often tempted to steal from him, David never allowed it, since it would have been unjust. This kindness, however, was not repaid, for, when David sorely needed meat for his men, Nabal refused.

"This selfish man must be punished," David said, and he ordered his army to assemble and march upon Nabal's large farm.

Nabal had a kindly wife named Abigail, who learned of her husband's selfishness and of David's wrath. She realized that it was wrong of Nabal to deny the very man who had protected him—but she also knew that David would be sorry before God if he killed her husband.

So, secretly, she called her servants and gathered up great quantities of food and wine. All of these she loaded onto donkeys, and set out to meet David and his troops.

Halfway up the road, the two groups met, and Abigail dropped to her knees before David.

"My lord," she said, "do not vent your anger on Nabal, my husband. He is selfish, I know, but some day you will be king and you must learn to control your feelings. Allow me to offer you this food and urge you to turn back and forget your wrath."

David listened and was deeply impressed. He accepted the food and promised not to harm Nabal.

Abigail returned to her house, and told her husband of his narrow escape. She also revealed how much food she had taken. Hearing this, Nabal had a heart attack and died.

Afterward, when David learned that Abigail was a widow, he sent people to comfort her, and bring her to him to become his wife. And she came to him and became his wife.

TRUE TO DAVID'S SUSPICIONS, Saul once again was on the march, swearing to capture his enemy. With thousands of men behind him, he went from tribe to tribe seeking David, bribing people to spy on his enemy—wearily and hopelessly trying to find the man who was to replace him on the throne.

David knew of Saul's movements. In fact, he followed the king to an open field near the Philistine border. Once again, David could have killed Saul and all his commanders. But instead, as before, he merely crept into the camp when everyone was asleep, and gently lifted the water jug that lay beside the king.

Then, in the morning, he called out,

"Once again, King Saul, I have spared your life. Let us live in peace!"

And, once again, Saul wept, and asked forgiveness. But David was still suspicious, so he took his troops back into the forest for safety.

Now the Philistines and the Amalekites joined to fight against Israel, and the land was filled with the noise of war. Terrible battles raged everywhere, and innocent people died cruel deaths, all because Saul forgot the mercy of God and hated David, without whom he could not beat his enemies. Slowly, the king saw his power and his glory slipping from his grasp.

"I must have help," he cried. "Bring me Samuel!"

But Samuel was dead. Had the king forgotten?

"True," Saul sadly replied. "He is dead." And he paused and thought a while. Then he jumped to his feet and exclaimed,

"Find me a sorceress who may bring the prophet back to life, so that I may consult him!"

The king's advisors were alarmed, for God prohibited sorcery in any form. Yet the king insisted.

Saul
Seeks
David
Again

169

The Witch of Endor

AFTER A FEW DAYS, a sorceress was found in the city of Endor. To her gloomy tent King Saul came in disguise.

"What do you wish?" asked the sorceress.

"Bring me Samuel, the prophet," answered the king, "and I will pay you well."

The witch began her incantations, and, before long, a curl of smoke appeared in the tent, and a figure seemed to rise from its midst.

The king believed that Samuel had risen from the dead. He fell on his knees, and begged the old prophet for guidance. But the words that he heard brought terror to his heart.

"Tomorrow you will die in battle," said the spirit, "you and your sons together; and the Philistines will triumph over Israel!"

Saul wearily left the tent and took up his sword. Then, like one who had lost his senses, he ran into battle on Mount Gilboa. Here, on every side, the enemy approached. Only a few brave men remained with their king, determined to fight or die.

Their brave hopes were shattered. Two soldiers suddenly appeared bearing the slain body of Jonathan in their arms. Seeing this, the king fell to his knees and tore his garments in grief.

Then, with tears in his eyes, he handed his sword to his servant and said:

"Kill me, lest my enemies find me."

But the servant was afraid, and the awful task was left to Saul himself.

Thus, by his own hand, the first king of Israel died, forsaken of God and man.

When the morning dawned, the Philistines found the bodies of Saul and his sons. They mistreated them in their vengeance—but Saul was at peace, and did not know of this final humiliation.

THE SECOND BOOK OF SAMUEL

(also known as the Second Book of Kings)

The Story of David the King; and of Absalom, His Rebellious Son.

David the King

THE NEWS of the death of Saul and Jonathan spread swiftly through the land. David had loved the king, in spite of their feud, and Jonathan had been his closest friend. Now he tore his clothing as a sign of grief, and lamented their deaths in these words:

> Saul and Jonathan were lovely
> and pleasant in their lives,
> and in their deaths they were not divided.
> They were swifter than eagles;
> they were stronger than lions.

> I am distressed for thee, my brother Jonathan:
> very pleasant hast thou been unto me;
> thy love to me was wonderful,
> passing the love of women.
> Oh how are the mighty fallen,
> and the weapons of war perished.

But now David knew that he would soon be king; he waited for the Lord's word. Then, with his family and his followers he marched into the land of Judah, to the city of Hebron, where God commanded him to await his destiny.

The people of Judah rejoiced that David had come to live among them, and they crowned him king at once. Meanwhile, in the northern part of the land, one of Saul's remaining sons, Ishbosheth, made himself king in his father's place. For several years he ruled, until, one day, his own soldiers killed him while he was sleeping.

Then the people of the north came to Hebron and cried:

"We want David to be king over all of Israel!" And they urged him to march into the city of Jerusalem.

But when the men who had slain Ishbosheth brought his head to David, expecting a reward, David was angered by this dreadful deed, and he commanded that they themselves be put to death. And David buried the head of Ishbosheth at Hebron.

Now the Philistines menaced Israel and sent an army toward Jerusalem.

"Guide me, oh Lord," prayed David. "Tell me what I must do."

And the Lord guided David to a resounding victory. So enormous were the Philistines' losses that they retreated beyond their borders, never again to bother Israel during David's lifetime.

With peace in the land, David had many great ambitions. He wanted to bring the Holy Ark to Jerusalem, and build a Temple and a palace in the midst of the city.

So he sent for the Ark, which had been kept in the home of a Levite for many years. When the sacred treasure returned, David rushed out of his palace and began to dance! That's how happy he was. Unfortunately, his wife, Michal, thought that this public display was undignified for a king, and she became angry and left the palace.

When the Ark was safely inside the Tabernacle and the city was quiet again, David set about making Jerusalem the most beautiful city in the world. Fine woods and beaten gold were brought from far-off places to decorate the palace. The streets were swept and lined with trees, and people lived a good life in peace.

The
Lame
Prince

NOW THAT DAVID was king he sought to do justice in the land. One day he asked his advisors if there might still be any one alive from King Saul's family. It was found that a certain servant of the king had survived; from this man David learned that Mephibosheth, the son of Jonathan, was also among the living.

David remembered his pledge to Jonathan that their children would live in peace, and he hurriedly sent for the young prince.

"Mephibosheth," cried David when he saw him.

With great difficulty—because he was crippled—the boy knelt before his king, and, lifting his eyes, he said:

"When I was a baby, my father Jonathan was killed in the war. My nurse, hearing of this, became alarmed and rushed from the palace with me in her arms. She was so frightened that she fell, and I was injured. That is why I am lame. However, we eventually escaped. I lived across the Jordan for many years until I heard that you were king. Now I have come to pay my respects and pledge my allegiance."

David was overcome with joy. He took the boy in his arms and declared:

"So long as I live, you shall be safe and happy, for you are the son of my dearest friend."

And so it was that Mephibosheth lived in the palace all his days as a trusted friend and advisor to the king.

David and Bathsheba

DAVID NEVER FALTERED in his duties as king. He loved God and followed the commandments. But, unfortunately he often made mistakes in the conduct of his personal life. Perhaps he thought that a king should have certain privileges denied to other men.

Such an idea must have been responsible for his attitude toward Bathsheba, a beautiful woman who lived in a house near the palace.

One evening, David was strolling on his balcony, when he happened to see Bathsheba in her garden. He fell in love with her at once, and inquired who she was.

To his surprise, he learned that she was married to Uriah, a captain in his armies. David had a disgraceful plan. He ordered Uriah to the front lines of a battle being fought against the Ammonites. On the first day, Uriah was killed. Then David promptly married Bathsheba.

Several people were unhappy about this marriage, including the prophet Nathan, who asked permission to see the king; he had a story to tell.

"There was a rich man," said Nathan, "with many sheep and goats. Next door to him lived a poor man who had one little lamb, which he kept as a pet and loved like a child. The rich man held a feast one day and invited many guests. Instead of killing his own sheep for the table, the rich man killed his neighbor's lamb, and served it for supper. What do you think of that, my king?"

David was angry indeed.

"What a greedy scoundrel!" he exclaimed. "Bring him here, and we will punish him!"

"You are that man!" cried Nathan. "You stole the wife of Uriah and saw to it that he was killed in battle. You, the king, acted like the rich man who stole the lamb; and, for this, God will punish you!"

Now David realized the evil of his crime. He prayed to God for forgiveness. But prayer was not enough.

Soon after, a son was born to David and Bathsheba and they loved him very much. Then, one day, as a part of David's punishment, the child grew sick and died.

But God is merciful, and, a few years later, another son was born. The happy parents named him Solomon, which means "man of peace." Solomon was destined to become the king of Israel after David.

BESIDES SOLOMON, David had many other sons, including Amnon and Absalom. Amnon was the oldest and therefore he believed that he should become the king. But Absalom had plans of his own.

Absalom was a shrewd, clever man—the handsomest in Israel. His glossy hair was exceedingly long, and he never cut it. Seated before his mirror, combing his famous long black hair, he would say to himself:

"I am handsomer than any other man in the land—and more intelligent. I deserve to be king, and I *will* be king, even if it means killing my own father and my brother Amnon."

Absalom was determined to destroy all who stood in his way. So he prepared a feast and invited his brother Amnon to attend. The deceitful Absalom told his soldiers to draw their swords on Amnon when he drank too much. And so he was slain as Absalom commanded.

Absalom ran away after this crime. David was, of course, enraged; and yet he wondered:

"Did I bring this on myself? Are all these troubles part of God's revenge for Uriah, the man I sent to his death?"

Thus believing himself partly responsible for Absalom's crime, David eventually permitted him to return to Jerusalem. But for two years he would not allow Absalom in his presence.

For his part, Absalom pretended to repent. His real plan was to build an army with which to attack the king and take the throne. For this purpose, he began plotting and scheming with court officials who hated David.

He was clever at this game. Every day, he stood at the entrance to the palace in Jerusalem and stopped the people who were on their way to visit the king.

"Whatever you ask him for," said Absalom, "I would give you double, if I were the king."

And the foolish people believed him and began to speak well of his plan to take the throne.

Absalom then asked David for permission to go to Hebron to offer a sacrifice. When he was in Hebron, however, he began to build the military force with which to overthrow the king.

"One day, you will hear a trumpet announce that I am king," he said. "Then we shall march on Jerusalem and take the throne."

Absalom's Conspiracy

How unbearable it was for David to know that his very own son was plotting against him. He realized again that God was punishing him for his earlier crimes, and he tried to repent.

But, one day, his chief minister Ahithophel joined the forces of Absalom. This treachery made David weep, and he called together his faithful men, and said:

"Let us leave Jerusalem. Absalom's forces are very strong, and he may march upon us at any hour."

And so the faithful followed their king out of the city, taking only their belongings and weapons.

One of the men who followed David was the wise priest Hushai, the new chief minister. When David saw him he said:

"Hushai, return to Jerusalem and pretend to be loyal to my son. In this way we may learn of his treachery."

Hushai agreed and went to Absalom.

"I am preparing a large army to attack the king," said the prince, "and I have many followers, as you can see."

"Indeed!" Hushai replied, and thought to himself, "Oh, how many treacherous people there are in the land."

Over and over again, the king learned that the men he had trusted were turning against him. His faithful supporters were angry, but the king was wise.

"My own son Absalom is trying to kill me," he said. "Why should I feel any worse because some stranger wishes to do the same?"

After David left Jerusalem, Absalom quickly entered the city. There he set himself up as king. Ahithophel was his chief advisor.

"Attack now!" the advisor said. "You can do it with twelve thousand men, for the king is weak."

Hushai, on the other hand, wished to delay Absalom and thereby give David time to raise a strong army. So he went to the prince and said,

"Wait a few days. Allow your men to refresh themselves, and then attack. David will be fooled by the delay and will come out of hiding."

Absalom believed in Hushai, and he agreed. Ahithophel was so offended that he hanged himself in shame.

Meanwhile, David prepared his armies. As his captain Joab was about to leave, he said to him:

"Avenge my honor and save my throne—but please deal gently with my son Absalom. Do not kill him, for I love him in spite of his treachery."

Joab agreed, and set off for war.

The king's troops were victorious, for the Lord was with them.

When the battle turned against him, Absalom fled. He leaped onto his horse and raced out into the forest. His long black hair, of which he was so proud, was now his undoing. As he galloped under a low-hanging tree, it caught in the branches. The horse kept on running, leaving the prince hanging by the hair. Soon Joab came upon the scene. Seeing his enemy thus defenseless, he joyfully stabbed him to death.

Across the river, David waited for news. In the early light of the dawn, he saw messengers running toward him from two directions. The first arrived and announced:

"We have won and the throne is safe!"

"And what of Absalom?" David asked. But the messenger had no further news.

"Let the other man tell you," he said.

"What of Absalom?" David said again, and the second messenger replied:

"May all the enemies of David be just as dead!"

Thus did David learn of his son's death, and he wept and cried out in grief:

"O my son Absalom! My son, my son Absalom!
Would God I had died for thee, O Absalom,
my son, my son!"

Then he went to the nearest building, and locked himself away from everyone.

Joab followed him and said:

"It seems you love your enemies and you hate your friends! I saved your life today, but Absalom tried to kill you. I can see that if Absalom had lived today and all of us who love you had died, you would have been perfectly happy. Go thank your army, or you will have neither kingdom nor friends."

David knew that Joab was right. He returned to Jerusalem and stood before his palace, so that he could thank each faithful man and forgive those who had briefly turned against him.

THE FIRST BOOK OF KINGS

(also known as the Third Book of Kings)

The Story of Solomon, the Wise and Splendid King; of the Divided Kingdom; of Ahab and the Wicked Jezebel; of Elijah, God's Mighty Prophet.

David Names His Successor

THE THRONE WAS SAFE, and David ruled in glory. For many years, he encouraged the growth of Israel. Prosperity and happiness ruled in the land. During this time, David called upon his captains to take a count of his armies, so that he might know their strength. By doing this, he displeased the Lord, for he showed too much dependence upon soldiers and not enough upon faith. There followed an epidemic in Israel, and David realized his mistake. He built an altar to God, and promised never again to rely on soldiers and spears for the glory of Israel.

Aside from this one difficulty, David was happy and was beloved by God.

Then, after many years, David knew that he was about to die. As soon as the news spread, there was trouble in the kingdom, and everyone asked:

"Who is to be David's successor?"

The Lord wished Solomon to be king of Israel after David. But Solomon had a younger brother, named Adonijah, who was very much like Absalom in many ways. He wanted to be king, and was willing to risk civil war in order to achieve his goal.

Bathsheba, Solomon's mother, remembered God's promise that her son was to rule. She went to David and said to him:

"There is talk that Adonijah will be king after you. But you have promised me that it will be our son Solomon. Therefore, I beg of you, do something before it is too late."

Her advice was sound, for, at that very moment, Adonijah was preparing a splendid feast, to which he had invited all the important people of the palace. It was his plan to make himself king at this dinner.

Joab, the captain, and other conspirators joined Adonijah in this celebration, and acted as though King David had already died.

But David was still very much alive and still very wise. He called the prophet Nathan and said:

"There is one way for me to make sure that my son Solomon rules when I am dead, and that is to crown him king *now*, while I am living. Therefore, Nathan, take Solomon to the Tabernacle and anoint him. Then place my crown on his head and let him sit on my throne. When this is done, send the trumpeters through the city to announce the news that Solomon is king. Thus will I protect my kingdom."

Nathan immediately obeyed, and led the young prince Solomon to his anointing.

Meanwhile, everyone at Adonijah's feast was having a wonderful time in expectation of victory. Suddenly, from the street below came the cry:

"God save King Solomon! Solomon is king!"

Adonijah was alarmed. He sent a messenger into the streets to find out what had happened. The messenger breathlessly returned.

"Solomon has been named king by David himself!" he cried. "He sits on the throne of Israel!"

Hearing this news, Adonijah rushed to the Tabernacle for safety.

But Solomon was kind and forgiving. He promised not to punish Adonijah or his followers so long as they lived in peace.

At first, Adonijah obeyed his king. But, after a while, he got ambitious again and tried to overthrow Solomon. This time, he was punished by death.

Solomon did not like this violence, but it was God's will that he be king. David knew this, and was content to see his son on the throne even while he himself was still alive.

Then, one peaceful day, King David closed his eyes for the last time. It had been fifty years and more since he had killed the giant Goliath and had become the rival of Saul and the friend of Jonathan. Now David slept with his fathers; and the people knew that a great man had lived among them and brought them greatness and peace.

SOLOMON WAS NOW KING in his own right. Young and courageous, he understood the great responsibility that had fallen upon his shoulders. He often prayed to God for guidance.

One night, he had a wonderful dream in which God appeared before him.

Solomon, the Wonderful King

"Ask me for anything and I will grant it," said the Lord, "for I wish you to be a very great king."

In his dream Solomon replied:

"I am young and inexperienced. The people look to me for leadership and strength. Therefore, dear Lord, I ask you to grant me only one gift, which I place above all others. Grant me wisdom."

God was pleased with this request, and promised Solomon long life, great wealth, and infinite wisdom.

Solomon was inspired. He set about his daily work with the knowledge that God was beside him. One day, he was put to a severe test of his wisdom.

It was the custom for people to appear before the king with their problems. On this occasion, two young women entered Solomon's chamber, accompanied by a soldier who carried a tiny baby in his arms.

"O mighty king," the soldier said, "both of these women claim to be the mother of this child. Neither can prove her claim, so they wish you to decide."

Solomon questioned each woman carefully. The first told him that she lived in the same house with the other woman, whose baby had recently died. That night, she continued, her neighbor took her child and left the dead baby in his cradle. That was one side of the story. The other woman insisted that she was the rightful mother.

"Her son is dead," she cried, "and my son is living!"

Solomon was perplexed. He prayed to God for wisdom and said:

"Bring a sword. Take the baby and cut him in two. Then each woman may have an equal part."

Upon hearing this, one of the women ran forward and threw herself before the king, crying:

"No! no! don't do that! Let the other woman have the baby, but he must not die!"

Solomon rose from his throne.

"This is the real mother," he said, pointing to the woman on the floor. "She would rather give up her child than see him die, and so she may have her baby."

180

The soldier immediately gave the child to his rightful mother. Everyone present knew that Solomon was in truth a wise, courageous king.

Indeed, no man knew more about nature than Solomon. He could name all the plants that grew in Israel. Like David, his father, he wrote beautiful poetry. He also fashioned clever proverbs. Some of his sayings are as famous today as when he uttered them. For example, he said:

A good name is better than great riches . . . The wicked flee when no man pursueth . . . He that spares the rod, spoils the child . . . Pride goeth before a fall.

These sayings, and many more, were uttered by King Solomon nearly 3,000 years ago.

The
Temple
of
Jerusalem

UNQUESTIONABLY, Solomon's greatest work was the Holy Temple that he built to God in Jerusalem. For many years, while David was still alive, plans had been drawn for such a building. But David did not wish to begin the project while he was still at war. So it was delayed until Solomon became king. As a man of peace, he was fit to revive God's sacred work.

Hundreds of years before, Moses had built the Tabernacle in the desert. It was beautiful and holy, but not permanent. Now, a permanent building dedicated to God's service would stand in the middle of Jerusalem. Solomon unfolded the plans and gave instructions.

"The Temple will stand on Mount Moriah," he said. "It will be made of stone on the outside, and on the inside lined with wood, all of which will be covered with pure gold leaf. The Holy Ark will stand by itself in a special room, and the altars and candelabra will be made of the finest bronze in Israel.

"From Lebanon," Solomon continued, "we shall bring precious cedar wood, and from the mountains of Galilee we shall carve the great blocks of stone that will encase our Temple. These stones shall be fitted together without the use of nails or cement, for God's Temple must be perfect and unblemished. Thus will all the world know His greatness and our devotion."

For seven years, thousands of laborers paved the courtyards and carved the pillars and wove the fabrics that adorned the Temple. Then the Holy Ark, of solid gold, was placed in its special sacred room, the Holy of Holies, which only the priests and the king might enter. Before the door of this room hung a huge veil, or curtain, of blue and crimson thread; and beautiful angels and flowers, carved of ivory and gold, ornamented the walls and ceilings.

Finally, on the day that the Temple was finished, thousands of people gathered in the courtyard before the huge bronze doors. There Solomon appeared, in all his finery, with the priests and leaders of the kingdom.

"We have come to dedicate this Temple to God!" announced the king. "May we always be worthy of God's blessing.

"But, if we sin," he continued, "may we then suffer His punishment. May we suffer if we turn to other gods and worship them; may our nation be defeated in war if we break the commandments given to us by our fathers. Let only the righteous and the faithful prosper and be at peace."

Then Solomon offered a sacrifice to God; and the sacred flame sprang up on the altar as in the days of the Tabernacle. The people knew that God was with them, and they rejoiced. Indeed, the Lord was very pleased with the magnificent Temple, and He descended in a brilliant cloud to fill the building with His glory.

WITH THE TEMPLE FINISHED, King Solomon turned to other tasks. He made Jerusalem the most marvelous city in the world, and his fame spread to many countries.

Far away, in the land of Sheba, the queen heard of Solomon and the glory of Jerusalem.

"I wonder," she said, "is it possible for a man to be as wise and rich as Solomon is said to be? I must go to Jerusalem and see for myself."

She set up a caravan of many camels, and ordered her servants to prepare many expensive gifts for Solomon. Then she crossed the desert toward Israel.

King Solomon was happy to welcome such a beautiful and famous visitor as the Queen of Sheba, and a royal reception was held. Everyone was dressed in gorgeous costumes. The banquet table was set with hundreds of delicious dishes served upon golden plates and eaten with golden spoons. Musicians played their instruments; beautiful slaves danced upon the marble floors; and great bouquets of flowers filled every corner of the palace.

When the dinner was over, the Queen of Sheba presented Solomon with her gifts, including treasures of gold and silver, fine spices and perfumes, rich thick velvets and shiny brocades—all the finest goods of Sheba. In turn Solomon gave his guest cedar chests ornamented with gold, strands of pearls, peacocks, and fine Arabian horses—indeed, all the best of Israel.

But the queen had not come for gifts alone. She wanted to test Solomon's wisdom and his faith in God. For hours they talked of many things, and, finally, she said:

"I had heard how wise you were, but I really couldn't believe it. Now I see that it is true. Every question I've asked you have answered, and every difficult idea you have explained. Your people are fortunate indeed to have such a king." Solomon was very flattered.

For years people talked about the visit of the Queen of Sheba and the wonderful gifts that had been exchanged.

AS SOLOMON GREW OLDER, he took more and more responsibility to himself, and, sometimes, he forgot the Lord. For example, he kept

Plate 46. SOLOMON AND THE QUEEN OF SHEBA,
by Konrad Witz (Swiss, about 1400–about 1446), Deutsches Museum, Berlin.

Plate 46. SOLOMON AND THE QUEEN OF SHEBA,
by Konrad Witz (Swiss, about 1400–about 1446), Deutsches Museum, Berlin.

peace with foreign kings by marrying their daughters. In those days, a wealthy man could have many wives—indeed Solomon married over seven hundred princesses, who all lived in the palace at Jerusalem. Most of these wives did not believe in the one true God and worshiped forbidden idols. Solomon allowed them to do so, in order to keep the peace, but God was angry.

"Solomon will be king of Israel as long as he lives," said the Lord, "but his son will only rule a tiny portion of the kingdom, and there will be much hardship in the land. For no man, however wise, can break the commandments of God."

The king ruled many years in peace. But, when he died, trouble arose in the kingdom, and the glory of Solomon vanished in the twinkling of an eye. Indeed, as Solomon himself once said:

"Vanity of vanities, all is vanity."

After King Solomon died, his son Rehoboam became the ruler of Israel. But another man also wanted to be king. His name was Jeroboam, and he had once served in Solomon's palace as an official. One day, an old prophet told him that he might be king if he would promise to obey the Lord.

"Solomon's son will lose his kingdom," the prophet said, "because his father has allowed idol worshipers in the palace. One of the tribes will remain loyal to Rehoboam; the others will follow you. Therefore, hide in Egypt until all is well; then return, and go to Shechem."

Rehoboam had heard rumors of trouble, but he was not concerned. Instead, he went to the city of Shechem to be crowned. As he was resting in his tent, a group of men approached him. They represented the ten tribes of northern Israel.

"Your father Solomon was a splendid king," they said. "But, in order to build the Temple and his palace, he had to tax the people very heavily. We want to know whether you plan to burden us with the same taxes and laws."

Rehoboam shrugged his shoulders.

"Give me three days to think about it," he replied.

For the next three days Rehoboam consulted with his advisors. The older and wiser men told him to lower the heavy taxes that his father had imposed and urged him to treat the poor people with kindness. He listened to their advice, but he did not seem impressed.

Instead, he turned to a group of his young friends and asked for their opinions.

"Increase the taxes," they told him. "This way we can all have more money for new clothing and fine horses. Tell the people that you will put a heavier burden upon them than your father did."

Rehoboam liked these suggestions. When the three days were up, he informed the men of Israel that he had no intentions of relieving their burdens.

"In fact," he said, "I plan to be very strict; worse than my father was. He beat you with whips, I will beat you with scorpions."

Hearing this, the men of Israel returned to their tents and called upon Jeroboam to become their new king. The tribes of Israel approved. They made Shechem their capital city, and broke all ties with Jerusalem. Only the tribe of Judah remained loyal to Rehoboam. They made him king of the southern portion of the land, which they called the new kingdom of Judah.

When he realized that he had lost much of his power, Rehoboam was very angry. He sent messengers into Jeroboam's kingdom to collect taxes. The independent people of Israel wouldn't hear of this, and stoned the messenger to death. Fearfully, Rehoboam hid himself behind the fortress walls of Jerusalem.

"We will form an army," he said, "and attack these traitors. Then the country will be reunited with me as king."

A wise prophet named Shemaiah heard about this plan and approached the throne.

"O mighty king," the prophet said, "God has decreed that this nation be split in two, with two kings forever. Nothing you do can change it—and you must not try." Rehoboam sadly obeyed.

Thus, for hundreds of years the Promised Land was divided into Israel in the north and Judah in the south. Each country had its own king and its own prophets—and there was hardship in the land.

*Idol
Worship
Replaces
the Worship
of God*

THE TWO KINGS were both evil men. Jeroboam was afraid that his people might stay in Judah when they went to visit the sacred Temple in Jerusalem, so he built two big temples of his own within the boundaries of Israel. These temples were not intended for the one true God, but for idols and statues made of gold. Jeroboam himself worshiped a calf of gold, and, before long, almost all Israel had forgotten God.

One day, a wise old prophet approached the king of Israel and said:

"Jeroboam, your descendants will not reign in Israel, and a good king named Josiah will eventually take your throne. All your false gods will crumble and split into many pieces. This is to be your punishment."

Jeroboam was very angry. He called his guards and ordered the prophet arrested. But, when he raised his arm, he felt as though it had turned to stone. At the very same moment, all the idols and altars in his temples crumbled into hundreds of pieces and rolled to the floor.

The terrified Jeroboam begged the prophet to forgive him and restore his strength. The prophet, believing that the king had learned his lesson, knelt and prayed to God.

When Jeroboam was able to move again, he invited the prophet to dine with him.

"The Lord has commanded me not to eat until I return home," the old man said. "Therefore, I cannot dine with you."

Jeroboam allowed the prophet to leave. But his heart was evil. He sent a wicked priest ahead who told the old man that God wished him to break his fast. The prophet was suspicious, but he accepted some food. For disobeying the Lord, he was killed by a lion on his way home.

For this treachery, Jeroboam was punished severely. His only son, prince Abijah, became seriously ill. Jeroboam's wife was so worried that she disguised herself and went to the home of another prophet who worshiped the one true God. The wise old man recognized the queen immediately. He told her that her son would die because of his father's sins. When the queen reached home, the child was dead.

In Judah, King Rehoboam also forgot the Lord. He spent large sums of money and enjoyed rich clothing and expensive food. He did not care when idol worshipers set up their statues in the very Temple of God.

The Pharaoh of Egypt realized that Rehoboam was weak, and he sent an army into Jerusalem. Many Judeans were killed and the treasures of the Temple were robbed. Rehoboam fell on his knees and prayed to God. Thus, his own life was saved. But, after the Egyptians had attacked, Jeroboam in the north also sent an army against Jerusalem. There was constant fighting for many years. Finally both Rehoboam and Jeroboam died, and their sons ruled the divided kingdoms.

Asa, Rehoboam's grandson, was a righteous man and worshiped God. When he became king, Judah prospered and was victorious in war. In fact, it seemed that the happiness and prosperity of David's time had at last returned.

But to the north, in Israel, an evil man named Baasha had taken over the throne. He was jealous of Judah's success. Furthermore, many Israelites were crossing the border into the southern kingdom, where life was easier.

Seeing this, Baasha ordered a wall to be built along the border, so that no one could sneak across. King Asa in Judah was very angry. He wanted all the people to return to the Temple of God in Jerusalem, and he knew that Baasha worshiped only idols made of gold.

So Asa called upon the king of Syria to help him by making war upon Baasha, thus causing him to halt his work on the dividing wall. Syria joined Judah, and Baasha's troops were defeated. But God was not pleased with Asa. He sent a prophet to speak to the king.

"You relied upon the king of Syria, not upon God," said the wise old man. "For this you will have trouble and disease."

Soon after, King Asa became crippled, and the kingdom of Judah fought many wars. Baasha meanwhile died in Israel and a new king, Elah, came to the throne. He was killed by a captain, Zimri, who was in turn killed by another captain, Omri.

AHAB, SON OF OMRI, later became king of Israel. Impossible though it may seem, he was worse than all the other kings who ruled before him. His queen, Jezebel, the daughter of a foreign king, was very beautiful, but she was also evil and cruel. First, she built a temple to the false god Baal. Then she ordered all the true priests of Israel to be slaughtered. Ahab was too busy forcing the people to give him their money to realize that Jezebel was the actual ruler of his kingdom.

One day, a strange-looking man appeared at the palace. His hair was very long, and white as chalk. His eyes were fiery and piercing. His clothes were torn.

"Who is this man?" the king wondered.

"I am Elijah, a prophet of God!" the old man said sternly. "I have come to warn you that Israel will be punished for your wickedness. Until I say so—by God's command—there will be no rain throughout this country and all the people will starve!"

Then Elijah lifted his eyes to God, and hurriedly left the king's chamber.

At first, Ahab was not concerned; all seemed well and prosperous in Israel. But, after a while, the prophecy came true. No rain fell on Israel, and the crops dried up. Indeed, a very severe famine set in. Ahab was enraged.

"Find that old prophet and bring him to me at once!" he ordered; and hundreds of soldiers went out into the countryside looking for Elijah.

Fortunately God had hidden His prophet in a wild and rugged place where only a few ravens dwelled. Here Elijah drank the fresh water of a tiny brook and ate food brought to him by the birds. But the shortage of rain was very great, and, soon, even Elijah's little brook dried up, and there was no more water. God instructed His prophet to head toward the city of Zarephath, where a widow would help him.

WHEN ELIJAH ARRIVED in the small village, he saw an elderly widow gathering firewood. He approached the woman and said to her,

Ahab and Jezebel

The Widow of Zarephath

189

"Can you help me find some water and food? I am very hungry."

The woman smiled and replied:

"I can give you a bit of water, though it is scarce. But I have only a tiny cup of flour and half an ounce of oil—just enough to bake some bread for me and my son."

Elijah said:

"Bake your bread; there will be enough."

And, true to his words, the widow found that there was enough bread for her son, for herself, and also for Elijah. As long as the famine lasted, there was enough flour and oil.

One day, sorrow befell the widow of Zarephath.

"Elijah! Elijah!" she called, as she came running from her house. "My son has taken ill! I think he is dying!"

Elijah ran to help the child, but it was too late. The widow was beside herself with grief, and begged Elijah for comfort.

The prophet lifted the boy and carried him to his chamber upstairs. There he knelt and prayed, while he tried to breathe life back into the widow's son.

The poor woman waited for hours alone in her kitchen. At daybreak, she suddenly saw Elijah standing at the door with her child in his arms—and the child was alive!

"You are truly a man of God!" the widow exclaimed, and she fell on her knees, joyously embracing her son.

Elijah Holds a Contest

THE FAMINE IN ISRAEL grew worse, and King Ahab was deeply concerned. He called his servant Obadiah, and the two went out looking for water in the desert. As Obadiah approached a desolate place, he saw Elijah kneeling in prayer. Obadiah, a God-fearing man, urged the prophet to flee, for Ahab had ordered his soldiers to kill him on sight. But Elijah was brave.

"I wish to see the king," he said. "Bring him to me."

"I am afraid," Obadiah cried. "If the king thinks I am your friend, he will surely kill me, too."

Elijah was firm, and, finally, Obadiah obeyed.

After a few hours, King Ahab and his soldiers approached the holy man.

"You troublemaker!" the king exclaimed. "You are responsible for this famine! I ought to put you to death on the spot."

"No!" said Elijah. "You have made the trouble. Israel is being punished for your crimes and your worship of the false god Baal. Now I will show you and all the people the power of the one true God." And Elijah ordered the king to assemble the people at Mount Carmel so that they might witness a contest between him and the priests of Baal.

The next day, thousands of people stood at the mountain as Elijah climbed to the top.

"You are all worshiping a false god!" the prophet announced, "and I shall prove it! Let the priests of Baal assemble here and offer sacrifices to their god. I shall offer sacrifices to mine. Then we shall see which altar is consumed by holy fire."

The people agreed, and the priests of Baal ascended the mountain alongside Elijah. There they built an altar to Baal and stacked it with wood and charcoal. Then they cut up a bullock and placed it on the grate. Elijah made an altar of stone. He also put wood, charcoal, and a fresh-killed bullock on his altar. Then he said,

"There are over four hundred priests of Baal—and I am one man alone in the service of God. Therefore, let the priests go first. Let them prove that their god is more powerful than mine."

And so the priests of Baal knelt and lifted their arms to the statue of Baal.

"Send us your fire to consume the sacrifice," they called.

But nothing happened. They tried again. Again there was no response. They danced, sang, and performed many strange motions, which they believed would achieve success. Elijah watched in amusement.

"Try harder," he said. "Maybe Baal is asleep, or perhaps he has gone on a trip and cannot hear you."

Over and over, the priests of Baal prayed and danced before their god, but no fire came from heaven to consume their sacrifice.

Finally, it was dark, and Elijah was impatient.

"Now it is my turn," he cried. "Bring me water. I shall drench my altar and soak the fuel so that no ordinary fire could possibly burn. And, yet, I say to you, God will provide a fire to consume my sacrifice."

And the soldiers poured water over Elijah's altar, over the wood, and over the bullock. Then the prophet raised his eyes to heaven, and prayed in a loud, clear voice,

"God of Abraham, Isaac, and Jacob, send Your holy fire to consume the sacrifice."

And, in that very instant, a flash of flame shot from the sky and burned up the wood and the coal and the bullock on Elijah's altar. The people fell to their knees in praise of God. So great was their repentance that they executed all the priests of Baal and tore down the statues of the sinful idol.

Ahab was amazed beyond words. He feared Elijah, and yet he also

Plate 48. ELIJAH AND THE WIDOW OF ZAREPHATH,
by Bernardo Strozzi (Italian, 1581–1644), Kunsthistorisches Museum, Vienna.

feared his wife Jezebel. Baal had been her god, and she permitted no other religion in Israel.

"I have seen the sacred fire," said the king to Elijah, "but the famine has not ended. The people will never believe in your God until they can eat."

Elijah spoke in an angry voice:

"Go back to your palace," he said. "There will be rain before daybreak."

Then Elijah climbed higher upon Mount Carmel with only one servant by his side. There he prayed for rain. When morning dawned he asked the servant to look toward the horizon, for Elijah was old and his eyes were weak.

"What do you see?" asked the prophet.

At first the servant saw nothing but the clear blue sky. Then suddenly, far off in the distance, a tiny cloud—no bigger than a man's fist—appeared on the horizon. Elijah rejoiced. From this small cloud a great rainstorm would grow, and the crops would thrive in Israel. And so it happened that day, and great torrents of rain fell on the land and the people praised God.

Jezebel's Anger

QUEEN JEZEBEL was enraged.

"My priests are dead!" she cried. "My precious god Baal is destroyed! I must have revenge on Elijah!"

Throughout the countryside, the word went forth—Jezebel means to kill Elijah. When the prophet heard of the threat, he decided that it would be best to leave the country. He took great care in his escape, for he did not want Jezebel's soldiers to follow him and bring harm to innocent people. He traveled by night, over rugged cliffs and through narrow valleys.

Finally, he arrived in Beersheba, the southernmost city of Judah. There he fell exhausted beneath a juniper tree.

While he was sleeping, an angel of God descended and stood by his side. When the prophet awoke he found food and water nearby. From this meal, he was able to gain enough strength to last for forty days. Then he climbed Mount Horeb, where Moses had died, and hid in a cave.

After a few days, Elijah grew discouraged. He thought about the wickedness of Ahab and Jezebel, and the sins of Israel.

"It is better to die," he said. "Even God's great power does not win respect."

Suddenly, he heard a rumbling in the earth, and he knew that God was present.

"Speak to me, Lord!" cried Elijah. "Give me encouragement."

And a loud wind blew across the sky.

"Was this the voice of God?" the prophet wondered. "Is it so fierce and frightening?"

Then all at once, the noise and the wind disappeared. There was not a sound, not even the fluttering of a leaf in the gentlest breeze. In this moment of perfect silence, a still, small voice was heard. Elijah knew that this was the voice of God. Never had he heard anything so beautiful.

Wrapping his mantle, or cloak, around him, he stood before the cave as God had instructed him.

"Return to Israel," said the Lord. "Many people there believe in Me, and they need your help. Along the way, you will find a young man named Elisha. Bring him to Israel, for some day he will take your place as My prophet. Be not afraid."

Elijah's heart was filled with courage as he returned to Israel. Along the way he met Elisha, who was tilling the soil. Placing his mantle on the young man's shoulders, Elijah said,

"Come with me. We shall spread the name of God throughout the land."

Ahab the Coward

IN SYRIA, King Benhadad prepared for war.

"We will attack Israel," he said. "We will enslave the people and take their gold. On top of this, we will tell them we're coming. Ahab, the coward, will be afraid and his army will run away."

Benhadad was right. When Ahab heard his threat, he became so frightened that he prepared to surrender even before the fight began. But a wise old prophet came to him and demanded courage in the name of God. He also promised that God would bring victory if Ahab obeyed.

OPPOSITE: Plate 49. ELIJAH IN THE DESERT, by Dieric Bouts (Flemish, about 1415–1475), Church of Saint Pierre, Louvain, Belgium.

That night, when Benhadad's troops were asleep after a feast, Ahab and a small army stole into their camp, attacked the sleeping men and killed their leaders.

Only Benhadad escaped. One year later, he assembled his armies again and headed toward Samaria, a chief city of Ahab's kingdom.

Once again God willed Ahab's victory; and all the Syrians fled leaving Benhadad behind. He was afraid to return home—and yet he knew he could not stay in Israel.

"Yes, you can," said one of his men. "Ahab will forgive you if you humble yourself."

So Benhadad dressed in torn clothing and went to Ahab to beg for mercy. Ahab complied. When the prophet heard of this meeting between Ahab and Benhadad, he approached his king and asked:

"If a soldier caught an enemy and let him escape, what would you do?"

And Ahab replied that he would punish the soldier.

"Exactly!" the prophet said. "That is why you will be punished, for Benhadad was an enemy of God, and you let him escape!"

Jezebel's Crime

AHAB TRIED to forget his troubles. He knew that he was a wicked king and he feared God's punishment—but he would not repent. Instead, he built himself a beautiful summer house in Jezreel, which he decorated with costly furniture.

Just beyond the gardens of this house was a fine vineyard that belonged to a man named Naboth. This vineyard was famous throughout the land for its luscious grapes and sparkling wine. Ahab wanted it for himself.

One day he approached Naboth, and said:

"I am your king, and I would like to have your vineyard for my own. How much do you want for it?"

Naboth was very polite. He informed the king that the vineyard had belonged to his family for generations, and that he had no wish ever to sell. Ahab was impatient, and offered his neighbor a very high price.

"I am sorry," Naboth replied. "The vineyard is my prized possession, my heritage. I cannot accept your offer."

Ahab returned to his palace angered beyond words.

Queen Jezebel saw that her husband was upset. He would not eat or sleep; instead, he sat on his throne for hours clenching his fists and mumbling:

"The vineyard. I want the vineyard."

Finally, Jezebel went up to him and asked what was wrong.

He told her about the beautiful vineyard and how Naboth refused to sell. Jezebel smiled, and urged her husband to forget his cares; she would obtain the prize.

Then Jezebel set out to commit a terrible crime. First, she got some evil men to lie about Naboth. Then she had Naboth brought to trial on false charges of blasphemy, and the people shouted for his death. In due time, as planned, he was executed, and the vineyard became the property of Ahab.

"I have obtained the vineyard," said Jezebel to the king. "Let us go and enjoy our new possession."

That evening the evil pair went strolling in the vineyard. Suddenly, they saw a strange figure lurking in the shadows.

"Who's there?" cried the king. "Come forward this instant!" Elijah the prophet stepped forth.

"You have done evil in the sight of the Lord," the old man said.

"You have stolen this vineyard and put an innocent man to death. For this, Ahab will perish in battle. Jezebel will be killed and her body thrown into the streets for the dogs to tear. That is God's commandment."

Ahab trembled with fear, but Jezebel was scornful, for she did not believe in the one true God.

However, a few months later, King Benhadad of Syria attacked Israel for the third time. In this battle, Ahab was killed by an arrow that went right through his heart. The first part of God's punishment had come true.

THE SECOND BOOK OF KINGS

(also known as the Fourth Book of Kings)

The Stories of Elisha's Miracles; of Jehu, Joash, and Other Kings; of Wars and Idol Worship.

Elijah's Miraculous Ending

QUEEN JEZEBEL ruled the country, even though her son Ahaziah was the actual king. Ahaziah was bedridden, having been badly hurt in a fall.

"Ask the god Baalzebub whether I shall recover," he said to his priests. "I am in great pain." And they left him to pray to the idol.

But Elijah stood on the road before the palace and he stopped the priests as they came his way.

"Why waste your time praying to a false idol?" he said. "Is there no true God in Israel? Pray to Him or Ahaziah will never get well and Jezebel will be thrown to the dogs, as I have already prophesied."

When she heard about this, Jezebel laughed in scorn. But, soon after, Ahaziah died, as Elijah had predicted, and his wicked brother Jehoram came to the throne.

By now Elijah was very old, and his time was drawing near. One day he set out, with Elisha, to bid farewell to his many friends. The two men traveled a great distance, and, finally, came to the river Jordan.

"I must go to the far shore," Elijah said. "There God will call me to heaven."

"But how will you cross the river?" Elisha asked.

Elijah smiled and dipped the hem of his mantle into the river. At that instant, the waters parted, as they had for Moses and Joshua. Elijah then turned to his young friend, and said:

"Leave me now, and return to Israel to preach the word of God."

But Elisha would not bid his beloved master farewell.

"Let me go with you!" he cried. Elijah was deeply moved. Taking the young man's arm, he led him across the Jordan on the dry path provided by God.

When they reached the far shore, Elijah asked:

"What can I do for you, Elisha, before I go?"

And his friend replied:

"Fill my soul with the Spirit of God, so that I may be like you."

But Elijah could not fulfill this wish, for it was a power that only God possessed. He said however:

"If God permits you to see my departure, you will know He has filled your soul with His heavenly Spirit."

Then Elijah lifted his eyes to God. At that instant, a flaming chariot, drawn by two shining horses, descended from the sky. Elijah embraced his friend, entered the fiery chariot, and, in a flash, was taken straightaway to heaven.

Plate 50. THE ASCENSION OF ELIJAH, by Peter Paul Rubens (Flemish, 1577–1640), Private Collection.

Elisha
and the
Mantle of
Elijah

ELISHA HAD BEEN PERMITTED to witness the miracle, and he fell to his knees calling:

"Father, my father. Now I must do your work."

Then he picked up Elijah's mantle and carried it to the Jordan. As his master had done, he dipped the hem into the sea, and the waters parted again. On the other shore, several pupils of the prophet waited.

"What has happened to Elijah?" they asked.

And Elisha replied that his master had gone to heaven. The pupils were not convinced. For three days, they searched in the forests for the vanished prophet. Finally, they had to admit that the beloved Elijah was no longer among the living.

Meanwhile, Elisha's fame had spread throughout the land. In Jericho, the city leaders came to him.

"We have a serious problem!" they said. "Our city is very fair, but the water is bad to drink, and many people become ill because of it. Will you help us?"

Elisha prayed to God and afterward commanded the people to bring him a box of salt. Then he threw the salt into the dirty waters. From that moment on, every drop was safe to drink.

Because Elisha had the power to perform God's miracles, many poor and deserving people were helped.

For example, one day the prophet heard that a poor widow was in danger of losing her home and that men to whom she owed money had taken her two small sons to sell as slaves. Elisha went to her and learned that her husband had left many debts when he died and that she could not pay them.

Elisha prayed to God, and then asked her:

"Is there anything in your cupboard?"

The woman replied that she only had a small cup of oil.

"That is enough," Elisha said. "Take all the empty jars you can find and pour oil from your cup into the jars until all are full."

The widow did not understand how she could fill many empty cups with such a tiny bit of oil. But she had faith and proceeded to obey the prophet.

To her amazement, she found that she could pour and pour all the oil she wanted from her little cup—and it never ran dry. So long as there was an empty jar to be filled, the oil kept flowing. What a miracle! By the end of the day, the poor widow had over fifty jars of precious oil. In those days, oil was like money. Thus, the poor woman could pay her debts and bring her sons home in safety. This was just one of the miracles that God enabled Elisha to perform.

Later, Elisha was staying in the town of Shunem. A kindly couple had furnished a room for him, so that he would be comfortable during his visit. God rewarded them by granting a son, even though they were very old. Years later, misfortune struck, and the little boy died. Tearfully, the mother ran to Elisha and begged him to help her son. Like Elijah before him, Elisha was able to revive the child and spare his parents much sorrow and grief.

All over Israel, Elisha journeyed, helping people and preaching the word of God. In the town of Gilgal, he saved the lives of some religious men who had accidentally taken poison. Later, he was able to feed many poor people with just a few loaves of bread. At another time, he helped a woodsman retrieve an axe that had fallen in the water. This axe was made of iron, and of course it could not float. But, with the help of God, Elisha made it rest upon the waters like a leaf, so that its owner could fetch it easily.

In spite of the miracles of Elisha and the proof of God's might, wars and treachery continued. King Benhadad of Syria invaded Israel again. Jehoram, king of Israel, was so afraid that he called upon Elisha; and the prophet prayed to God. That day, the Syrians were defeated.

When Benhadad learned of Elisha's power, he sent soldiers to capture and slay the prophet. But when they approached Elisha's home, God struck them blind and they could not see. Jehoram's soldiers immediately prepared to kill their enemies, but Elisha was merciful, and allowed the Syrians to live, with their sight restored, and return home.

Jehoram did not approve of this mercy, and he began to hate Elisha. When famine came to the land, he blamed the prophet. Elisha predicted that there would be plenty of food, in due time, for everyone except the unbelievers. Then the Syrians attacked again, and brought their supplies and weapons to a camp near the Jordan river. During the night, God created a terrible storm that sent the soldiers fleeing for their lives. The next day, some poor beggars found the food and weapons that the Syrians had left, and the whole city was able to eat—all except the unbelievers.

Ashamed because of his defeat, King Benhadad lay dying. A servant of his, named Hazael, sought out Elisha and said,

"I have heard you can see into the future. Tell me what will happen to Benhadad?"

And Elisha replied,

"Someone will kill him and then become king. That man will bring sorrow and ruin to Israel."

"Who is the man?" cried Hazael.

And Elisha replied in a solemn voice:

"That man is you!"

Hazael returned to the palace of King Benhadad. The next morning, when he was alone with the ailing monarch, he held a thick cloth over Benhadad's face and killed him. Then Hazael made himself king, and began again the wars against Israel.

Naaman's Sickness

IN SYRIA THERE WAS a famous soldier named Naaman, who had led many of King Benhadad's invasions. He lived quietly in the country with his wife and an Israelite servant girl, whom Naaman treated very kindly.

But sorry days befell the Syrian soldier. He became afflicted with leprosy, a disease in which the skin becomes white and full of sores. Nothing that he did could relieve his condition.

"I know who can help you," the Israeli servant said. "When I was a little girl in Israel, there was a miraculous prophet named Elisha, who could cure any disease. Go to him, and I am sure that he will help."

Naaman's wife agreed, and the soldier was encouraged.

"I shall ask our king for permission to leave the country," he said.

The king of Syria gave Naaman permission, and sent a letter to Jehoram, king of Israel. No mention was made of Elisha. The letter simply read: Please try to cure Naaman, for he is a righteous man.

When Jehoram read this letter, he thought the Syrians were trying to play a trick on him.

"I am no doctor," he said. "This is an excuse for them to start a war."

He told Naaman to return to Syria.

But the king's advisors were wise. They remembered Elisha, and urged Naaman to pay him a visit. The poor sick man went directly to the prophet's home. There he waited in the shadows while a servant approached the house. Leprosy is an ugly disease, and Naaman did not wish to offend Elisha.

"Tell your master to go to the Jordan river," the prophet said. "There he must splash himself seven times with water. Then the leprosy will be gone. But he must remember that his cure comes from God, the one true God of Israel."

When Naaman heard about this proposed cure, he was furious.

"Did I travel all the way from Syria to splash in the Jordan?" he cried. "Aren't the rivers of Syria better than all the waters of Israel?"

But Naaman's servant was wise.

"Master," he said, "if Elisha had given you a difficult cure, you would not have complained. The fact that it is so simple should encourage you."

Naaman finally agreed, and went to the Jordan. He walked into the shallow water and splashed himself seven times. When he had finished and the water had flowed over his body for the seventh time, a miracle happened. All the white spots and sores disappeared, and he was cured!

With tears in his eyes, Naaman fell to his knees on the shore and cried out:

"Hail to the God of Israel. He is the only God of all!"

The Treacherous Servant

CURED AND HAPPY, Naaman went to Elisha's home with many wonderful presents and much silver. He begged the prophet to take these offerings of thanks. But Elisha refused.

"God did this for you, not I," he said. "The only thing I ask is that you respect Him."

Naaman swore that he would worship God and destroy his Syrian idols. Then, gathering a quantity of earth, he said:

"And I will build an altar to God with this soil of Israel."

Naaman then departed with all the presents he had brought from Syria.

Inside Elisha's house there was a servant named Gehazi. As he watched Naaman disappear down the road, he thought to himself:

"All those wonderful presents; how I would love them. Elisha is a fool for refusing them. I would not, if I were he."

Gehazi dreamed about the gold and silver until he could stand it no more and he dashed from the house in order to catch up with Naaman.

"Wait! Wait!" he shouted as he ran along the road—and Naaman pulled the reins of his horse to a halt.

"What is it?" he asked.

"My master Elisha has changed his mind," said the wicked servant. "He has decided to take your presents, as you first offered them."

Naaman was delighted. Generously, he loaded up Gehazi's arms with all the gold and silver that he had brought from Syria. Then he bade the servant good-by, and continued his homeward journey.

Gehazi returned to Elisha's house like a thief. He hid the precious gifts and pretended that he had not left the house.

But Elisha knew the truth, and he approached the treacherous servant and said:

"You have taken Naaman's gifts under false pretense. You wanted riches more than honor. Well, you may have them. But you will also have Naaman's leprosy from this time forth, until you repent your selfish crime."

And, that night, Gehazi was stricken with the frightful disease of which Naaman had been cured only a short time before.

The Death of Jezebel

THOUGH THE EVIL JEZEBEL and her son Jehoram still ruled the land, Elisha knew that God was greatly displeased with them, so he set out to find a new king for Israel.

He chose Jehu, a brave captain in the army. Elisha also sent one of his pupils to anoint Jehu with holy oil, as was the custom.

Newly proclaimed king of Israel, Jehu set out with an army for Jezreel. On the way, soldiers and townspeople joined his troops, for they were tired of Jezebel's wickedness.

Jehoram went out in his chariot and met Jehu. He asked if he came in peace. Jehu answered:

"There will be no peace while your evil mother lives."

Jehoram was afraid and turned to flee, but Jehu drew his bow and sent an arrow through Jehoram's heart. Then Jehu had the body thrown into Naboth's vineyard, which Ahab had stolen years before.

Inside the palace at Jezreel, Jezebel heard what had happened and she awaited the coming of Jehu.

"I will dress in my finest robes," she said to her servants. "Then Jehu will know I am queen."

And so she dressed herself in gold and silver, and then went to the window of her chamber and called down to Jehu:

"I am Jezebel, queen of Israel. Do you come in peace?"

But Jehu would not be fooled by this wicked woman. He called to the servants inside the palace and said:

"If you are on my side, then throw this evil woman out of the window, so that we may trample her beneath our feet. Otherwise, I will spare no one in the palace."

When the servants heard this threat, they rushed upon Jezebel and immediately tossed her out of the window.

Her body remained in the dirt all day. That night a pack of wild dogs devoured it, as Elijah had predicted long ago. Such was the fate of Ahab's evil family.

But there were other sons left in Ahab's family and Jehu wrote them and warned them of his intention to be king. Later, he had them slain, until not a man was left of Ahab's house, as Elijah had once prophesied.

Now Jehu reigned as king. He was brave and strong, but not always righteous, and, after several years, he, too, passed away. A long line of monarchs followed in Israel. Some were good; most were bad. Eventually, God decided to end the kingdom.

IN JUDAH, THERE WAS ALSO trouble and wickedness. Since the days of Rehoboam, the son of Solomon, idol worship and war had ruined the country. Once in a while, a good king appeared, such as Asa, the man who tried to break down the boundary wall built by the Israelites.

His successor Jehoshaphat was also a righteous man. He loved God and tried to restore the Temple. But he made one fatal mistake; he allowed his son to marry Athalia, the daughter of Ahab and Jezebel.

Athalia was as evil as her mother. More than anything else, she wanted to rule over Judah. When her husband died, she had all his children killed. She even murdered her little grandchildren, lest one of them be named ruler of the land. Then, with everyone dead, she assumed the throne and crowned herself queen.

For six years, Athalia ruled with an iron hand, worshiping idols, stealing the people's money, and behaving in a shameless fashion. Little did she know that, hidden in the Temple of God, there was a small boy named Joash, the only living heir to the throne. When he was a baby, a kindly priest named Jehoiada had wrapped him in a blanket and secretly hidden him in the Temple. The priest knew that Athalia would never come there to worship, and that the child would thus be safe from her murderous plans.

For six years, the little boy lived and played unknown to the world. Then, one day, Jehoiada decided to gather many people together in the Temple, so that he could anoint Joash and proclaim him king. He divided his supporters into three groups and assigned them to different places in the Temple, so that they could effectively protect the boy and carry out the coronation. Each group was well armed and bolstered by soldiers who had joined the righteous cause.

At the appointed time, thousands of people filled the streets around the Temple. The queen's soldiers thought that they were simply going there to pray, and paid no attention. But suddenly a great shout was heard throughout the city. "Hail! King Joash! the true king of Judah!"

Athalia was on her balcony when she heard this cry. She rushed to the Temple and pushed her way through the crowd. There at the altar she saw Jehoiada standing with Joash. On the little boy's head was the crown of Judah, and around him stood his protectors.

Queen Athalia screamed in anger:

"This is treason! Stop this treason!"

But no one came forward to do her bidding. Fearfully, she rushed from the Temple into the streets, where a crowd of angry people beat her to death.

From that day on, the seven-year-old Joash was king of Judah. Because he was so young, Jehoiada was actually in charge of all affairs. He was a righteous man who worshiped God, and, as long as he lived, things were peaceful in the land.

But, when the old priest died, Joash, who had become a lazy young man, began to rule in a wicked way. At first, he repaired the Temple of Solomon, which was a righteous act, but soon after he turned to idol worship. As he grew older, he became less interested in the people and in God. Many men were jealous of him, and realized that he was weak without Jehoiada. One day they gathered together and bribed the young king's servants to murder him. So it happened.

His son, Amaziah, became king and slew the men who had murdered his father. Later, Amaziah fought a war with Jehoash, the king of Israel, and was defeated. Many of the treasures of Jerusalem were taken by Jehoash to Israel. The people of Judah grew more and more displeased with Amaziah. He fled from Jerusalem, but he was found and killed.

THE BOOK OF ISAIAH

and Additional Stories from the Second Book of Kings and the Chronicles

The Story of Isaiah, the Prophet; of Hezekiah, the King; of the Fall of Israel; of the Good King Josiah of Judah; and of Nebuchadnezzar, the Assyrian.

AFTER JOASH came several wicked kings. One of them, named Uzziah, sinned greatly and, as a punishment, fell ill with leprosy. Leprosy was such an ugly disease that the king was obliged to live alone in a tower for the rest of his life.

A good man named Jotham became king in Uzziah's place. Though he worshiped God, he found that he was without the power to control the wickedness of the people.

"Dear Lord," he prayed. "Send me help, so that I may do Your bidding."

Help came in the form of a wise and courageous man, Isaiah, the prophet. Isaiah spent his life preaching to the people and warning them of God's great anger. When he was very young, an angel had touched his lips with purity, so that he could speak only the truth. But, sometimes, the truth is frightening, and, when the people heard Isaiah, they were afraid.

"Great enemies will descend upon this land," he would tell them. "They will come here and make us slaves, because we are wicked and sinful. Our beautiful cities will be overgrown with weeds. Our wells will run dry. Even Jerusalem will fall, and the holy Temple will crumble. Believe me, this is the wrath of God."

But no one would believe Isaiah. Instead, the people continued to live selfish and ungodly lives.

Then King Ahaz came to the throne. He was wicked, and would not listen to Isaiah's warnings. Often he fought with his neighbors and joined with the enemies of God. He even went so far as to turn over the precious gold and silver of the Temple to his new-found heathen allies.

The Great Prophet Isaiah

For this crime, God cut short King Ahaz's reign, and he was replaced by a good man named Hezekiah.

By then Jerusalem had become a wicked city, and the Holy Temple was neglected and falling apart. The precious gold and silver had been given away by Ahaz, and the beautiful tapestries and carved wood ceilings were dirty and abused. King Hezekiah was sad to see this sorry condition. He called the best craftsmen in Judah, and ordered them to repair the Temple and make it fit for God.

When the Temple was restored and the city walls were sturdy again, Hezekiah and the priests celebrated with a holy sacrifice. Many people were inspired, and abandoned evil ways. They even joined together for the feast of Passover, which had been forgotten for so many years; at the proper time, hundreds of people came to Jerusalem to celebrate the Exodus from Egypt. Even the people of Israel were invited, and many came. This was to be the last time that the Israelites enjoyed such happiness, for their country was soon to cease existence.

The Fall of Israel

ELISHA WAS STILL ALIVE in Israel. Like Isaiah and other righteous men, he had fought a lifelong battle against wickedness. Now he was sick and weary, and he knew that he was about to die. So he called Jehoash, the king of Israel, to his bedside and said:

"Take your bow and shoot one arrow out of the window. This will be a sign that you will defeat your enemies the Syrians, and they will be utterly consumed.

"Then, in time," the prophet continued, "God will abandon Israel because of all its wickedness and sin."

These were Elisha's last words.

Soon after, true to his prophecy, a great war broke out, and the nation was in turmoil. A wise man named Amos tried to take up the mission of Elisha, but he, too, was ignored. Hosea, another prophet of God, also attempted to preach the way of righteousness. Once again, the people scorned the word of the Lord.

Then, in time, a fierce Assyrian king attacked the land of Israel. He was mighty, and his armies were very strong. Israel, on the other hand,

had become weak with sin and easy living. In a very short time, the Assyrian horsemen overran the countryside and tore down the walls of thirty cities.

The Israelites were in panic. Grabbing their belongings, they began to flee in every direction, weeping and praying, but to no avail. Many were captured and made slaves. Others disappeared or became mixed with the people of Assyria. Eventually, the entire population of Israel dwindled to a mere handful of beggars.

So it was that, after 250 years, the great kingdom of Israel was ended and the words of Amos, the prophet, came true.

"You and your children will die in foreign lands," he had said, "because you have abandoned the way of God."

The Defeat of the Assyrians

THOUGH THE KINGDOM of Judah still remained, war and turmoil filled the land. The good king Hezekiah was, therefore, sorrowful, and he called Isaiah the prophet to his side.

"I have tried to keep peace with Assyria," he said, "but I cannot succeed. No matter how much gold and silver I give the Assyrian king, I know that he will soon attack us."

Isaiah counseled the king to be brave, and trust in the Lord.

In Assyria, King Sennacherib plotted war, as Hezekiah feared. Many times, he had threatened Judah with an invasion, because he wanted the gold and treasure of the Temple. Now he called his generals and said:

"I have heard that the God of Judah is very powerful. We shall see, for tonight 185,000 Assyrian troops will attack Jerusalem with all our force. Go, then, and prepare for war!"

That night, the great Assyrian army began the march on Judah, clad in heavy armor and armed with terrible, destructive weapons.

Behind the walls of Jerusalem, King Hezekiah could see the approaching horde.

"How shall we be saved?" he cried to Isaiah. The prophet replied:

"God will send an avenging angel against the Assyrians, and they will fall back like a man before a burning furnace. All this will happen if we have faith in God."

Below, in the fields, the Assyrians prepared their invasion. Each bowman aimed his bow and arrow. The banners were flying, the chariots were ready, the spears were raised, when, suddenly, as if from nowhere, there came a flaming wind out of heaven. It was the angel of God. He descended on the enemy, as Isaiah had predicted. The soldiers fell back choking and charred, their armor burned, their weapons turned into lumps of melted metal. The Assyrian troops fell dead like flies as the avenging angel swept through their midst.

Sennacherib, the mighty king, fled in fright, only to be murdered later by his sons when he returned to his own kingdom.

But Judah was saved that night, and Hezekiah raised his voice in thanksgiving and homage to the Lord.

SOON AFTER THE ASSYRIAN WAR, King Hezekiah became ill and was put to bed. Isaiah came to him, and sadly told him that he would die. Hezekiah was afraid. He began to plead with the prophet for a few more years of life.

"I have been a good man," he said, "and I have many more things to do in this life. Pray to the Lord for my recovery."

Feeling pity for the king, Isaiah prayed to God that Hezekiah's life might be spared.

The Lord was merciful, and the king recovered. He lived many years and grew very rich. But, in time, he forgot the Lord and became boastful and proud. Isaiah was angry.

"One day this great kingdom of Judah will disappear," he cried, "and all its wealth and its people will be dispersed throughout the world. This is the punishment for arrogance and pride."

Within a few years, Hezekiah died. His young son Manasseh came to the throne and ruled longer than any other king in Judah. His son was Ammon, who ruled a very short time. Then came the good king Josiah.

More than two hundred years before the birth of Josiah, a prophet had foreseen the day when a king of Judah would take revenge against God's enemies. Josiah was this king. As a young man, he ordered his soldiers to destroy idols and to clear the streets of all sinful altars. Then he had the Temple restored and made fit for God.

While the workmen were repairing the Temple, a priest found some ancient scrolls of the Law buried in the deepest cellar of the ancient building. These scrolls had been written by Moses himself, but they had been lost and forgotten for many hundreds of years. When Josiah learned of this discovery, he was truly inspired, and he spent many days reading and studying the documents.

"I have read the scrolls," he said, "and they have saddened me. For, now, I see how greatly we have sinned these many years. Worst of all, I see what terrible punishments the Lord has planned for us as a result."

*Good
King
Josiah*

Plate 52. THE DEFEAT OF SENNACHERIB,
by Peter Paul Rubens (Flemish, 1577–1640), Pinakothek (Picture Gallery), Munich.

But the prophets of God had comforting words for the king. They told him to take heart, since the Lord would not punish the people so long as Josiah ruled.

Determined to save his kingdom, King Josiah called all the priests and elders of Judah to his palace, and there he read them the long-lost scrolls of Moses.

"Let us obey these laws," he pleaded, "and we will be spared the final judgment."

JOSIAH CONTINUED to enforce the holy laws. He turned the gardens of Baal into cemeteries. All the foreign altars were destroyed and the feast of Passover was celebrated for the first time in many, many years. Not since the days of Samuel had the people lived so close to God.

Then the Egyptians decided to march through Judah in order to invade Assyria. Josiah knew that this invasion spelled great danger to the Hebrews, so he prepared for war. At Megiddo, dressed as a common soldier, he went into battle and was struck by an enemy arrow. The king's soldiers quickly carried him home to Jerusalem; but it was too late. He died and was buried with great honor and tribute. Jehoahaz, his son, became king.

The Pharaoh of Egypt did invade the land, as Josiah had feared. He placed a weakling named Jehoiakim on the throne of Judah, and forced the people to pay heavy taxes to Egypt and to worship Egyptian gods.

Far away, in the land of Babylon, the great king Nebuchadnezzar decided to attack Judah, defeat the Egyptians who ruled there, and take the treasures of the Temple for himself. Jehoiakim offered little resistance, and so it was that Nebuchadnezzar and his armies eventually came to Jerusalem. They took great loads of treasure and many captives back to Babylon.

Nebuchadnezzar Comes to Judah

THE BOOKS OF JEREMIAH AND THE LAMENTATIONS

The Story of Jeremiah's Prophecies; of the Fall of Judah and the Captivity of the Jews.

Jeremiah

NEBUCHADNEZZAR WAS the true master of Judah, for King Jehoiakim was weak, and did as his Babylonian master commanded. Once again, the people turned to idol worship.

In a small town near Jerusalem, there was a good man who had been born during the times of King Josiah. Though the son of poor, hard-working people, he was to become one of the greatest prophets of the Lord. His name was Jeremiah, and in his soul there was a passion for justice, and a sorrow for the sad condition of his nation.

Jeremiah grew up a lonely and shy young man. But, when King Jehoiakim came to the throne and the Babylonians entered Jerusalem, Jeremiah took courage and went out to preach.

At first, no one listened to the youthful prophet, who was timid and unsure of himself. But as time went on, the Lord strengthened his heart and gave him wisdom and strength.

With new determination, Jeremiah went to the Temple of Jerusalem and climbed to the top of the high marble staircase. There he called to the people below, and said:

"Turn from your wicked ways, or the kingdom of Judah will surely perish!"

There was no response; the people merely shrugged their shoulders and walked away. Feeling that he had failed, Jeremiah decided to dramatize his words, and he placed on his shoulders a heavy wooden yoke, such as oxen wear in the fields. Again he came before the people.

"Unless you turn to God," he cried, "our enemies will place the yoke of slavery upon our people even as this yoke is on my back today."

But everyone merely laughed at the sight, and ignored the prophet.

Time after time, Jeremiah tried to warn the people of their doom. One day, he brought a sack of pots and dishes to the Temple. Standing before the crowd, he smashed the dishes against the wall and shouted:

"Our people will be dispersed like the shattered pieces of a broken plate, unless we turn away from wrongdoing."

The people thought that Jeremiah was insane, and, again, they laughed and turned away. But the brave prophet of God kept on. He stood in the doorway of the Temple and stopped the people as they entered.

"Do you think you can wash away your sins," he asked, "just by going to the Temple once in a while? God sees all. He knows our hearts. The humblest man who prays at home is more loved by the Lord than those unbelievers who come to the Temple."

When the soldiers of the king heard this, they arrested Jeremiah for treason. They said that he was preaching against the law of the land. But the princes of the palace were afraid to harm a righteous man. They released him with a warning never to enter the Temple again.

ALONE AND WITHOUT FRIENDS, Jeremiah continued his preaching. Then he heard the voice of God:

"I will give you many new laws for the people to obey," said the Lord. "You must write them in a book. I will also prophesy many punishments that will befall the kingdom of Judah. Preach My word to all men, so that they may be saved, for, if the people listen, I will not destroy Jerusalem."

Jeremiah immediately set about to prepare the book of God's Holy Word. He called upon a man named Baruch, who was trained in writing. Through many nights and days, Jeremiah spoke the words of God while Baruch wrote them down.

When the book was completed, Jeremiah told Baruch to bring it to the Temple and read it to all the people assembled there, because Jeremiah himself was no longer allowed to visit the sacred building. Baruch obeyed, and, standing at the head of the great staircase, he read aloud the words of God that foretold the doom of Judah.

When the people heard him, they were angry and afraid.

"Tell us who wrote these terrible words!" they shouted. Baruch admitted that the prophet Jeremiah had written the book.

Some people ran to tell the king, and others, friendly to Baruch, warned him and Jeremiah to hide themselves from the wrath of Jehoiakim.

The king was merely curious about this troublesome book, and he ordered it brought to the palace and read to him. Seated before his roaring fireplace, the king listened while the doom of Judah was read aloud.

"This is miserable nonsense!" he cried. "Give me my knife!" And he took his knife and cut the pages from the book, one by one. Then he hurled them into the fire. He continued to do this until the whole book was burnt. Many people were afraid when they learned of this sacrilege.

Jeremiah
Writes
God's
Word

Jeremiah was not alarmed. Again, he called upon Baruch, and again he patiently uttered the words of God as Baruch wrote them down.

In spite of this new book the king and the princes paid no attention to the prophet, and continued to live contrary to God's commandments. Then, one day, the great armies of the Chaldeans, under Nebuchadnezzar, marched into the city. They captured the fortress; they ruined the Temple; and they put the king in jail. Through all this misery, Jeremiah begged the people to be brave.

"Even if we are taken as slaves," he cried, "let us not forget our God. Even in captivity we may worship him, for He is all over the world and not just here in Judah."

This was a new idea, and the people didn't understand it. They thought that Jeremiah approved of Nebuchadnezzar's invasion and that he wanted Judah destroyed. Many hated him, and blamed his book for all their troubles. Jeremiah was arrested and put in jail.

When Nebuchadnezzar was victorious, he placed a man on the throne of Judah who would do just as he was told. This man was named Zedekiah, and he was to be the last king of Judah's history. At first, Zedekiah listened obediently to the Babylonian king. But Zedekiah rebelled when Nebuchadnezzar returned to his own land. For a few short years, Judah seemed strong again. Then Nebuchadnezzar decided to teach his enemies a lesson. Once again, he led the great Chaldean army toward Jerusalem.

Fearfully, Zedekiah called for the prophet Jeremiah, and said to him,

"What is to be our fate? Will the Chaldeans be defeated? Answer and say they will not come."

Jeremiah was firm.

"I cannot make up words to please you," he said. "It is the will of God that Judah be destroyed unless the people repent."

Hearing this terrible warning, Zedekiah ordered Jeremiah thrown back into prison.

But, after several months, Jeremiah was freed by friends, and he continued to preach the word of God.

"The enemy is coming!" he announced. "And he will defeat us. Those that remain in this city shall die by the sword, but he who goes forth a captive, he shall live. This is God's plan, and, if we are worthy, some day we can return to Judah as righteous people.

"Therefore, obey the voice of the Lord," he cried, "and peacefully surrender!"

When the king heard that Jeremiah was actually telling the people

HIEREMIAS

OPPOSITE: Plate 53. JEREMIAH, by Michelangelo (Italian, 1475–1564),
Sistine Chapel, The Vatican, Rome.

to surrender and accept captivity, as it was God's will, Zebediah ordered the arrest of the prophet.

Jeremiah in the Muddy Pit

THE KING'S SOLDIERS captured Jeremiah while he was preaching. Secretly they dragged him to a dungeon and lowered him by a rope into an old well, which was filled with mud. There the great prophet prayed to God, even though surrounded by filth.

But Zedekiah had accomplished nothing by his cruelty to Jeremiah, for Nebuchadnezzar's armies were closing in. It seemed that there was no hope in all the land.

A servant in the king's palace knew of Jeremiah's misery. He was a Negro named Ebedmelech. He went to the king and said:

"Release Jeremiah from the pit, or else he will die."

The king did not desire his death, and he ordered thirty soldiers to remove Jeremiah from the muddy pit. Carefully they raised the prophet by ropes strapped under his arms. When he was cleaned and rested, he was taken before the king.

"It is God's will that Jerusalem shall fall," he said. "But the Lord is merciful, and He will spare the lives of all the people in Judah, your own included, if you do not resist."

Zedekiah didn't know what to do. He kept Jeremiah in the palace under guard, so that the prophet would not excite the people. Then, fearfully, he watched from his window as Nebuchadnezzar's enormous army massed outside Jerusalem, waiting to attack.

Months passed and nothing happened. Every day, the food supply diminished and the people were miserable and hungry. Finally, King Zedekiah decided to escape. But it was to no avail. He crept out of the palace by a secret door, only to find himself surrounded by the enemy. This was all the Chaldeans needed as an excuse to attack. They blinded King Zedekiah, killed his sons, and set fire to the city.

Now Jeremiah rushed to the streets, and cried to the people:

"Surrender and live, so that you may repent in captivity, for it is better to live and worship as a captive abroad than to die here in Jerusalem!"

Many obeyed the prophet and were led away as captives. Others perished as the Chaldeans plundered the city. When the destruction was complete, and the great Temple lay in ruins, only Jeremiah and his Negro friend were allowed to go free.

Thus, after almost 350 years, the great kingdom of Judah was destroyed, as had been prophesied.

Who had been at fault? Surely the people were not entirely to blame. They had been ruled by weak and sinful kings. Now, at last, the kings were gone and a governor named Gedaliah was placed by the Babylonians over the remnants of Judah.

Jeremiah chose to stay behind with those too old or too sick to travel all the way to Babylon. Sitting on the broken walls of the burned-out Temple, he surveyed the ruins of his city and wept. All day and night he wept and he lamented:

How doth the city sit solitary,
that was full of people!
how is she become as a widow!
    she that was great among the nations,
    and princess among the provinces,
how is she become tributary!
She weepeth sore in the night
    and her tears are on her cheeks:
Among all her lovers
    she hath none to comfort her:
    all her friends have dealt treacherously with her,
        they are become her enemies.
Judah is gone into captivity because of affliction
    and because of great servitude:
She dwelleth among the heathen,
    she findeth no rest.

A few years after the destruction of the Temple, there seemed to be some hope again in the land of Judah. Groups of determined people, led by Jeremiah, began rebuilding the countryside. Gedaliah, the governor, was a kindly man and helped as best he could. But treachery was everywhere. One day, Gedaliah was secretly murdered by men from a neighboring kingdom. When the people learned of this, they were afraid.

"Nebuchadnezzar will put the blame on us," they said. "We must escape."

Jeremiah urged them to be calm.

"Do not run away," he pleaded, "or Judah will surely become a wasteland forever."

But, once again, the people would not listen to their prophet, and, in fear, they fled this way and that, many ending up in Egypt. Jeremiah was taken along to Egypt against his will. There, according to tradition, he was put to death by his detractors.

THE BOOK OF EZEKIEL

The Story of Ezekiel's Visions While in Captivity.

THE KINGDOM OF JUDAH had perished, but the people were still alive. The many thousands taken as prisoners into Babylon came to be known as Jews. They were destined to remain together for two hundred years, even without a country of their own. But their unfortunate neighbors, the Israelites, had vanished completely.

In Babylon, which lay many miles to the east of Canaan, the Jews were strangers. Fortunately, they were treated with kindness by their masters, and, very often, they rose to positions of wealth and dignity.

In spite of this, they kept away from other people because they worshiped the one true God and their Babylonian neighbors worshiped idols. The Jews, in their sadness and in their captivity, had finally become the people of God. But they missed their homeland and often wept:

> If I forget thee, O Jerusalem,
> let my right hand forget her cunning.
> If I do not remember thee,
> let my tongue cleave to the roof of my mouth;
> if I prefer not Jerusalem above my chief joy.

One of the most remarkable Jewish prophets of this time was Ezekiel, who was brought to Babylon during the earliest days of the captivity. He was a man of visions, to whom the Lord spoke in many puzzling ways. Ezekiel was able to predict the fall of Jerusalem and the destruction of the Temple months before the events occurred. How did he know? Here are his words, as he wrote them:

"This is what I saw in the heavens; four creatures, each with wings; and the one had the face of a man, the second the face of a lion, the third the face of an ox, and the fourth was in the likeness of an eagle. And the sky behind these creatures was the color of fire and ice.

OPPOSITE: Plate 54. THE VISION OF EZEKIEL, by Raphael (Italian, 1483–1520), The Pitti Palace, Florence.

"Then they let down their wings and I was lifted up, and they took me away for many miles, and they brought me even to Jerusalem, and the Lord showed me the wickedness of Jerusalem and its abominations."

Ezekiel could also see the armies of Nebuchadnezzar suddenly descending upon the city, setting fire to the walls and ruining the sacred Temple. All this he saw in his vision.

The next day, Ezekiel went among the Jews who had just been brought into Babylon. They were sad, and they waited by a river, wondering if they might not have done better to have remained in Judah.

But Ezekiel described his vision and told them that many hundreds would die and that Jerusalem would crumble; even the sacred Temple would be destroyed. He said it was better that they had fled, as Jeremiah had instructed.

Soon after, news came that confirmed all of Ezekiel's predictions. The people knew that a man of God was in their midst. From that time on, they listened when he spoke of his visions.

"I have seen a chariot of fire drawn across the heavens," he said. "There were wheels within wheels, and they all went around and around, as it is God's will that we survive and live and worship Him."

These words gave comfort to the sad and lonely Jews. They asked Ezekiel again and again to tell them of his visions.

"I see a field filled with old, dry bones," he said, "and the Lord commands the dry bones to rise up like men, and soon the bones are covered with flesh, and they become whole again and they breathe and walk and they are revived!"

"What does it mean?" the people wondered.

"We, the Children of Israel, we are like old, dry bones," the prophet said. "We seem hopeless and destroyed. But someday, God will breathe the breath of life back into our nation, and we shall return to our homeland once more.

"Behold," Ezekiel continued. "I have a stick in each hand. One is marked Judah, the other Israel. See, they move together. They have become one by the will of God. This means that our divided nation will join again, and that our people will return to the Holy Land if we are righteous and deserving."

From these wonderful words of Ezekiel, the Jewish captives took hope and comfort for many years. Indeed, they lived to see their enemies crumble—in Egypt, in Philistia, and in Babylon itself. They lived to return briefly to the Holy Land—always under the oppression of a foreign king. And then, in our very own time, within the memory of many people who read this book, Ezekiel's prophecy came true at last, and the nation of Israel was reestablished after thousands of years!

THE BOOK OF DANIEL

*The Story of the Wise Man Daniel, Who Was Thrown
to the Lions and Delivered by God; of the Return to Judah
by the Children of Israel.*

KING NEBUCHADNEZZAR WAS the most powerful man in the
world. His kingdom extended far and wide. His wealth was very great,
and he had many slaves. Nevertheless, Nebuchadnezzar was generous
and just. He thus commanded his soldiers to go among the Jewish captives and select a group of strong young men who could be trained to
become leaders in Babylon. Nebuchadnezzar was willing to educate
these young men in the language of Babylon, and to give them high
positions and wealth if they proved qualified.

Four young Jews were selected for this special opportunity. They
were brave and handsome. Above all, they were quick to learn; and,
soon, they could speak the Babylonian language as easily as their own.
Before long, they dressed and talked exactly like Babylonians.

Three of these boys changed their names as well. They became
Shadrach, Meshach, and Abednego. The fourth young man was called
Belteshazzar, but he refused to give up his Hebrew name.

"I am Daniel," he said, "and that is how I wish to be known." He
was so insistent that the king allowed him to keep his Hebrew name.

While Daniel and his three friends were learning the ways of Babylon, they lived in a special house, and every day Nebuchadnezzar sent
delicious food for them to eat. Unfortunately, this food was not prepared according to the Laws of Moses, and Daniel would not eat it.

"Bring us lentils to eat and water to drink," he asked the servants
of Nebuchadnezzar, "for we do not wish to eat any foods forbidden by
our religion."

At first the king's men were afraid to carry out this request.

"If you don't eat properly," they said, "you will grow pale and thin,
and the king will hold us responsible."

"Let us try it for ten days," Daniel said. "If we become thin, then we
will eat the king's food, and he will never know."

The servants agreed and every day they brought the lentils and
the water to the young Hebrews. As the days went by, Daniel and his
friends grew stronger and healthier than all those people who ate the
Babylonian food. The king's servants were no longer afraid. In fact, they

*Four
Hebrew
Boys*

were complimented by Nebuchadnezzar himself for taking such good care of the young Jewish men.

After three years, Daniel and his friends were the best-looking and most intelligent young men in the kingdom. God had given them wisdom and strength, for they worshiped Him alone and never disobeyed His commandments.

Nebuchadnezzar Has a Dream

ONE NIGHT, King Nebuchadnezzar suddenly awoke from his sleep. He had just experienced a very strange dream that had greatly bothered him. Hurriedly, he called his wise men together, so that they might explain its meaning. But then, to his great annoyance, he found he could not remember the dream.

"I want you to discover the meaning of my dream," he said. "It troubles me greatly."

"But how can we interpret your dream, if you have forgotten it?" the wise men asked. "In all the world, no man can do that."

Nebuchadnezzar would not listen to reason. He sent out an order for all the wise men in Babylon to be executed unless they could discover his forgotten dream.

When Daniel heard of this, he went directly to the king.

"Instead of killing innocent men," he exclaimed, "allow me the chance. If I fail, you may kill me alone. All I ask is a little time to pray."

Nebuchadnezzar agreed, and repealed his order of execution. Then he waited for Daniel.

The young Hebrew meanwhile went to his three friends and urged them to join him in prayer, so that God would reveal the nature of Nebuchadnezzar's dream. After many hours in silent devotion, Daniel exclaimed:

"I know the dream! God has given me the solution."

Then he rushed to the palace and stood before Nebuchadnezzar.

"Oh, mighty King," he said. "No wise man on earth could tell you what you had dreamed. Only God could do that, and He has seen fit to reveal the secret to me. Now you will know that the God of Israel is the one true God of all the world."

"Yes, yes," said Nebuchadnezzar impatiently, "but tell me my dream."

Daniel continued:

"You have been worried about the future. With this in mind, you went to bed one night and dreamed that you saw what appeared to be a mountainous statue. Its head and shoulders were made of gold and its arms of silver; its body of brass. But its legs were formed of iron, and its feet were partly made of clay."

"Yes," cried the king, "that was my dream! Now you must tell me what it means."

Daniel explained that the statue represented the vast empire of Babylon led by Nebuchadnezzar himself, symbolized by the head of gold. The other nations, which formed his kingdom, were made of either brass or silver. The danger was that the feet that held up this mighty kingdom were merely made of clay. Therefore, in the dream, when a great stone rolled down from Heaven and smashed into the statue, it crumbled the feet of clay, and the entire kingdom crashed to the ground, breaking into thousands of tiny pieces. The stone then began to expand; it grew very large, until it had filled the statue's place.

From this, Daniel drew a grave conclusion.

"God is warning you that even your great power will end," he said, "and that His power alone will cover the earth."

Nebuchadnezzar was so amazed by the accuracy of Daniel's description of his dream, and so frightened by the prophecy, that he fell to his knees and exclaimed:

"Daniel, you are a god!"

"No," Daniel insisted. "The one true God of Israel alone was responsible for my revelation. I beg you to rise and give proper thanks to the Lord."

The king agreed. He then bestowed great honors upon Daniel, and also upon Shadrach, Meshach, and Abednego, whom he made governors of his lands. For a time, Nebuchadnezzar actually seemed to believe in the one true God of Israel. But he was to change his mind very rapidly.

"BUILD A STATUE of me, ninety feet tall, and cover it with gold," commanded Nebuchadnezzar one day. "Then set this statue on the plain of Dura, and there all the people of the kingdom must come and worship me."

When Nebuchadnezzar's subjects heard this strange command, they were fearful, and quickly obeyed. They built the statue, covered it with gold, and set it high on the plain of Dura.

Then the word went forth: "Everyone must fall on his knees before the statue of our king as soon as the trumpets are heard. Anyone who disobeys this command will be burned in a fiery furnace."

Tens of thousands gathered on the plain of Dura to worship the idol of the king. When the trumpets were blown, they fell to their knees

The Fiery Furnace

and groveled. Even the princes and high officials of Babylon worshiped in this fashion.

Only Shadrach, Meshach, and Abednego refused to bend their knees to an idol made of gold. Their enemies immediately reported the news to the king. Nebuchadnezzar was enraged.

"Is it true," he said to Shadrach, Meshach and Abednego, "that you refuse to worship my image?"

And they nodded.

"Very well," answered the king, "I will give you one more chance. The next time you hear the royal music, you will bow down to the image on the plain of Dura. If you do not bow down you will be cast into the

Plate 55. THREE BOYS CONDEMNED TO THE FURNACE, by Matteo Rosselli (Italian, 1578–1650), Academy of Fine Arts, Florence.

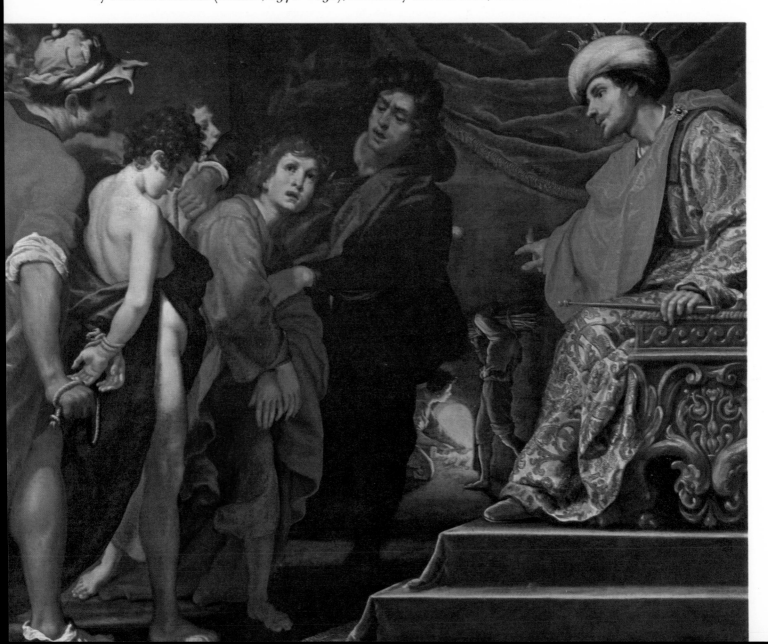

fiery furnace. Who is that God who can deliver you from my hands?"

"We shall not obey," answered the three young men. "And we will trust in our God to deliver us from your punishment."

"Take them to the furnace and make it seven times hotter," cried the furious king.

Daniel was out of the country at this time, and it seemed as though no one could save the three young men. They were bound with rope and led to the fiery pit. Then, when the heat had become unbearable and the flames leaped higher and higher, Nebuchadnezzar ordered Shadrach, Meshach, and Abednego tossed into the furnace.

"That is the end of them," said the king.

But suddenly the door of the furnace, which had been sealed, swung open wide, and there, in the fiery pit, Nebuchadnezzar could see Shadrach, Meshach, and Abednego walking about unharmed—and with them was another figure in flowing robes.

"Did we not throw three men into the flames?" the king questioned in surprise.

"That is true," his soldiers replied.

"But I see four!" Nebuchadnezzar exclaimed. "One is like an angel, and is protecting the others, so that they will not burn."

It was true. Shadrach, Meshach, and Abednego were completely safe even in the midst of the flames, and with them was a strange figure who had joined them in prayer.

Nebuchadnezzar was frightened and trembling. He ordered the prisoners removed from the furnace at once, and, when they were brought before him, he could see that not even a hair of their heads had been singed. Only the ropes that bound them had burned away.

"Surely the God of Israel has saved these men," cried the king. "Blessed is the Lord of Shadrach, Meshach, and Abednego. From this day forth, no one may threaten these men or deny them the right to worship their God as they desire. If anyone disobeys, he shall die and his house shall be destroyed."

And then Nebuchadnezzar gave Shadrach, Meshach, and Abednego great gifts and high honors in his kingdom.

FOR A LONG TIME, Nebuchadnezzar tried to worship God, but his power and enormous wealth made him boastful and vain. He knew that he was greater than any man in his kingdom, and, soon, he believed himself greater than God. One night, he had a disturbing dream, and he called Daniel to his chamber.

The Madness of Nebuchadnezzar

"I dreamed that there was an enormous tree standing in a field," said the king, "and suddenly a voice from heaven commanded, 'Cut down that tree; scatter its branches; and leave only its stump standing for seven years.' Then the tree was cut down and fell to the ground and the voice said, 'God, not man, rules the earth.' What does this mean?"

Daniel was silent for a long time; then he spoke with a heavy heart.

"The Lord is warning you of your downfall, for he will cut you down like a tree, and scatter the branches of your kingdom. Then, for seven years, you will live like a beast in the fields unless you worship Him and lead a godly life."

Nebuchadnezzar was at first alarmed. But, after a time, when he saw that nothing unusual had happened, he became bold again and walked about his palace boasting of his greatness and wealth.

Then, one day, the soldiers in the palace were horrified. There in the fields, on his hands and knees, was the great king Nebuchadnezzar, and he was eating grass and growling like an animal.

"The king has lost his mind," the people cried. "His kingdom has been taken away from him by the will of God."

And so it was for seven years, as Daniel prophesied, that King Nebuchadnezzar lived like a beast in the grass, his hair grown long, his fingernails shaped like claws. No one could tell whether he was a man or a lion.

But, after seven years, God in His mercy restored Nebuchadnezzar's sanity. The king repented and lived a godly life until his death.

The Handwriting on the Wall

WHEN NEBUCHADNEZZAR DIED, his son Belshazzar came to the throne. He had inherited all his father's wealth and power, but none of the respect for God that the old king learned toward the end of his life. So it was that Belshazzar was a fun-loving, sinful king who liked nothing better than big parties and too much wine.

One night, he gave a banquet to which he invited hundreds of wealthy friends. Food and wine were abundant, and the entertainment was splendid, indeed. During the meal, the king and his guests drank and ate from the precious cups and plates that Nebuchadnezzar had taken from the sacred Temple in Jerusalem. Beautiful gold dishes that once held the holy bread of the Temple were now smeared with the unholy food of idol worshipers.

Such a turn of events greatly pleased King Belshazzar, who thought of himself as the most powerful man in the world. Full of merriment, he rose from his throne and held up his goblet of wine.

"I wish to make a toast," he laughed.

But, as he lifted his cup, a cold wind blew through the hall and a strange light filled the room. Belshazzar was alarmed. He turned and looked over his shoulder to see what had happened. There, hovering in mid air, was a human hand tracing four strange words across the wall in letters of fire.

"Mene, Mene, Tekel, Upharsin," wrote the mysterious hand.

The king was horrified, and fell into his chair.

"What does this mean?" he cried to his guests.

But no one knew. Even the wise men trembled, for they could not offer an explanation; and they tried to sneak out of the room.

"What does it mean?" the king cried again.

Finally, the queen came forward and said:

"Years ago, your father called upon a wise Hebrew named Daniel to interpret his dreams. Perhaps this same man can explain the meaning of the handwriting on the wall."

Belshazzar ordered his soldiers to find Daniel at once.

"If he can tell me the answer," he said, "I will give him fine robes and a chain of gold."

Then the king remained on his throne, afraid and trembling, as the magical words continued to glow on the wall.

When Daniel arrived in the palace, he was brought before the king.

"I have heard that you are a wise man," said Belshazzar. "Very well, tell me the meaning of these glowing words on the wall, and I will make you rich and powerful."

"I don't wish to be rich," Daniel replied. "I shall pray to God, and discover the meaning of these words without reward."

Then Daniel studied the handwriting and said:

"You inherited a great kingdom from your father, but you, Belshazzar, have sinned, and worshiped idols, and you have taken the sacred goblets and plates that were brought from the Temple in Jerusalem and have used them for your unholy food. Therefore, God has sent down His judgment, in these words:

"Mene. This means that God has numbered the days of your kingdom and brought them to an end.

"Tekel. This means that you have been judged by the Lord and found wanting.

"Upharsin. This means that your kingdom will be divided up among the Persians and the Medes. This is God's punishment for all your sins."

Belshazzar was terrified. Nevertheless, he gave Daniel a chain of gold as he had promised, and he appointed him a ruler in the kingdom.

ABOVE: Plate 56. BELSHAZZAR'S FEAST, by Rembrandt (Dutch, 1606–1669), Private Collection, England.

OPPOSITE: Plate 57. DANIEL IN THE LION'S DEN, by David Teniers, the Elder (Flemish, 1582–1649), Bavarian State Picture Collection, Munich.

But, even at that moment, God's judgment was being carried out. Outside, all around the city, the great army of Medes and Persians was preparing to attack. At midnight, they charged. When morning dawned, all Babylon had been captured, King Belshazzar was dead, and a man named Darius, from the eastern kingdom of the Medes, was placed on the throne. From that day on, the great empire of the Babylonians belonged to the Persians and the Medes, as Daniel had prophesied.

Daniel in the Lion's Den

DARIUS WAS a noble king who treated his subjects with kindness. He had a special liking for Daniel, whom he considered very wise and very brave. For this reason, the king made Daniel his chief minister, so that the Hebrew was second in command throughout the Persian kingdom. Daniel's high position made many Persian princes jealous, and they began to plot against him.

"We must catch Daniel in a mistake," they said, "so that the king will get rid of him. But, alas! he does no wrong, and we can find nothing against him to report!"

It was true. No matter how they tried, the jealous Persians could not accuse Daniel of any mistakes. They thought up a clever plan, however, and went to the king.

"O mighty Darius," they said, "you are like a god among the people. We believe that everyone in this land should worship you and no other god for thirty days. Anyone who disobeys should be tossed into a den of lions."

King Darius was flattered by this idea, and, after much persuasion, signed the decree making himself a god. Such a decree could not be revoked once it was signed—a fact that the evil Persians knew, for it was their intention to catch Daniel worshiping the one true God of Israel, and, thus, cause him to be thrown to the lions.

Their plan worked well. Daniel would not obey the king's decree, and worshiped God three times a day as he had always done. When they saw this, the wicked Persians rushed to the king with the news.

"Daniel has disobeyed your decree," they cried. "He must be punished."

King Darius was very upset. He admired Daniel, and did not wish to do his friend harm. But the law was the law, and it could not be changed.

Sadly, Darius called Daniel to his chambers.

"I have signed a foolish decree," said the king, "but I cannot call it off. Therefore, you must be tossed to the lions this very night. I know that your God will protect you, however, and even I shall pray for you."

Daniel was then taken and lowered into a dungeon filled with hungry lions.

All that night, King Darius prayed in his chambers, refusing to eat or drink in sorrow for his friend. Then, in the early morning, he rushed to the dungeon and called:

"Daniel, Daniel, are you safe?"

At first, there was only silence from the den of the lions. Again the king cried out:

"Daniel, answer me!"

And from the bottom of the dungeon, Daniel replied:

"I am unharmed, O King, for God has protected me, knowing that I am innocent. Last night, He sent an angel from heaven into the dungeon, and, though the lions were fierce and hungry, they made no attempt upon my life. Indeed, they are as gentle as a flock of sheep."

Darius was overjoyed, and he ordered Daniel's immediate release. Then he arrested the wicked Persians who had plotted against his friend. They were thrown to the hungry lions, who devoured them on the spot.

"From this time forth," decreed the king, "all the people of my kingdom shall worship the God of Daniel, for He is the one true God in all the world; and His kingdom will endure forever and ever."

The people accepted this decree, and, when Darius died, the new king, Cyrus, continued to lead a righteous life, with Daniel as the chief of all his ministers.

FOR MANY YEARS, Daniel served the kings of Persia as advisor and friend. But he never forgot his own people, the Jews. Over and over, he could hear them praying for the day when they might return to their homeland in the west.

Many years before, Jeremiah had prophesied that, after seventy years, the captives would be freed and allowed to leave Babylon. It was almost that time, and Daniel decided to devote his old age to the task of helping his people return to their homes.

Thus, he prayed and fasted every day, wearing sackcloth instead of his fine garments, and covering his head with ashes as a sign of humility. For many months, Daniel prayed to God in this fashion.

Then, one night, he saw an angel descending from heaven in a halo of light. At first, the prophet was unable to speak, and he fell face down to the ground in fear and wonderment.

Daniel's Prophecies

But the angel said:

"Do not be afraid, for I have come to help you and reveal many wonderful prophecies of God."

Then the angel took Daniel to the river front, and, in the reflections of the water, he revealed the following things that were to happen to the People of Israel:

First, the Jews would return to their homeland and rebuild the sacred Temple. Then they would become guilty of sinful wickedness once again, and strangers would come and take away their land. After many, many years they would return, under foreign rule, and the Messiah would come into the world to relieve their sins. All these things would happen in the distant future.

When Daniel awoke the next day, he wrote all the angel's words in a book, and he rejoiced in his heart, for he knew that his people would be free. Indeed, King Cyrus soon after sent a proclamation throughout the land, in which he said:

"The Lord has ordered me to rebuild the Temple of Jerusalem. Therefore, I shall free the Jews to return to their homes and undertake this task. I shall also give them all the precious treasures that Nebuchadnezzar took from their Temple. This is as the Lord commands. Therefore, let all those who wish to go assemble at the river."

Over forty thousand Jews eagerly and happily packed their belongings, and prepared for their return to Judah. They were led by a brave young man named Zerubbabel, who was to become the ruler of Jerusalem under King Cyrus' command.

But not all the Jews wanted to return, for some had become very prosperous in Babylon. Instead, they sent money and presents to help those who were heading back. Many other generous people in Babylon gave money and food to the departing Hebrews.

And so the people set out, bravely, to rebuild Jerusalem and the sacred Temple. As for Daniel, he would wait behind and pray. In the words of the Bible: "Happy is he that waiteth . . . for he shall rest at the end of his days."

THE BOOKS OF EZRA
AND NEHEMIAH

*The Story of the Rebuilding of the Temple and the Walls
of Jerusalem; and of the Second Covenant with God.*

"TODAY WE SHALL LAY the cornerstone of the Temple," commanded Zerubbabel, "and tomorrow we shall start the foundation here on Mount Zion. Let us work until we have finished our sacred task."

The Jews rejoiced. For years, they had been captives in Babylon. Now they were home at last, and prepared to rebuild not only the Temple but all of Judah, as well. And so the Jews—young and old—began to clear the rubble and weeds from the ruins of Jerusalem.

To the north of the city lived the idolatrous Samaritans. When they heard that the Jews had returned and intended to rebuild their Temple, they became envious and decided to make trouble. Pretending friendship, they went to Jerusalem and sought out Zerubbabel.

"We are your neighbors from the north," they said, "and we would like to help you rebuild your Temple."

Zerubbabel was suspicious, and informed the Samaritans, in a very polite way, that only the Children of Israel were supposed to work on the sacred building, as ordered by King Cyrus of Persia. The Samaritans were annoyed. They sent presents and bribes to the high officials of Persia along with the following message:

"Do what you can to stop the Jews from rebuilding their Temple."

The wicked Persian officials went to King Cyrus and bothered him every day, urging him to delay the reconstruction. But though the Samaritans interfered with the progress of the sacred work, the Jews nevertheless managed to rebuild at least the foundation of their Temple.

Finally, King Cyrus died, and a man named Artaxerxes came to the throne. He was more receptive to the urgings of the Samaritans, for he believed their evil warnings against the Jews. One day, he ordered all work halted on the sacred Temple. While Artaxerxes lived, only the foundation stood on Mount Zion.

When Artaxerxes died, a second King Darius came to the throne. Like his ancestors and namesake, this new king was generous and understanding. He ordered the Samaritans to leave the Jews alone so that they might complete their sacred work. Unfortunately, the Jews themselves no longer wished to rebuild the Temple.

*Rebuilding
the Temple
of Jerusalem*

A prophet named Haggai now appeared in Jerusalem. He climbed upon the foundation of the building and cried:

"You have built yourselves beautiful homes, but the House of God still lies in ruins. Unless you finish this sacred work, all of Judah will be afflicted."

For years, Haggai preached to the lazy people, and then, at last, when sorrow and affliction came upon Judah, the Jews repented. Immediately, they began to gather wood and stone so that they might complete the reconstruction. To strengthen their cause, King Darius sent a decree threatening severe punishment against anyone who interfered with the important work. Furthermore, the Samaritans, who had caused so much trouble, were ordered to provide food for the priests of Israel so long as the Temple was under construction.

Thus, after many months, the great building was completed, and the people gathered for a solemn celebration. Offerings were made to God, and holy men, such as the prophets Haggai and Zechariah, joined in prayer and song. The Jews were so inspired that they held the feast of Passover for the first time in many years.

Ezra and the King of Persia

WHILE ARTAXERXES was king of Persia and Babylon, a righteous Jew named Ezra lived near the palace. Every day, he heard reports that the Jews who had returned to Judah were having great trouble in keeping the law and the proper worship of God. Ezra had devoted himself to studying the Laws of Moses and felt that he might be able to serve his people in Judah. He therefore asked permission to see the king.

When he arrived before the throne of Artaxerxes, he pleaded for a chance to return to Judah with all those Jews still living in Babylon. The king was sympathetic to his plea and ordered safe conduct for Ezra and his followers. In addition, the king gave the departing Jews many expensive gifts and food.

The courageous Ezra was put in charge of the journey home. He was also responsible for keeping the law. For this reason, he established among the Jews a group of judges who would enforce the commandments of God.

For three days, the Jews prepared for their departure and prayed for guidance. But some of them grew worried in spite of their prayers. They went to Ezra.

"We have no army to protect us in the desert," they said. "It is a long trip to Judah, and there are many bandits and robbers along the way. Let us ask for an army so that we may be safe."

Ezra replied:

"We must trust in God to protect us. If we ask for an army, King Artaxerxes will lose respect for the power of the Lord and His people, and may not allow us to go free."

The people agreed.

Thus, without protection, the Jews began their journey. True to Ezra's words, the Lord safeguarded His people, and, after many months, they arrived in Jerusalem. Ezra was most unhappy with what he found. For one thing, the sturdy walls, which had once protected the city from invaders, were now in ruins. No one had bothered to repair them. Another source of Ezra's unhappiness was the fact that many young people had forgotten God and were marrying out of their religion. Ezra wished to preserve the Jewish faith, and prohibited any marriage to a stranger. After a time, the people came to respect Ezra, and they looked to him for spiritual guidance.

Far away, in Persia, another Jew was turning his eyes toward Jerusalem, in order to help his people. His name was Nehemiah.

Nehemiah and the Walls

AS CUPBEARER to King Artaxerxes, Nehemiah had a very important position in Persia. He was responsible for the king's wine, which meant that he had to be a trustworthy man—if someone tried to poison the king, Nehemiah would know. During the time in which he served Artaxerxes, Nehemiah was very loyal.

One day, bad news reached Nehemiah. The Jews of Jerusalem were having great difficulties in rebuilding the city, and the protective walls that once had encircled Jerusalem were still in ruins. Nehemiah knew that the Jews would be open to an easy attack if their enemies decided to invade. Determined to help his people, he approached King Artaxerxes, and asked permission to enter Jerusalem for the purpose of rebuilding the city's walls.

The king was very fond of Nehemiah, and did not wish him to leave Persia.

"How long do you think this journey will take?" he asked.

And Nehemiah replied,

"About two years. During this time I will need Your Majesty's protection and letters of permission to complete my task. I hope that I may have them."

Artaxerxes was generous and gave Nehemiah permission to rebuild the walls of Jerusalem. He also sent letters to his subjects throughout the kingdom urging them to help the Jews in their task. Gratefully, Nehemiah accepted the king's good wishes, and, with a small group of soldiers, he left Persia.

After many months, Nehemiah arrived at the outskirts of Jerusalem. There he found the walls in ruins, just as he had been told. Sadness filled his heart to see the glory of his people in such destruction; and he became more determined than ever to fulfill his mission. On the following day, he called all the elders of the city together, and said to them:

"Without strong walls to guard Jerusalem you are weak and open to attack by your enemies. Therefore, let us work swiftly and without stop, as commanded by the king, until every stone is safely in place."

The Jews were enthusiastic. Under Nehemiah's leadership, they set to work immediately. But, as usual, there was trouble. Certain foreigners who lived near Jerusalem were unhappy with the idea of a well-protected city. Others were jealous of Artaxerxes' friendship toward the Jews. These troublemakers made fun of the walls, hoping to discourage the Jews.

"These walls will crumble if a fox walks over them," they said, and laughed. "What a waste of time!"

But the Jews would not be discouraged. Seeing this, their enemies turned to stronger measures, banding together to invade Jerusalem while the walls were still incomplete. But God had spoken to Nehemiah and prepared him for treachery. Thus, when the invaders approached Jerusalem, they found an army of Jews waiting for them. The enemies turned back without trying to attack.

From then on, half the men of Jerusalem repaired the walls while the other half kept guard with spears and swords. For nearly two months, the work went on at a feverish pace. The Jews were nearing completion of their walls, when trouble began all over again, this time among the people themselves. A group of poor men went to Nehemiah, and reported:

"We have worked so long on these walls that our money is running out. Because of this we have had to borrow from our wealthier neighbors. Now they want to be paid or they will take our children as slaves."

Nehemiah was furious. He forced the rich to withdraw their threats and made them swear before the priests of God that they would not take advantage of their poorer brethren. When the foreigners outside the city heard about this trouble, they took heart.

"We will invite Nehemiah to meet with us," they said, "and, when he is outside the city, we will kill him."

And so they sent messages to Nehemiah inviting him to attend a feast that they were giving. But he knew it was a trick, and refused.

"I have more important work in Jerusalem," he said.

The enemies tried to threaten him.

"We will report you to Artaxerxes," they said. "We will tell him that you are planning to make yourself king of Jerusalem."

"Tell him what you like," Nehemiah replied. "He will know that it is false."

Several times the foreigners tried to lure Nehemiah outside the city, but they always failed. Finally the great walls were complete and the bronze gates inserted. Now Jerusalem would be safe.

To celebrate their success, the Jews held a day-long parade, which started at the walls of the city and continued to the Temple of God. All day, silver trumpets were heard in joyous fanfare, and the people danced in the streets.

Nehemiah was pleased that his task was completed, and he prepared to return to Persia. Before leaving, he established a system of sentries for the wall, so that no enemy could sneak up on the city.

140. The Second Covenant

NOW EZRA, WHO WAS very old, called all the Jews to the main gate of the wall and there he unfolded a long scroll, which he read to them line by line, without skipping a word. It was the Law of Moses, which had been forgotten for many years. When the people heard God's commandments, they realized how greatly they had sinned, and they wept and repented.

"Let us rededicate ourselves to the Law," said Ezra to the people. "We shall have a second covenant with God, as did Abraham, our father before us. And, to prove our faith, let us each sign a scroll pledging obedience to God and the conduct of a righteous life."

Everyone agreed, and solemnly signed the second covenant. Then Nehemiah departed for Persia, leaving behind him a well-protected city and an upright people.

Some time later, Nehemiah received permission from Artaxerxes to return to Jerusalem. Ezra was dead and the Temple had not been kept holy nor was the Sabbath being properly observed by the people. Nehemiah was sorely grieved at this lack of faith, and he commanded that the Temple be cleansed, and that the proper ceremonies should once again be held there. Then he ordered the gates of the city be shut on the Sabbath so that merchants and traders could not come and go with their wares, and do business in Jerusalem on the holy day. And Nehemiah always strove to keep the children of Israel in the ways of the Lord, and did all he could to keep them from straying.

THE BOOKS OF ESTHER, JONAH, AND JOB

Stories of the Jewish People in Foreign Lands; of Esther, Who Became a Queen; of Jonah, Who Was Swallowed by a Whale; and of Job, Who Kept His Faith in God.

Esther Becomes Queen of Persia

KING AHASUERUS OF PERSIA was mighty, and his palace in the city of Shushan was the center of a gay and exciting life.

Giving large parties was a passion with King Ahasuerus. One party lasted a whole week, and everyone in Shushan—both great and small—was invited. According to custom, the women dined in the palace and the men in the courtyard of the palace garden. Ahasuerus' wife, Queen Vashti, was hostess to the ladies.

Toward the end of the feast, the king became very gay. Holding his goblet in his hand, he called for the queen, and commanded that she appear before him with her crown upon her head. He wished to show his beautiful wife to all the men of Persia.

But Vashti was furious. She did not want to be put on display, and she refused to obey the king's command.

"My wife will not do as I ask," said the angry king. "How shall I punish her?"

"Take away her crown," answered his advisors. "If she is not severely punished, all the women of Persia will think that it is proper to disobey their husbands; and that will be terrible for us."

The king agreed, and proclaimed throughout the land that Vashti was no longer his queen. He also called for a contest among the women of Persia to see which one should fill her place.

"I will seek out the most beautiful maiden in all the land," said the king. "She will become my wife and my queen."

At this same time, there was a Jewish man named Mordecai, who was a gatekeeper at the palace of the king. He heard about Queen Vashti's disgrace and the search for a beautiful maiden. Eagerly he ran home to his cousin, Hadassah. Since her early childhood, Mordecai had raised the dark-eyed girl as though she were his very own daughter. Now he believed that, because of her beauty, God had chosen her to become Ahasuerus' queen.

Hadassah dressed in her finest robes and placed myrtle leaves in her raven hair. Then she prepared to go to the palace for the contest. Before she left home, Mordecai took her aside and said:

"It would be better if you did not reveal that you were Jewish. In fact, we will change your name, for Hadassah is a Hebrew word. From now on you shall be called Esther, which means beautiful. Now go, and God be with you."

Esther took her place in line with the other women who had come for the contest. After a while, King Ahasuerus entered the chamber. He passed from one contestant to the other without showing any interest. But, when he saw Esther, his heart rejoiced. At once, he proclaimed his love for the Hebrew maiden, and in due time she became his queen.

WHILE ESTHER LIVED in the palace as Queen of Persia, her cousin Mordecai remained gatekeeper to the king. No one knew that they were related or that Esther was Jewish.

The queen greatly admired her cousin, and often visited him as she strolled in the royal gardens. She relied on him to tell her about the poor people of the kingdom, and about her own kinsmen, the Jews.

One day Mordecai, while at the royal gate, overheard two men plotting against the life of the king. It was their plan to surprise him at a feast and stab him to death. Mordecai immediately sent a message to his cousin with a warning for Ahasuerus.

The laws of Persia were very strange. No one could enter the king's private rooms without his permission. Anyone doing so faced the possibility of death. This law applied to Esther, the queen, as well, and she dared not risk her husband's wrath. So she waited until he passed her chambers, and then she told him of the plot.

"The gatekeeper Mordecai discovered this treachery," she said.

The king was very grateful. He had the traitors arrested and he inscribed Mordecai's name in the royal book of good deeds.

IN THE PALACE of Ahasuerus were many princes who sought favor with the king. None of these was more cunning and ambitious than Haman. Year after year, Haman made himself humble and did just as the king desired. Then, one day, he found himself promoted to the highest position in the land.

Now the boastful Haman strutted about in his fine robes and jewels, demanding obedience from all. In fact, a law was passed that every-

Mordecai
Overhears
a Plot

Haman
and
Mordecai

241

one should bow down to the ground whenever Haman appeared. One man refused to obey—Mordecai the gatekeeper. Every time Haman appeared at the gate, Mordecai rose to his feet while everyone else dropped to his knees.

"How dare you disobey my command?" Haman cried. "Who gives you that right?"

And Mordecai replied:

"I am a Jew; I bow only to God."

From that day on, Haman hated Mordecai and all the Jews. Each time he passed the gate, Mordecai refused to bow. One day, Haman conceived a terrible plan.

Calling together some friends, he broke straws into various lengths and held them in his hand.

"Choose one of these," he said to his friends. "I want to determine the day and the month in which I shall put all the Jews to death."

Thus, by casting lots in this fashion, Haman decided to wipe out the Jewish people on the thirteenth day of the twelfth month, Adar. He then dressed in his finest robes and went before the king. Ahasuerus trusted his chief advisor and was glad to see him.

"I have important news," said Haman to the king. "Living in Persia is a group of wicked people called Jews. They worship their own God and refuse to obey our laws. I say, put them all to death!"

The king was at first unsure. But Haman continued:

"Then, after we have destroyed them, we may take their homes and money and make ourselves rich."

Ahasuerus was greedy, and approved the plan. He gave Haman his royal ring and told him to do as he pleased. The evil minister quickly ran to his scribes, and decreed the mass execution of the Jews for the thirteenth day of Adar.

Copies of this evil decree were sent throughout the land. Mordecai found one of them near the palace gate. When he realized what Haman was planning to do, he tore his clothing in grief and put on sackcloth and ashes. Then he bowed in prayer before the palace gates, hoping that Esther would somehow hear of her people's terrible danger.

The very next day, one of Esther's trusted maids came into her chamber and said:

"I have seen Mordecai, the gatekeeper, wearing sackcloth and covered in ashes as a sign of grief. What can be wrong?"

Esther was puzzled and alarmed. She gave her maid fine garments for Mordecai and told her to deliver them. But the maid returned with the garments and said:

"His grief is so great that he could not raise his head."

Esther was very upset. This time, she sent a trusted messenger to Mordecai in order to learn the source of his grief. Mordecai handed the messenger a copy of Haman's decree.

"Show this to the queen," he said, "and tell her to plead for the Jews before the king."

When Esther received the news she was overcome with sorrow and fear. She loved her people, but she knew the temper of Ahasuerus. Calling her faithful messenger again, she wrote a letter to Mordecai.

"I have received the evil news," it said, "but I am afraid to appear before the king. You know the law. If I enter his chamber and he does not hold out his golden staff, it means that he is angry and will put me to death. Dare I go before him?"

Mordecai was determined. He sent the following reply:

"You face death in any event, for our enemies are ruthless. They will kill even you, the queen. Therefore, I urge you to go before the king and save your people. God foresaw this moment when he made you Queen of Persia."

Esther was convinced. She told Mordecai to order a fast among all the Jews of Shushan.

"For three days I will fast and pray," said the queen, "and then I will go before my husband, even on pain of death."

For three days, the pious Jews fasted and prayed for their queen. Then, on the fourth day, Esther put on her finest robes and her crown, and she walked through the inner court of the palace into the private chambers of the king.

There was Ahasuerus on his golden throne looking grim and very stern. Esther's heart skipped a beat as she waited for the signal that would mean life or death.

Slowly Ahasuerus raised his eyes. At first, he seemed surprised to see his queen. But she looked so lovely and so brave that he smiled and extended his golden staff as a sign of his pleasure. Greatly relieved, the brave Esther approached the throne.

"I have come to invite my lord to a feast," said the queen, "and I wish your minister Haman also to attend."

The king was delighted and accepted.

"Have you no other requests?" he asked.

And Esther replied:

"I shall ask you a very special favor tomorrow, at my feast, and I hope that Your Majesty will grant my request."

The king promised to give Esther whatever she asked, even if it were half of his kingdom. The beautiful queen left the royal chamber and returned to her rooms.

244

OPPOSITE: Plate 58. MORDECAI LAMENTING AT THE PALACE GATES, by Sandro Botticelli (Italian, about 1445–1510), Collection Pallavicini, Rome.

BELOW: Plate 59. THE WRATH OF AHASUERUS, by Jan Steen (Dutch, 1629–1679), Barber Institute of Fine Arts, Birmingham, England.

Esther's Feast

WHEN HAMAN HEARD that he had been invited to dine with the king and queen, he became more boastful than ever. He strutted about and called attention to his fame. But every time he saw Mordecai, his anger returned.

"I shall never be happy," he thought, "until every Jew is dead—especially Mordecai."

At home, Haman complained about Mordecai again. His friends suggested that he ask the king to execute the Jew by hanging him on a special gallows. The evil minister thought this a splendid idea, and ordered a huge gallows built in the palace yard. Then Haman walked to Ahasuerus' private chambers in order to make his vengeful plea.

That night, the king could not sleep. Instead, he occupied his mind by thumbing through the pages of his royal book on good deeds. While reading, he came upon the account of Mordecai who had saved his life by reporting the assassin's plot.

"This man has never been rewarded," noted the king. "I shall correct that immediately."

At this very moment, Haman entered the room and bowed. He had come to request permission to hang Mordecai on his gallows. But the king spoke first.

"Tell me, Haman," he said, "how should I reward a man who has done me great service?"

The boastful Haman thought to himself, "He refers to me. Whom else could he mean?

"O great King," Haman exclaimed, "to honor such a man I would seat him on the king's white horse, dress him in the king's robe and crown, and command one of the noble princes to lead him through the city in triumph."

"So be it," said the king. "Take my robes and my crown to the loyal Mordecai; and you, yourself, lead him through the streets as you have described."

Haman was horrified. But he dared not disobey the king. Gathering the royal robes, he went to his hated enemy and carried out the royal decree. Thus, Haman had to lead the resplendent Mordecai through the city streets—Mordecai, the very man whom he wished to hang on the gallows!

Ashamed and bitter, Haman returned to his house and hid. He was so upset that he forgot about Queen Esther's banquet, and had to be reminded by a messenger. Quickly, he dressed and rushed to the palace.

For a time, Ahasuerus, Esther, and Haman ate in silence while the musicians entertained them. Finally, the king leaned over to his wife and tenderly said:

"You wish to make a request of me? Do not be afraid, for I will grant you any favor."

Esther rose from her place and in a quavering voice she exclaimed:

"I am a Jew, and an evil man has sent forth a proclamation ordering all my people killed, including me. I therefore beg you to save us and to punish the villain."

Ahasuerus was amazed.

"Who ordered such an evil decree?" he demanded.

Bravely, Esther pointed to Haman and cried:

"Haman! He is the man!"

The king became furious. He rose to his feet, overturning the banquet table in rage.

"How shall I punish him?" he asked.

"There!" cried one of his guards, pointing to the window. "Someone has built a gallows in the courtyard."

"Excellent," shouted the king. "I order that Haman be hanged there this very morning. Only then will I be satisfied."

That morning, the wicked Haman was hanged on the gallows that he had prepared for Mordecai. But his evil decree to execute the Jews was still in effect, and, according to Persian law, it could not be repealed.

Mordecai went before the king.

"Arm the Jews with swords and spears," he said, "so that they may defend themselves before their enemies. Then let everyone know that we are no longer defenseless and weak. That will save us."

Ahasuerus agreed. When the thirteenth day of the twelfth month dawned, no one in all Persia dared harm the Jews. Instead, a great celebration was held throughout the land, and the people cheered the brave Queen Esther and the wise Mordecai. To this day, the feast of Purim is celebrated in honor of the beautiful Jewish maiden who was the queen and kept her people from being destroyed.

IN THE PROVINCE of Galilee lived the prophet Jonah. He was a righteous man who often preached about God's eventual judgment. The Lord was pleased with Jonah, and decided to send him on a mission to the great city of Nineveh, in the kingdom of Babylon.

"Arise and go to Nineveh," said the Lord. "The people there have sinned, and I will punish them severely. You must tell them of My anger."

Jonah was surprised. The people of Nineveh were not Jews, he thought. Why should God be concerned with them? Besides, Nineveh

*A Fish
Swallows
Jonah*

was a very wicked city, far from home, and Jonah was unwilling to risk his life just to save some heathens. Therefore, instead of obeying the Lord, Jonah secretly boarded a ship headed in the opposite direction.

When the ship was in the middle of the sea, one day out from shore, a terrible storm arose. Darkness, thunder, and lightning filled the air, and a great wind fiercely rocked the ship, so that its mast creaked and swayed as though it would break. The sailors and passengers on the ship were terrified. They threw part of their cargo overboard, hoping to lighten the load, but still the boat rocked dangerously in the waters amid great waves.

Finally, the captain of the ship issued a command.

"Let everyone fall to his knees and pray to his gods," he said. "In this way we may be saved—for surely someone on this ship has sinned and offended his god."

Far below, in his cabin, Jonah paid no attention to the storm. Instead, he curled up in his bunk and fell asleep. When the captain learned this, he rushed to Jonah and said:

"Wake up, you sleeper! Pray to your God! Perhaps he can save us from this storm."

After the captain left his room, Jonah began to fear that he was the cause of the storm. His fears were confirmed when he heard the sailors crying:

"Someone has sinned on this ship, and God is punishing him."

To find out who it was, the sailors drew lots among themselves and all the passengers. The shortest lot fell to Jonah, proving his guilt.

"Who are you, and what sin have you committed?" cried the sailors. Jonah confessed.

"I am a Hebrew," he said, "and I have disobeyed the Lord. If you want to be saved, you must throw me overboard and let me drown."

The sailors did not want to kill Jonah, and tried to outrun the storm. But the harder they tried, the more imperiled they became. Finally, begging forgiveness from God, they threw Jonah over the side of the ship into the dark and dangerous waves.

As soon as the prophet hit the water, the storm subsided and the dark clouds disappeared. The grateful seamen knew that Jonah's God was very powerful; nevertheless, they regretted having drowned the prophet.

But Jonah did not drown. As he sank below the waves, an enormous fish, as big as a house, swallowed him in one gulp. Alone in the dark belly of the fish, Jonah knew that God wished him to live so that he might go to Nineveh and preach. For three days and nights, Jonah crouched within the fish, praying to the Lord for forgiveness.

Plate 60. JONAH CAST INTO THE SEA, by Peter Paul Rubens
(Flemish, 1577–1640), Museum of Nancy, France.

Jonah in Nineveh

ON THE FOURTH DAY, Jonah felt the fish heaving and tossing in the waters. Then, suddenly, the prophet was cast out of the belly of the fish onto dry land. Looking around, Jonah saw that he was on the outskirts of a large, strange city. He brushed himself off and began walking toward the center of town.

"Where am I?" he asked some passers-by.

"This is Nineveh," they replied.

At last, Jonah realized that he could not escape his mission. With determination in his heart, he set out to preach the word of the Lord in the streets and byways of the city.

"Prepare to meet your God!" he cried. "For the Lord will destroy Nineveh in forty days as punishment for all its sins and wickedness."

When the king of Nineveh heard this warning, he became afraid. Knowing the God of Israel to be powerful and mighty, he sent a decree ordering the people to fast and pray in repentance for their sins. The people of Nineveh, even though they were not Jews, believed in the power of God and truly repented.

For weeks, no one danced or made merry in Nineveh, and the murmurs of prayer could be heard throughout the streets. God was pleased. But the prophet Jonah was annoyed and he said to God:

"I warned these people that in forty days they would be doomed. Now You have forgiven them, and I look like a fool. It would be better if I were dead."

Then, pouting like a little child, Jonah took leave of Nineveh. He walked up into the mountains to a spot overlooking the entire town.

"Perhaps the Lord will change His mind and destroy the city after all," the prophet thought. "I shall wait and see."

Jonah then built himself a small hut and waited. After a time he became very uncomfortable, for it was terribly hot in the sun. Complaining of the heat, Jonah lay down to sleep. When he arose in the morning he found that a luxurious palm tree had grown up right over his shack, providing him with shade. He was grateful, indeed. Still he could not be completely happy, for there was Nineveh stretched out before him, and the Lord had not yet destroyed it.

The next day Jonah awoke in dismay. His luxurious palm tree was all shrunken and dead, for a worm had eaten its roots. Now without shade, Jonah began to suffer in the heat. Before long, hot winds came up out of the east and beat upon his head. He turned red as fire, and was in such agony that again he called on God to strike him dead.

But the Lord replied:

"You are angry because the palm tree wilted and died. But this was not your palm tree; you did not make it. If a dying tree can cause you such sorrow, why have you no mercy on Nineveh? Here is a great city of thousands of people, thousands of cattle, and many buildings. Why should they be destroyed if they repent?"

Tears of pity filled Jonah's eyes. He realized at last that God was merciful to all the people of the earth, and that the salvation of even one man, in a distant city, was worth every effort of the Lord.

ONCE, IN THE LAND OF UZ, there lived a good man named Job. Great wealth and comfort were his, and he had a large and happy family. No one prayed more earnestly than Job. He prayed for his children lest they sin unknowingly, and he was kind to his neighbors, to strangers, to beggars, and to all the poor.

In Heaven, God sat upon his lofty throne and the angels clustered at His feet. Among the angels was Satan, the devil, who had crept into the sacred company. With mischief in his heart, he rose to speak before God.

"I have been roaming upon the earth," the devil said. "And I do not think that Man loves God."

The Lord replied,

"There is one man who is righteous above all others. His name is Job. Have you not seen him?"

And the devil laughed.

"Why shouldn't Job be righteous and good? You have given him all manner of wealth and happiness. See what happens if he should lose his livestock and his house and his children. He will surely curse You to Your face."

God knew the heart of Job. He ordered Satan to undo all Job's wealth and happiness.

"We will see if he will curse Me to My face," said the Lord. "Try your evil. But do not lay a hand upon Job to harm him."

Then Satan quickly departed to do his work.

NOW GREAT MISFORTUNE fell upon Job. While he was sitting in his house a servant came running breathlessly through the door and shouted,

"Tribesmen from the east have attacked your cattle and carried them off. They have killed our herdsmen—all of them. Only I escaped to tell you."

Job:
The
Prologue

The
First
Ordeal

Job was astonished. Before he could recover from the news, another servant rushed into the house crying,

"Lightning has struck the sheepfold and burned it down. All the sheep are dead, and the shepherds with them. I alone escaped to tell you."

Misfortune followed upon misfortune. In the same afternoon, Job learned that his cattle had been destroyed, his sheep burned, his camels and asses plundered, and all his servants killed. By the time the sun had set, it seemed no greater sorrow could befall the once happy man. But now a servant came running up the path, crying:

"Job, Job! Your children were seated together in the field when a tornado came out of the sky and killed them all in one blow. I alone escaped to tell you."

Job fell to the floor and tore his cloak in grief. But his faith was strong. Instead of crying out against God, he said:

"The Lord has given, and the Lord has taken away. Blessed be the name of the Lord."

The Second Ordeal

WHEN SATAN LEARNED of Job's great faith, he immediately returned to the throne of God. The Lord was pleased with Job and said:

"You have tried to break the faith of My servant Job, but he has remained steadfast."

The devil laughed:

"The misfortunes that befell him did not directly cause him pain. See what will happen if he should become ill and miserable. He will surely curse You to Your face."

The Lord had faith in Job. He instructed the devil to afflict Job with illness and with pain. Satan quickly went about his evil work.

From that day on, Job became desperately ill. His skin broke out in painful boils. The hair fell from his head. His teeth rattled in his jaw. He was so miserable that he placed sackcloth upon his body and sat among the ashes as a sign of grief. His wife came out of the house. She saw her husband's painful condition, and she cried out in despair:

"How can you have faith in God after all this misery? Curse Him, and maybe He will have mercy and let you die."

But Job would not speak against God.

"When the Lord is good to us," he said, "we do not complain. Should we not accept evil when the Lord chooses to send us evil?"

Thus the days dragged on, and Job sat among the ashes in pain and suffering, and his faith began to falter. Then, one day, three of his friends came down the path to visit him and comfort him. They were Eliphaz, Bildad, and Zophar. When they saw Job's miserable condition, they began to weep. So great was their sympathy that they could not even speak. They simply sat silently watching their unhappy friend. Then, at last, Job lifted his eyes and cried out in anguish:

"Perish the day on which I was born, the night when they said, 'The child is a boy.' May that day be blotted out from memory. May it be cursed and forgotten, because mine is a life of meaningless misery. I am greatly afflicted. I sigh and groan. I have no peace, no rest."

When Job's friends heard him speak, they tried to comfort him. This is how it went:

ELIPHAZ: If we try to have a word with you, will you mind? We look at you, once happy and once so good, and we wonder. Have you perhaps lost your faith through sin? Perhaps that is why you are suffering. Think! What innocent person suffers like this? Man himself makes his own mischief, just as sparks fly upward. If I were you, I would appeal to God and try to find out how you have sinned against Him.

JOB: I am overwhelmed with more trouble and pain than there is sand in the sea. Your words are, therefore, no comfort. Can you think of any sin I have done against you or any man? Have I ever been insincere or given to falsehood? You say that I have lost my faith in God. But I have never spoken against Him in all this anguish, for I know that man cannot live forever. What is man that God should pay him any heed?

BILDAD: But it must be that you have sinned, for God does not punish without reason. Repent, and once again the Lord will fill your mouth with laughter and your lips with rejoicing.

JOB: God is wise and mighty in strength. He makes the mountains and He can destroy them. He commands the sun and seals up the stars. Therefore, He must know what He is doing in so afflicting me. Perhaps it is His will to afflict the innocent and reward the guilty. For I am innocent, and I know it. But you do not believe me. Even if I laid aside my sadness in spite of my pains, you would not believe that I am innocent. You would say that I have challenged God.

254

ZOPHAR: And yet you do challenge God by refusing to seek the cause of your punishment. Do this, and you will be freed from your misery. Your pain will wash away like water.

JOB: You offer useless remedies to me, for I am innocent, unless being human is a sin. Man, born of woman, is short-lived and full of trouble. Is any man, therefore, free of sin?

ELIPHAZ: There! You have said it. There *is* some sin upon your soul. Perhaps you have wronged an innocent man. Were you ever unkindly to a beggar? Did you steal unknowingly? Think of all the wicked things that you may have done.

JOB: You do not comfort me. You ask me to think about my sins. Have I not enough to think about? My wealth is gone; my children are dead; and I am wracked with illness. I cannot sleep without the fear of awful dreams. I cannot eat. And yet you come to make it worse for me.

BILDAD: We have spoken as we see fit to speak. If a man is so severely punished, then there must be a reason.

JOB: Why don't you pray for me, instead of all these unkind words? Or if not, leave me. I never asked you to come.

ZOPHAR: Only a wicked man would speak like this to his friends.

ELIPHAZ: Only a sinner who has angered God.

JOB: You talk like this of a man who once was honored and loved throughout the land. A man who once had happy children and a happy home! Don't you see? God has afflicted me for no reason at all. Therefore, I complain. I tear my clothing and I weep. For, in all my life, I never did any man harm, nor was unkind, or cruel. I always worshiped God and loved Him. Why am I punished?

WHEN JOB HAD SAID these words, he closed his eyes and bowed his head. Then another man named Elihu stepped forward. He had been listening to the conversation among Job and his friends, but, being younger than the rest, he felt that it was not proper to speak until they had finished. His words were none the less disturbing to Job. He too accused him of a sin against God. He also criticized the others.

"You have not helped Job," he said. "You point out that he has sinned, but you have not helped him find his sin, so that he might be forgiven. Behold, God is great, and we know him not."

God's Reply

255

The friends began to argue among themselves, while Job cried out in pain:

"Why, why, am I so afflicted?"

Then, all at once, a storm brew up out of the heavens, and God spoke to Job with the voice of the wind:

"Is this Job who asks so ignorant a question?" said the Lord. "Has Job lost his faith and courage? You seek many answers to explain your suffering, and you want to know the ways of God. But you do not know how the earth was created, and yet it does exist. You do not know the mysteries of the oceans, and yet the oceans continue to turn and toss. You did not create the stars in the sky, and yet each night they appear and each morning they fade with the sun. You know nothing of man or beast, and yet man lives and moves and breathes. Of all these things you are ignorant, and yet these things exist, for I alone understand My purpose and My plan."

Job then lifted his eyes and answered the Lord most humbly:

"It is true. All these things You can do, and there is a purpose behind Your every deed. Such truth I have always known, but pain and suffering have made me weak. I repent ever doubting the justice of Your deeds. I ask forgiveness and will accept my fate in perfect faith."

The Lord was pleased. He spoke to Eliphaz, and scolded him and the others for being cruel to Job in accusing him of sin.

"I have My reasons for all things," said God. "And man does not always understand them."

Eliphaz and his friends begged Job to pray for them, so that God might forgive their ignorance. Job fell on his knees, still aching with pain, and prayed for his erring friends.

Then, slowly but surely, the boils disappeared from Job's body and the pain vanished, and health was restored to the once-suffering man. At the same time, the warm sun shone forth and Job's fields began to flourish with wheat and corn. His flocks increased. Within a year he had more cattle than ever before. And, in due time, seven strong sons and three beautiful daughters were born to him in perfect happiness.

For many, many years Job lived in peace and in comfort such as he had never known. In all of this, he remembered the greatness of God.

"The Lord gives and the Lord takes away," he exclaimed. "Blessed be the name of the Lord."

THE APOCRYPHA

THE BOOKS OF TOBIT, JUDITH, SUSANNA, AND THE MACCABEES

Stories of Tobit and His Son Tobias, and of Sara, the Unhappy Bride; Stories of the Brave Widow Judith, Who Slew General Holofernes; Stories of the Righteous Susanna, Who Was Accused by the Elders in Babylon; Stories of the Brave Brothers Maccabee, Who Freed Their People from Bondage.

TOBIT LIVED IN NINEVEH in the days of the captivity. He had been brought from the hills of Galilee in Israel with his wife Anna and their small son Tobias.

For a time, the family led a pleasant life under King Shalmaneser. There was enough food, and the Jewish people were treated fairly. Tobit made it a practice to visit his brethren who were sick, and he was often responsible for seeing that the poor were decently buried when they died.

But evil days fell upon the Jews in Babylon when King Sennacherib came to the throne. He passed a strict law that said: if any Jew died or was killed on the streets, his body was to be dragged outside the city walls and left for the vultures and the wild dogs. Tobit was horrified by this news. Stealthily at night, he crept out of the city and, single-handed, buried the dead according to the Hebrew law. All this he did at the risk of his own safety.

For many years, the cruel Sennacherib ruled in Babylon and Assyria. All this time, Tobit saw to the proper burial of the dead. He was often under suspicion for his deeds, and eventually, soldiers came to his house and took away his furniture and valued belongings. They also prevented anyone in Nineveh from giving him employment. His wife Anna complained:

"What good have they been, all these righteous deeds in the name of God? You have lost your money, and now we may starve."

Tobit felt sorry for his wife, and promised to stay in the house and avoid trouble. But, one day, his son Tobias rushed up to him and said,

Tobit and His Son

"One of our Jewish neighbors has been strangled by the enemy, and his body lies in the street with no one to bury it."

Tobit could not allow such a disgrace, and he left his house and immediately proceeded to bury his neighbor. On returning from his errand of mercy, Tobit realized that he could not enter his house for his hands were still unclean, after the burial. It was late, so he decided to sleep in the garden. In the morning, he awoke with a burning pain in his eyes. During the night some bird lime from a swallow's nest in an overhanging tree had fallen on his face. Now poor Tobit was blind.

He went into his home, where his weeping wife tried to take care of him. In all his suffering, he prayed to God for the strength to continue his charity among the Jews.

The Unhappy Bride

IN THE DISTANT KINGDOM of the Medes, Tobit had a cousin named Raguel. Raguel's daughter Sara lived under a terrible curse, for a demon named Asmodeus was in love with her, and mysteriously murdered every young man who tried to marry Sara. The townspeople could not see Asmodeus, for he was invisible. Therefore, they blamed Sara for the murders, and she had to hide in her room for fear of unjust punishment.

God conceived a plan to help both Tobit and Sara, the daughter of Raguel. He sent the Angel Raphael to earth disguised as an ordinary man. Raphael journeyed to Tobit's home and waited on the road. He knew that his services would soon be needed.

Inside the house, the blind Tobit called Tobias, his son, and said:

"We are poor and without money. But, years ago, I provided for such a time. I left a great quantity of silver in trust with my friend Gabael in the land of the Medes. Now you must journey there and bring back our money, so that you may marry and be prosperous."

Tobias agreed; but he was unsure about the route, and was afraid that he might get lost or even robbed and murdered, far from home. Tobit decided to hire a guide for his son, and instructed Tobias to seek an honest man who knew the route to Media.

At the same moment, there was a knock on the door. Outside stood Raphael, the angel, who had come to offer his services as a guide. Tobit was satisfied with the stranger's qualifications and agreed to hire him.

"What is your name?" Tobit asked.

And Raphael replied:

"I am Azarias, and we are distantly related, you and I."

"Go then, Azarias," said Tobit. "Take my son to the land of the

Medes and see that no harm comes to him. When you return I will pay you well."

Then Tobit blessed his son and sent him off with Azarias. Anna wept to see her son go off on such a long journey, and Tobias' little dog also whimpered and scratched at the door until he was freed to follow his master.

When they had traveled several miles, Tobias and Azarias decided to rest by the banks of a river. While Azarias prepared a fire, Tobias laid aside his clothes and jumped into the water in order to bathe.

Suddenly, a strange fish came swimming toward Tobias with its fearsome jaws opened wide.

"Help me, Azarias," called the young man. "A fish has attacked me!"

Azarias ran to the shore and cried:

"Grab the fish by his fins, and he will become helpless."

Tobias obeyed. In a flash, the fish became limp and helpless. With the catch in hand, Tobias dashed out of the water and huddled near the fire that Azarias had kindled.

"This fish will be good to eat," the angel said. "But, first, you Tobias, must cut it open and remove its heart, liver, and gall. Wrap these in cloth and put them in your pocket. Who knows? These may be useful, some day."

Tobias followed Azarias' instructions. He opened the fish, removed the heart, liver, and gall. Then he and his guide ate the fish.

In the morning, Tobias, the angel, and the little dog joyfully continued their journey toward Media. As they walked, Tobias questioned his friend.

"Of what importance are the heart, the liver, and the gall of the fish?" he asked.

And Azarias answered:

"The heart and liver, put on burning coals, will drive away demons, for they are afraid of the smell. The gall is an excellent cure for certain kinds of blindness. All these things we shall learn of presently."

By midday, the two were in Media, and went directly to the home of Raguel, Tobit's cousin. Before they entered the house, Azarias took Tobias aside and said:

"Raguel has a lovely daughter who is most unhappy. She will make an excellent bride for you, and I shall speak to her father on your behalf."

Tobias was, at first, delighted. But then he remembered the stories that he had heard about Sara of the land of the Medes.

"Is she not the girl who is supposed to have murdered seven husbands?" questioned Tobias in alarm.

The angel smiled, and assured Tobias that all would be well, if he kept faith in God.

IN DUE TIME, the wedding between Sara and Tobias was arranged. Raguel approached the day with mixed emotions. On the one hand, he was happy to see his daughter engaged to such a fine young man. On the other, he believed that Tobias would die on his wedding night, like all the others. Sara, too, was unhappy. She loved Tobias but feared for him, for the evil Asmodeus had sworn to kill every husband whom Sara brought into her house.

On the night of the wedding, Azarias took Tobias aside and said:

"When you and your bride are alone in the bedroom, take the heart and the liver of the fish. Place these on the fire. The smoke will frighten the demon Asmodeus away, and he will never return. Then you will live happily ever after with your bride."

Tobias did just as he was told, and, that night, while Sara was preparing for bed, he threw the heart and the liver into the flames. In a moment the demon Asmodeus appeared.

"What have you done?" he exclaimed. "I cannot stand that smoke! Take it away!"

But Tobias would not take it away. The smoke grew very thick and filled the room with a terrible stench that caused Asmodeus to choke and cough until he could stand it no more—and, in a flash, he disappeared, never to be seen again.

In the morning, Raguel waited fearfully at the door of the bedroom, for he thought surely Tobias was dead. But to his delight, when the door opened, there stood bride and bridegroom in perfect happiness.

"We will hold a great feast!" cried Raguel.

Tobias then sent servants to Gabael, his father's friend, with an invitation to the feast. At the same time, Gabael was to bring the silver that he had kept for Tobit so many years.

The celebration for Tobias and Sara lasted fourteen days. Raguel

Tobias Marries Sara

OPPOSITE: Plate 62. TOBIAS AND THE ANGEL, School of Verrocchio, (Italian, 15th century), The National Gallery, London.

was so happy for his daughter that he would not permit the feast to end. Every time the food and drink ran low, he cheerfully ordered new supplies. But he finally blessed the couple and allowed them to depart.

Tobias Returns Home

BACK IN NINEVEH, Tobit and his wife Anna did not know what had happened, and they feared that their son Tobias was dead. Poor, blind Tobit lost all will to live. One day, when their hope was almost exhausted, the old people heard footsteps on the path. There, at last, were Tobias and Azarias his guide. They were both running toward the house.

Tobit rose from his chair and groped his way to the door, stumbling in his blindness. At that same moment, Tobias entered. Leading his father back to the chair, Tobias withdrew the gall of the magic fish. Carefully he applied the juice of the gall to his father's eyes, just as Azarias had told him. A moment later, the old man cried out in joy:

"I can see! I can see! Praise be the Lord!"

Happiness followed upon happiness. Tobias now told his parents of Sara, his bride, who even at that moment was approaching in her caravan. The dutiful son also produced the great quantity of silver that he had received from Gabael in Media. So great was Tobit and Anna's joy that they ordered a feast and celebration that lasted for seven days.

When the feast had ended, Tobit called his son to him and said:

"We must now pay Azarias his wages as we promised, so that he may go about his business."

Tobias agreed. He had become very fond of Azarias, and asked his father to reward him with half the quantity of silver that Tobias had brought from Media. Tobit was pleased to do so and called Azarias to his side.

"I am so happy with your services," Tobit said, "that I wish to reward you many times over. You have protected my son, brought him a good wife, and, through your wisdom, helped cure my blindness. Please take this silver with my thanks."

But Azarias would not take the silver; instead he drew Tobit and Tobias aside and declared in ringing tones:

"Behold! I am Raphael, one of the seven holy angels who stand before the throne of God. Tobit has served the Lord, and the Lord is pleased. Therefore, I came here to help you and bring you peace. Your goodness is the only reward that I need."

When the others heard this they fell on their knees, and buried their faces, for the room suddenly became filled with glorious light. In that same instant, Raphael unfolded his wings and departed to heaven. Tobit lifted his eyes:

"Praise be to God," he said. "He has brought us wonderful works and we will bless Him for ever and ever."

AFTER THE JEWS RETURNED to Jerusalem from the Babylonian captivity, there was trouble in the Eastern world. The king of Assyria, offended by the ambassadors of certain smaller countries, decided to teach them a severe lesson. For this purpose, he called upon Holofernes, the fiercest general of his armies.

"Lead your troops against our enemies," said the king. "If they surrender and join you, let them live. If they resist, spare no one, neither man, woman, nor child."

Holofernes was pleased with this order. He loved war and enjoyed the prospects of victory. In the months that followed, he led the powerful Assyrian army in triumph over the smaller countries of the Middle East. Finally, he faced Judah, and the city of Jerusalem.

"Tell the Jews to surrender," he ordered his men. "Tell them to march out of their cities and bow down to me and to my king, or we will kill them all."

The messenger soon returned. They reported that the Jews refused to surrender and were in deep prayer to their God for protection and deliverance. Holofernes was surprised. Never before had he come upon a nation that dared oppose his army and his strength.

"Who are these people?" he asked.

A man named Achior stepped forward to answer the general.

"These are the same people whom Moses led out of Egypt," said Achior. "Many miracles took place in those times, for these Jews have a very powerful God. When they are righteous and pure, their God is kind to them, and gives them victory. When they sin, He turns His wrath against them. Now they are in prayer and they are fasting. Surely their God will help them and grant them victory even over your great strength."

When the soldiers heard Achior they grew afraid and there was much dissension in the ranks. Furiously, Holofernes turned on Achior and accused him of being a Jewish spy, who had come purposely spreading alarming and unreliable stories. As a punishment, he had Achior bound with rope and led back into the hills of Judah.

"Tell your friends that we mean to destroy them all, every man, woman, and child!" said the general.

Achior was tied to a tree on a hillside near the city of Bethulia, and left there by the Assyrians. He was found and released by some Jewish soldiers who took him into the city.

"The fierce general Holofernes is about to attack your city," he announced. "And he will kill me and everyone else whom he finds!"

The people of Bethulia became panicky. From their fortress, they could see Holofernes' enormous army. They could also see the general's tent, surrounded, as it always was, by an armed guard of a hundred men.

"Surely they will defeat us," said the Jews. "Either they will hurl their armies against us or they will starve us out. It would be best for us to surrender."

And so they decided to surrender in five days, unless God came to rescue them.

The Widow Judith

IN BETHULIA there lived a widow, Judith, the most God-fearing woman in the entire city. For three years she had lived in mourning for her husband, who died while working in the fields. Now she heard of the plan to surrender, and she came before the elders of the city.

"You are tempting God," she told them, "by saying that you will surrender in five days unless He rescues us. Have you no greater faith? Perhaps God chooses to help us on the sixth day, or on the tenth. We must pray for our own deliverance."

Then she told the elders that she had a secret plan to defeat the enemy. She asked permission to leave the city that night with her maid.

The elders were impressed with Judith's speech, and agreed to her wish. But they wondered what she, an ordinary woman, could do to save the nation.

Judith returned home, and spent the rest of the day in prayer. Then she removed her widow's weeds and dressed in her most beautiful garments. Upon her head she set a jeweled crown, and upon her arms she placed many bracelets and beads. After this, she called her servant and prepared a large sack of food, for she would not eat anything forbidden by her religion. When she was fully prepared, she walked to the city gates. The elders were amazed to see her beauty, and, though they still did not know what she planned to do, they wished her well, opened the gates, and allowed her to leave.

Judith and her servant roamed the countryside near the Assyrian camp. In the darkness, they could see campfires and the tents of Holofernes' army. As they watched from a clump of trees, a group of soldiers came up behind them.

Plate 63. JUDITH ABOUT TO SLAY HOLOFERNES, by Tintoretto
(Italian, 1518–1594), The Prado Museum, Madrid.

"What are you doing here?" they demanded.

Judith explained that she and her servant had deserted the Jewish
city since they knew that Holofernes would be victorious. Now, Judith
continued, she wanted only to serve the great Assyrian general. The soldiers were impressed with Judith's beauty and charm, and they decided
to bring her to their general.

There, in his tent, Holofernes was resting beneath a luxurious can-
opy. When Judith saw him she fell on her knees.

"O great Holofernes," she said, "I am your servant. I have left my
people because they are weak, and I know that they will be defeated by
your army."

Holofernes was impressed with the beautiful woman and urged her
to rise.

Judith continued:

"I am a righteous woman and favored by God. If I pray to Him, He
will tell me when the Jews have sinned and when He will abandon
them. Then you may attack and easily win."

Holofernes remembered that Achior had told him that God would abandon the Jews if they were wicked. Thus, he believed Judith. From that moment on, he declared, she was to come and go as she pleased within the Assyrian camp.

For three days, Judith prayed silently to God. On the fourth day, Holofernes invited her to a feast in his tent. She accepted, but asked permission to bring her own special food. Holofernes agreed.

When Judith arrived in the general's tent she looked more beautiful than ever before. As she ate, Holofernes admired her.

"Drink now, and be merry with us," he said. He was sure he had nothing to fear from Judith.

"I will drink gladly," the Hebrew woman replied.

For hours Holofernes ate and drank, all the while boasting of his coming victory over the Jews. By the end of the evening, he was so drunk he fell down fast asleep on his couch.

This was the moment that Judith had awaited. Stealthily, she lifted the general's heavy sword from its place, and, with two mighty strokes, cut off his head at the neck. She then put the head in the bag that had carried her food, and quietly, with her servant, left the Assyrian camp undisturbed and hurried toward Judah.

When Judith arrived at Bethulia the elders were surprised to see her alive. But she had no time to explain, and she urged them to call all the people into the streets. When everyone had assembled, Judith mounted the stairs and withdrew the severed head of Holofernes. Holding it aloft she cried:

"God has delivered us from our enemy because we kept our faith in Him!"

The people shouted for joy and grew bold in their hearts. The Assyrians, meanwhile, having found the headless body of their general, were in complete confusion. It was, therefore, easy for the Jews to defeat them and drive them away. When the battle was won, a great celebration was held throughout the land. The hero of the day was the beautiful widow Judith, who had so bravely slain the fierce Assyrian general.

Susanna and the Elders

IN BABYLON, ONE DAY, a man named Joiakim came to the prophet Daniel with a painful story. Joiakim's wife, Susanna, had been accused of unfaithfulness by two respected elders of the city. Now, the court had condemned her to death without listening to what she had to say. Daniel was angered by so high-handed a procedure, and went to hear Susanna's story from her own lips.

"For many days," she told him, "two of the city's elders came to my husband's house to discuss business. I noticed that they often watched me as I walked in the garden with my maids. I felt uncomfortable whenever I saw them, but said nothing.

"It was very hot a few days ago, and I decided to bathe in my garden. I told my maids to lock all the garden gates, so that I would not be disturbed. They set a basin of water before me and brought me many fine oils and soap. Then, because they had other work to do, they left me and returned to the house. When I was alone in my bath, I suddenly saw the two elders, who had come out of hiding. They declared their love for me, and when I shrank from them, they said:

"'You can't avoid us. If you try, we will say that you have been meeting in secret with a young man here in the garden. Since there are two of us, we shall be believed and you will be condemned as an unfaithful wife.'

"I was afraid, but had faith in God, so I told them not to touch me, and I screamed for help. My maids came running back. The elders immediately accused me of unfaithfulness. They said that I had been entertaining a young man who had broken away from them and left by the garden gate. I was taken to prison—though I am innocent—and now I have been condemned to die."

Daniel heard the story with much compassion, and was convinced of Susanna's innocence.

Filled with indignation, he went to the court where Susanna had been tried, and demanded the right to question the elders. Since he was highly respected, the judges agreed. Daniel then took one of the elders aside, so that the other could not hear. Only the judges were present as Daniel said:

"You testified that Susanna met a young man in her garden and sat with him beneath a large tree. Tell me, what kind of tree was it?"

And the elder replied:

"It was a gum tree."

Daniel then called the other elder before the judges.

"Tell us," he said, "under what kind of tree did Susanna sit with the young man?"

And the second elder replied:

"It was a holly tree."

Then Daniel turned to the entire court and exclaimed:

"These men have lied! This one says it was a holly tree, the other, a gum tree. They made up the entire story because they tried to dishonor Susanna and she would have no part of them. Therefore, let them be punished severely, and let Susanna reclaim the respect and dignity that she rightly deserves."

The court agreed. The elders were put to death, and Susanna and Joiakim were happily reunited.

THE HISTORY OF the ancient world is full of war and conquest. One great empire conquered another, enslaving thousands and sending great armies into the field. Egypt was the first of these conquering empires. For a long time, Egyptian power was unchallenged. Then the Assyrians and Babylonians conquered Egypt, and took over all its territories. Israel under Solomon had a brief period of imperial glory—soon ended by Assyria under King Nebuchadnezzar. During the time of the prophet Daniel, the Persians and the Medes conquered Assyria. Under such kings as Darius and Cyrus, the Persian Empire covered most of the known world. From 333 to 327 B.C., Alexander the Great of Greece conquered the Persian Empire and all its holdings. Judah, also called Judea, was part of Alexander's vast empire.

Under Greek rule, the Jews fared well. They were free to worship God and follow the Laws of Moses. Unfortunately, Alexander the Great died when he was very young. There followed great turmoil in the world. Civil wars broke out and various families took control of Alexander's far-reaching empire. First, the Ptolemies ruled Judah. They were followed by the Seleucids, a cruel family of kings who persecuted the Jews and caused much hardship and grief.

Antiochus was a Seleucid king who seemed to take pleasure in persecuting the Jews. First he desecrated the Temple in Jerusalem. All the precious treasures were removed and the holy objects smashed and defiled. Then he ordered severe punishment and death to all those who continued to obey the Laws of Moses. The Jews were once again a broken and sorrowful people. Their sanctuary was laid waste; their feasts were turned into mourning; their Sabbaths were dishonored. They were forced to witness sacrifices made to idols, and all manner of uncleanliness and profanation was put upon them.

OPPOSITE: Plate 64. SUSANNA AT THE BATH, by Albrecht Altdorfer (German, about 1480–1538), Pinakothek (Picture Gallery), Munich.

"I told my maids to lock all the garden gates, so that I would not be
disturbed. Then they set a basin of water before me
and brought many fine oils and soap into the garden."

As this persecution continued, the Jews grew stronger in their faith. Many went to their deaths rather than eat forbidden food or break the Holy Laws. One family of seven sons suffered the cruelest tortures because they would not eat pork, which the Jews considered unclean. While their aged mother looked on, each of the seven sons was put to death in hideous fashion. But their bravery became a legend, for each son grew more defiant as he saw his brother die. And the aged mother was bravest of all.

"Do not break the faith!" she cried to her sons. She preferred to see them die as Jews and patriots rather than bend to the will of the evil Antiochus. For this, she too, was put to death.

In all this suffering and persecution, the Jews did not weaken. Instead, they began to form secret groups of resistance.

One such group was headed by the High Priest Mattathias, who had five sons. Antiochus was wary of Mattathias, who was rich and very influential. One day, the king ordered the priest to renounce his Jewish faith publicly. Mattathias gathered his family and faithful followers and escaped to the hills in northern Judea.

"We will resist the evil tyrant and reclaim our country," announced Mattathias, "even if we must live like beasts in the hills."

Indeed, Mattathias and his sons and their followers did live like beasts in the hills, eating what they could find, while they prepared to attack the enemy.

To lead the Jewish army, Mattathias chose Judas, one of his sons. Because of his great strength and courage, Judas was called Maccabeus or "the hammerer." Soon the entire army became known as the Maccabees.

At first, Judas and his men suffered defeat at the hands of Antiochus. With each setback the Jews retreated to the hills, where they hid and regrouped their forces. Antiochus was not familiar with the hills of Judea and dared not venture out of his cities. For a long time, the rebels were silent, and the tyrant thought that he had conquered them. But Judas and his brothers were gathering new strength.

"We will fast and pray," said Judas to his men. "Then upon my

OPPOSITE: Plate 65. THE TRIUMPH OF JUDAS MACCABEUS, by Peter Paul Rubens (Flemish, 1577–1640), Museum of Nantes, France.

signal, we will strike at the cities of Antiochus and reclaim Jerusalem."

Judas was a brilliant commander. With only six thousand men, he attacked several well-fortified cities and defeated the enemy troops. Then he prepared to invade Jerusalem, the stronghold of Antiochus. For days before the battle, Judas prayed and sacrificed to God in the company of his followers.

Meanwhile, the king, having seen the might of the Maccabees, became afraid and sick with worry. He gathered many of the treasures that he had taken from the Jews and fled the city. But guilt and illness weighed him down. Surrounded by the sacred treasures he had stolen, Antiochus died in agony. He was succeeded by his very young son. This child was no match for the Maccabees. After nearly two hundred years of persecution and enslavement by their enemies, the Jews finally triumphed. Judas led his men into Jerusalem and freed the city.

In order to celebrate their victory, a solemn rededication of the holy Temple was held. For eight days, the grateful people offered sacrifice and homage to God for their deliverance. This great holiday was called the Rededication, or "Chanukah"; and it is celebrated today by the Jews as a remembrance of the brave Maccabees.

For nearly a hundred years thereafter, the Jews were independent and free of foreign rule. Judas became leader of the nation. In due time, he was followed by his brothers and their descendants. But to the west another great empire was forming under a man named Julius Caesar. This was the great Roman Empire that conquered almost the entire world. By the year 66 B.C, Rome had conquered Judea as well, and set up a new family of kings of whom the first was Herod Antipater. These kings were not Jews, but descendants of Esau, and they took their orders from Rome. For centuries thereafter, the Jewish people were under foreign rule or lived dispersed in many parts of the world.

In 1948, during our own times, the State of Israel was proclaimed on the site of ancient Canaan. Once again, the Jews returned to their homeland after great hardship and persecution. Once again, they faced hostility from their neighbors in the Middle East. But, in the spirit of rededication, they rebuilt Jerusalem and the other cities of the Holy Land. Thus, after thousands of years, the Covenant of God with Abraham was fulfilled in the Lord's own words:

> I will establish My covenant between Me and thee and thy seed after thee in their generations, for an everlasting covenant, to be a God unto thee and to thy seed after thee. And I will give unto thee, and to thy seed after thee, the land wherein thou art a stranger, all the land of Canaan, for an everlasting possession; and I will be their God.

THE NEW TESTAMENT

THE GOSPELS OF MATTHEW, MARK, LUKE, AND JOHN

Stories of Jesus, Called Christ. The Events in Judea in the Time of Herod the Great; the Birth of Jesus; His Life; His Miracles; the Parables He Told; His Death and Resurrection.

DURING THE DAYS of the Roman Empire, the country of the Jews was known as Judea. A family of kings named Herod ruled over the land, but above them was a Roman governor with a Roman army to enforce his will. The Emperor of Rome allowed Herod to hold court and live in a beautiful palace, but the Roman governor actually passed the laws and carried them out.

The Jews of those days worshiped in synagogues, which were small buildings combining religious study and prayer. Since their great Temple was again in ruins, the synagogues were the only places in which they could congregate to recall the days of their greatness and the deeds of their forefathers.

In their synagogues, the Jews discussed their hope of a Messiah, a Saviour who would come from God to relieve the sufferings and injustices of the world. They had read about this Messiah in the prophecies of Isaiah and Daniel, and it seemed to many that the time was at hand for such a Redeemer to appear.

Of course, there were various groups who had various ideas of how this Messiah would look and what would happen when he arrived. The Pharisees were a group of Jews who strictly followed the Torah, the Books of Moses, to the last letter. They were studious men, and their teachings were rigid. The Sadducees were another group, many of them well-to-do, who adapted themselves to a more political way of life, and readily accepted the Roman rule. The Pharisees and the Sadducees often quarreled, and accomplished little as a result. Besides these two parties, other groups formed. Some were pious and secluded. Others wandered from town to town preaching, like the early prophets. By and large, few Jewish people belonged to any of these groups. They only yearned for the day when the Messiah, the Redeemer as they called him,

The Jewish People and Rome

277

would miraculously free them from oppression and ease their suffering.

Herod, though a partly foreign king, tried to gain respect from the Jews by rebuilding their holy Temple. With permission from Rome, he created a splendid building of white stone covered with silver and gold. Many Jews thought this Temple too elaborate and unlike the original Temple of Solomon. For that reason, they preferred to worship in their simple synagogues.

Some accepted Herod's building with open arms. These men were close to the king, and sought his favor. He, in turn, made them priests of the Temple, and dressed them in beautiful robes. Many of these priests became very rich and powerful.

But, even with the Temple, most Jews had little comfort. They were forced to work at simple jobs that earned them little money. On top of this, they had to pay taxes to Rome, to Herod, and to the priests. It was small wonder that poverty existed in the land, and that misery afflicted family upon family in Judea.

Zacharias was the head of a family of priests. Nevertheless, he was poor and humble. With his wife, Elisabeth, he lived quietly in Jerusalem, performing the duties of his religion in a righteous way. Though Zacharias and his wife were well past their youth, they had no children. Every time the good man went to the Temple, he prayed for a son. The years went by, but no child was born. Even so, Elisabeth and Zacharias served God with great devotion.

Then, one day, when he was alone preparing the altar in the Temple, Zacharias saw an angel of God. Fearful and bewildered, the humble priest fell to the floor, and buried his face in his hands. But the angel spoke reassuringly.

"Do not fear me," he said. "God has heard your prayers for a son and will grant your plea. In due time, a boy will be born to your wife Elisabeth. You shall call him John, and he will be filled with the Spirit of God, like the prophets of old."

Zacharias was dumfounded. How could he, a man so old, and his wife, also well past her youth, have a son?

"Please give me proof of your prophecy," he asked the angel.

"I am Gabriel, one of the angels of God," replied the visitor. "And I regret that you ask me for proof. Because of your doubt, you will not be able to utter a single word until the birth of your son. Then you will know that I have spoken the truth."

The angel disappeared, leaving the bewildered priest alone in the Temple. After a while, some people came to inquire why he tarried. When he tried to answer, he found that he could not speak. The angel's prediction had come true.

ONE DAY in spring, the Angel Gabriel appeared in the city of Nazareth, in the hills of Galilee. There lived the maiden Mary, who was betrothed to marry Joseph, the carpenter.

It was a peaceful day. Mary was seated quietly in her house, reading her prayers.

"Hail," the angel said to her. "The Lord is with thee; among all women art thou most blessed."

Mary humbly lowered her eyes, for she did not understand. Then Gabriel prophesied that Mary would soon give birth to a son—the Hope of the World—and that this son would be called Joshua, or, as we know him, Jesus.

"He shall be great," said the angel, "and he shall be called the Son of the Highest; and the Lord God shall give unto him the throne of his father, King David. And he shall reign for ever and ever, and unto his kingdom there shall be no end."

Mary bowed her head and replied:

"Whatever the Lord God commands, I will gladly do."

Then Gabriel disappeared, and Mary remained at her prayers in the quiet of her room.

The
Annunciation

ELISABETH, THE WIFE of Zacharias, was Mary's cousin. She sent word to the younger woman that, by a miracle of God, she was expecting a son. Mary had been told by Gabriel that Elisabeth would so conceive, and she was overjoyed.

Filled with the Spirit of God, Mary journeyed to her cousin's home for a visit. When Elisabeth saw her, she was stirred by Mary's beauty and serenity, and she said:

"Surely you are blessed among all women and blessed is the fruit of your womb."

Mary lifted her voice in thanks to God for her great fortune.

"My soul magnifies the Lord," she said, "for He has blessed me. And though I be humble, all generations from this time forth will call me blessed, for there is no single thing that the Lord cannot do."

Mary stayed with her cousin Elisabeth for three months, and the two women often talked of the wonders of God and His blessings upon the Children of Israel.

Then Mary returned to Nazareth and wed Joseph the carpenter. Though he was a humble man in a humble trade, Joseph was descended from the royal house of King David. He too was visited by an angel in a

The
Visitation

ABOVE: Plate 66. THE ANNUNCIATION, by Rogier van der Weyden
(Flemish, about 1399–1464), The Louvre Museum, Paris.

OPPOSITE: Plate 67. THE VISITATION, by Mariotto Albertinelli
(Italian, 1474–1515), The Uffizi Gallery, Florence.

dream and was told of the wonderful child that Mary was to bear. Being a pious Jew, Joseph was overjoyed to know that the prophecy of Isaiah would be fulfilled, for it said that a Saviour would be born to the family of the House of David in the city of David and that the birth would be like no other in all the world.

The Advent of John

NOW ELISABETH was about to give birth. Many friends and relatives gathered in the house of Zacharias to celebrate the great event.

"What will they name the child?" the neighbors wondered.

"Zacharias, of course," one man said. "It is the custom to name firstborn sons after their fathers."

But Elisabeth interrupted, and announced:

"My husband wishes the boy to bear another name that an angel told him long ago. But, since he has lost his speech, we do not know what that name will be."

Zacharias was listening. He beckoned the guests to his side and then with his pen he wrote the name *John* on his writing table. And, in the same instance, his speech returned.

"John shall be his name," said the father joyously.

The people of Judea heard, with wonder, about the birth, and said, "What manner of child will this be?" For they knew the hand of the Lord was upon him.

And filled with the Spirit of God, Zacharias prophesied:

"Blessed be the Lord God of Israel, for he has visited and redeemed his people. He has raised up a horn of salvation for us in the house of his servant David; as he promised by the mouth of his holy prophets from of old that we should be saved from our enemies, and from the hand of all who hate us, to perform the mercy promised to our fathers and to remember his holy covenant: the oath which he swore to our Father Abraham to grant to us, that, being delivered out of the hand of our enemies, we may serve him without fear in holiness and righteousness all the days of our life.

"And you, child will be called the prophet of the Highest; for you will go before the face of the Lord to prepare his ways, to give knowledge of salvation to his people by the remission of their sins, through the tender mercy of our God, whereby the dayspring from on high has visited us, to give light to those who sit in darkness and in the shadow of death, to guide our feet into the way of peace."

And the child grew, and became strong in spirit, and was in the deserts till the day of his appearance to Israel.

THE PROPHECY of the angel Gabriel was about to be fulfilled, for Mary was soon to bear her son, the infant Jesus. At this same time, a decree went out from Caesar Augustus, the Emperor of Rome, that each man in Judea was to return to the city of his birth so that a census might be taken.

Joseph the carpenter had been born in Bethlehem, a small city some distance from the town of Nazareth, where he and Mary lived. Obedient to the emperor's decree, Joseph gently placed Mary on a donkey and began the long journey to his childhood home.

When they reached Bethlehem, they found the city crowded and bustling with people, all of whom had come in answer to the emperor's decree. Joseph was concerned, for Mary was close to the time of her delivery, and he went from place to place, seeking shelter. But there was no room for them in the public places.

At one inn the owner told Joseph:

"You may stay in the stable tonight."

So Joseph led his wife into the stable among the horses, the sheep, and all the other gentle creatures. There she gave birth to her son and wrapped him in swaddling clothes and—lacking a cradle—she laid him in a feeding trough, called a manger. Thus was Jesus born.

Not far away, in the peaceful hills, certain shepherds were tending their flocks, when suddenly they saw a glowing angel appear.

"Fear not," he called to them, "for behold, I bring you good tidings of great joy, which shall be to all people. For unto you is born this day in the city of David, which is Bethlehem, a Saviour; Christ the Lord. And this shall be a sign unto you; you shall find the baby wrapped in swaddling clothes, and lying in a manger."

The shepherds rejoiced. At last the long awaited prophecy was at hand and, as they rushed toward Bethlehem to see the newborn child, a brilliant new star shone in the deep black night, and a multitude of heavenly voices exclaimed:

"Glory to God in the highest and on earth peace, good will toward all men."

LIKE A BEACON, steady and bright, the star of Bethlehem pointed the way to the stable where Mary and the baby were sleeping. Joseph watched over them in the light of a little fire he had kindled. How beautiful was the child and how peaceful was the night!

"Let us now go even unto Bethlehem and see this thing which has come to pass," said the shepherds.

The Birth of Jesus

The Adoration of the Shepherds

283

ABOVE: Plate 68. THE NATIVITY, by Piero della Francesca
(Italian, about 1416–1492), The National Gallery, London.

OPPOSITE: Plate 69. THE ADORATION OF THE SHEPHERDS, by El Greco
(Spanish School, 1541–1614), The Metropolitan Museum of Art, New York.

Then, outside, quietly and reverently, the shepherds approached the barn, and saw the infant resting in the manger as the angel had described him. Kneeling, they prayed to God and gave thanks for the hope that was now in their hearts. This was the world's first Christmas.

For some time after, Mary and Joseph stayed in the stable caring for the newborn child. Then, after Jesus was circumcised, they journeyed to Jerusalem, so that the baby Jesus might be presented in the Temple. It was the custom in those days for a firstborn Jewish son to be blessed by the priests while his father made the proper sacrifices to God. Joseph obeyed this law, and offered a pair of turtledoves, or pigeons, upon the sacred altar.

The Elderly Couple in the Temple

WHILE JOSEPH AND MARY were thus in the Temple with their son, an old man named Simeon was praying off in a corner of the building. Every day, he came to pray for the Messiah, believing that he would not die until he had beheld the Saviour of the world. Now, as Simeon prayed, he lifted his head and saw Mary carrying Jesus from the altar. Immediately he knew that this was the Holy Child, and he approached Mary and said:

"This child is to be our Saviour. I know it in my heart. Therefore, I pray, let me hold him for a moment, so that I may depart in peace knowing my salvation."

Mary was very kind. She placed her baby in the old man's arms. An aged widow, Anna, also fondled the child, and the two elderly people had tears of happiness in their eyes.

All the while, Mary was somewhat puzzled. She remembered the angel Gabriel and the wonderful things he had said about her child. Yet she wondered; how would this little baby be the Saviour of the world? Did God intend the Messiah to be like everyone else, to be born like a man, to grow up and go to school and to do all the things that other men do? Mary could not answer. Taking her child from Simeon, she returned with Joseph to Bethlehem.

The Visit of the Wise Men

FAR TO THE EAST of Judea, there lived certain wise men called Magi. These wise men (according to tradition, there were three), looked up into the heavens and saw a brilliant, new star. They knew this star represented the birth of the new king of the Jews, and they decided to pay him homage.

So they gathered up many fine gifts and treasures and set out for Judea. All the while, they followed the brilliant star. But, when they came to the gates of Jerusalem, they could not be sure if the star pointed in that direction or just slightly beyond.

"We will ask King Herod," they said.

Herod had not heard about the newborn child. When the noble wise men came before him they asked:

"Where may we find the new king of Israel, so that we may pay him homage?"

The wise men referred to Jesus as a king, not in the sense of one who sits upon an earthly throne, but as a king of goodness and peace. Herod did not understand this. He became immediately fearful that some child had been born who would one day take away his power. But he did not show his fear. Craftily, he said to the wise men:

"The prophets have written that this child would be born in Bethlehem, which is very near. Go there and find that child; then send word where he is, so that I may follow and pay my respects."

Herod had no intentions of paying his respects to the newborn king. In fact, it was his plan to murder Jesus as soon as he found where he lived.

The wise men did not suspect Herod of such an evil plan, and departed toward Bethlehem. Above them, the star shone brightly, ever leading the way to the spot where Mary and Joseph watched over the baby.

"Here at last is the place," said the wise men.

They loaded their arms with wonderful gifts, and came before Mary and Joseph and the child. For some time, they paid homage to the infant Jesus and placed their precious treasures at his feet. Then they planned to return to Herod with the news of Jesus' whereabouts. But as they slept, that night, an angel appeared to each of them in a dream and warned them of Herod's plan. Quickly, the wise men loaded their horses and left the land of Judea, so that Herod could not find them.

That same night, an angel appeared to Joseph and said:

"There is danger here. Take Mary and the baby, and flee into Egypt, for Herod means to murder the child."

Indeed, King Herod was filled with wrath, for the wise men had not returned, and the baby's whereabouts still remained unknown to him. He then conceived a terrible plan.

"I must find this child and destroy him," he thought. "If every baby under two years of age is killed, then surely this child will be among them."

So he ordered his soldiers to slaughter hundreds of innocent chil-

dren in Bethlehem. By this time, however, Jesus was safely on his way to Egypt in the arms of his mother.

There, in Egypt, the Holy Family stayed for a time. Then word came that the evil Herod was dead. Joseph knew he could safely return to Judea. But, instead of going to Bethlehem, Joseph led his family north to the hills of Galilee and the town of Nazareth, where he and Mary had lived before. Thus, they avoided Herod's son, who was now the king in Jerusalem and who was just as wicked as his father had been.

IN NAZARETH, Joseph followed his trade as a carpenter. His shop was next to the house where Mary and the baby Jesus spent the day. But, as Jesus grew up, it came time for him to learn his father's trade. Often, he would help Joseph at the carpenter's bench, planing wood and mending chairs.

Besides learning a trade, Jesus went to school. Every Jewish boy was obliged to learn the Torah, or the Five Books of Moses, so that he might fully obey the laws of God. Jesus found this training very easy. He "waxed strong in spirit, filled with wisdom," as the Gospel says.

On the Sabbath and on holidays, Jesus and Joseph went to the synagogue in Nazareth to pray and study. Once again, Jesus proved most learned and devout. When he was twelve years old, his parents decided to take him to Jerusalem for the Passover festival.

Jesus had been in Jerusalem as a tiny baby, but he remembered nothing of the great city and the awesome Temple. Now, for the first time, he gazed upon the place that had been home to King David and King Solomon. His heart was filled with the love of God.

Many times before, the boy Jesus had felt a strong passion for God and for religion. But it seems that he was not yet aware of his role in the world. From what we know, neither Mary nor Joseph, nor any of the angels of God came to him and told him, "You are the Saviour." It was Jesus' task to learn this himself, as he lived and suffered like any other man. Nevertheless, by the time he was twelve, he *had* discovered one

Jesus
as a
Boy

OPPOSITE: Plate 70. THE PRESENTATION IN THE TEMPLE, by Hans Memling (Flemish, about 1430–1495), The Prado Museum, Madrid.

ABOVE: Plate 71. THE ADORATION OF THE MAGI,
by Albrecht Dürer (German, 1471–1528), The Uffizi Gallery, Florence.

OPPOSITE: Plate 72. THE FLIGHT INTO EGYPT,
by Giotto (Italian, about 1276–about 1337), Arena Chapel, Padua.

most important truth: that all good men might call themselves the sons of God and live a perfect and righteous life by doing as God would do if He Himself lived on earth.

In Jerusalem, Jesus spent little time at the festivities. Instead, he went to the Temple, and entered the study rooms where many learned rabbis and aged teachers sat conversing and discussing the Law. To their

amazement, this mere youth of twelve seemed quite well versed in the teachings of Moses. After a while they sat in surprise as he instructed them on the deeper meanings and the inner truths of what he knew in his heart.

Mary and Joseph did not know that Jesus was in the Temple conversing with the priests and teachers. Nervously, they searched for him in the streets where the other boys were playing. But he could not be found. Nightfall was coming.

"Let us look in the Temple," said Joseph wearily.

There in the midst of the learned men, sat Jesus, discussing the most difficult points of religion.

"How worried we were," his mother said to him. "We did not know where to find you."

Jesus was surprised.

"Where else should I be," he said, "but in my Father's house, attending to His business?"

Mary was puzzled. She did not understand that Jesus referred to God as his father and had meant no insult to Joseph. The three returned silently to Nazareth. For many years Jesus led a quiet life, studying, growing wise, and every day coming nearer to the truth of his great identity.

The Baptism of Jesus

YOUNG JOHN GREW into manhood, and was filled with great religious fervor. Later, when he was about thirty years old, he went into the desert of Judea and lived alone, wearing a rough coat of camel's hair and eating only locusts and honey. His beard grew long, and his eyes shone with inspiration.

Occasionally, hecklers and wicked men came to make fun of John. He always knew when they were present, and raising his voice, he would cry:

"Repent! For the kingdom of Heaven is at hand!"

Because of his zeal, many thought that John was the Messiah. But the strange prophet always disclaimed that great distinction.

"I am not worthy to untie the laces of His sandals," he would say. "I am only His prophet, and I lead the way."

Nevertheless, hundreds of Jews, seeking comfort from their sorrows, followed John and joined him in the worship of God. To purify their souls and to wash away their sins, John instructed them to immerse themselves in the cold, clear waters of the river Jordan. This was the act of baptism, and, as a result, people called the prophet of the Lord, John the Baptist.

One day, as John was baptizing some of his followers, Jesus, now about thirty years old, came from Galilee to the River Jordan. Though Jesus and John were cousins, they had met only as children, for John spent most of his life in the desert. Nevertheless, the prophet recognized Jesus at once. Falling on his knees, he exclaimed:

"Behold! This is the One greater than I who will cleanse the world of its sins!"

Everyone was amazed. But Jesus said nothing. He advanced to the shore of the river and asked John to baptize him.

"*You* must baptize me," said John in reverence.

Jesus insisted, for he wished to know the experiences of all other men. So John baptized Jesus with the waters of the Jordan; and, as he did so, the clouds in the sky drew apart, a great burst of sunlight filled the scene, and, high above, a voice from Heaven could be heard proclaiming:

"This is My beloved Son, in whom I am well pleased."

NOW, MORE THAN EVER, the Holy Spirit filled Jesus, and he realized his mission in life. In order to prepare and purify his soul, he went into seclusion for forty days, deep within the barren wilderness of Judea.

While Jesus was fasting and at his prayers, Satan, the devil, came up from the lower depths to tempt and torture him.

"You think you are the Son of God," Satan said. "Then prove it to me. Turn these stones into loaves of bread and ease your hunger."

But Jesus remained at his prayers and quietly said:

"My prayers are more important to me, for man shall not live by bread alone."

The devil laughed.

"Well then," he said. "If you are really the Son of God, throw yourself off the highest steeple of the Temple, and we will see if you are saved."

Jesus remained at his prayers and simply said:

"It is wrong to test God's powers by such a reckless act."

The devil was becoming impatient. Intent upon trapping Jesus and ruining his soul, he devised another plan.

"Worship me!" he pleaded, "and I will make you master over all the cities of the world, and over all the wealth within those cities."

Then, through his magic trickery, Satan caused an image of all the glittering cities of the world to appear in the barren desert.

Jesus did not hesitate a minute. Sternly, he exclaimed,

The
Temptation
of Jesus

Plate 73. THE TWELVE-YEAR-OLD CHRIST IN THE TEMPLE,
by Luca Giordano (Italian, 1632–1705), The National Gallery, Rome.

"Away, Satan, away! God and only God will I serve!"

With these strong words, the devil was cast down to the lower depths whence he had come. Then the angels of God descended and brought food and comfort to Jesus, who had proved, beyond all doubt, his purity and his love of God.

When he was refreshed, Jesus prepared to return to the River Jordan to find his cousin John. But then he heard some sorry news. The new king Herod had arrested John for preaching against the sins of Herod's wicked wife. John was now in prison, perhaps being readied to die.

Jesus knew that it was best for him to return to Galilee and begin his ministry. He went to Capernaum near Nazareth. There he preached in the synagogue to the poor of the town.

"Repent!" he announced, "for the Kingdom of Heaven is at hand!"

Plate 74. THE BAPTISM OF CHRIST, by Andrea del Verrocchio (Italian, about 1435–1488), The Uffizi Gallery, Florence.

Jesus and His Followers

AFTER THE ARREST of John the Baptist, many of John's followers went into hiding. They were alone, now that their leader had gone. But some of the men remembered Jesus of Galilee, and recalled that John had said:

"This is the One greater than I."

John had also referred to Jesus as the "Lamb of God," which meant that Jesus would take upon himself the sins and sufferings of the world, like a lamb sacrificed upon the altar.

The followers of John who remembered these things were now prepared to follow Jesus.

Two of these men, Andrew and Simon, were brothers who earned their living as fishermen on the sea of Galilee. One day, as Jesus was walking by the shores and meditating, he saw these brothers casting their nets into the waters.

Andrew recognized Jesus and was eager to follow him, but Simon was more reserved. As they were talking, a group of men and women came to the shore to hear Jesus preach. Often, persons met in out-of-the-way places to listen to this young man of Nazareth, who seemed so filled with authority and holiness.

That day, the crowd was very large. Jesus turned to Simon and asked him if he might stand in the fishing boat, so that everyone could see him and hear better. Simon agreed.

After the sermon, when the crowd had dispersed, Jesus advised Simon to row out a bit farther and lower his nets. There he would find many fish, which Simon needed, for he had not been lucky in his catch that day. Simon followed this advice. To his amazement, he caught so many fish that his net was full and his boat so heavy that it almost sank. The following day, when he saw Jesus, Simon threw himself on the ground and cried:

"I am a sinful man because I hesitated to follow you. Now I know that you are the one for whom we have all been waiting, and I wish to do your bidding."

Jesus helped Simon to his feet and told him to come with him and with Andrew and the others who were eager to find salvation.

"I will make you fishers of men," he said.

Now the word spread that the teacher Jesus of Nazareth was calling the faithful to abandon their old lives and follow him to bring the message of God to the world. John and James, the two sons of a man named Zebedee, joined the group, to be followed by Philip and a man named Nathanael. In time, they were all to be known as the disciples, or those who teach. Tirelessly, they toured the cities of Galilee with Jesus, spreading the word of God.

IN THE SMALL TOWN of Cana, there was to be a wedding. Among the honored guests were Jesus, his mother, and several of the disciples. In those days, a wedding feast took many days, and much food and wine was consumed.

Jesus only attended briefly, for he was busy preaching. He arrived toward the end of the feast, when all the wine had been drunk. Mary was a close friend of the host. She knew that he was greatly embarrassed to have no more wine, since an important official from the city was coming to pay his respects.

So Mary turned to her son, Jesus, and said:

"I know that you possess great powers. Can you help these friends? They have no wine and they expect an important guest."

Jesus had not yet performed any of the miracles that lay in his power. He did not wish to attract a following of those who would be impressed only with magic and sorcery, for his message appealed to the soul. Nevertheless, out of respect for his mother, Jesus decided to help the host. He told the servants to fetch six large pitchers.

"Fill them with water from the well," he said.

The servants obeyed. Jesus had them carry the pitchers to the table. By this time, the high official of the city had arrived and was asking for a glass of wine.

The guests knew that there was no wine, and were amused when the servants brought the water pitchers to the table. But, to their amazement, when the colorless water was poured it turned into clear red wine. Everyone filled his cup and drank.

"Wonderful!" said the high official. "This is the finest wine I have ever tasted."

All the guests agreed, and complimented the host for saving the best wine until last. But the disciples of Jesus knew that a real miracle had occurred, and their faith and reverence for their master increased.

NOW THAT HE HAD changed the water to wine, Jesus was becoming famous in the area of Nazareth. He journeyed with his disciples to Capernaum again, and there he preached in the synagogue. It was the custom for learned men to give sermons and read lessons on the holidays.

While Jesus was preaching, a man in the congregation started to shout and call out insults and blasphemies. This man was unhappy and ill, but the people of the village simply thought he was insane and paid him no mind. Jesus came down from the pulpit, where he was preaching, and gently placed his hand on the angry man's shoulders. Then he

The
Wedding
at Cana

Jesus
Preaches
and
Heals
the Sick

Plate 75. THE TEMPTATION OF CHRIST, by Duccio
(Italian, about 1255–1319), The Frick Collection, New York.

lifted his eyes to God, and, soon, the man who had been shouting, his face red with rage, became quiet and calm. Everyone was deeply impressed, and the word spread fast that Jesus had the power to heal the sick with prayer.

Simon the fisherman, who had joined the disciples, was in need of Jesus' help. His mother-in-law lay ill with a serious fever and no doctor could relieve her. Jesus entered the house and straightaway cured the

Plate 76. THE MARRIAGE AT CANA, by Gerard David (Flemish, about 1450–1523), The Louvre Museum, Paris.

elderly woman. All the curious neighbors who had crowded into the house were overwhelmed with astonishment. But Jesus wanted no praise. He left the cured woman and went to a solitary place to pray. There Simon followed him and declared himself a faithful disciple forevermore. With Jesus, he journeyed through Galilee preaching in the synagogues.

But it is always true that a famous man gathers enemies as well as friends. Many men of power became jealous and angry at the news that Jesus of Nazareth could heal the sick and cause great multitudes to follow him and accept his ideas.

One day, Jesus was preaching in the streets, when he heard a commotion nearby. The people were hurrying away in all directions because a leper was coming. A leper is afflicted with a terrible disease that causes flaking and scabbing of the skin. In those days it was thought that this disease was very contagious, and lepers were not allowed to mingle with other people. But this poor man wanted to be cured, and he dared venture into the streets to find Jesus.

"Make me clean again," the leper pleaded, "for no one will help me, and my life is meaningless."

In his great compassion, Jesus stretched forth his hands and touched the leper on the head. In that instant the horrible disease miraculously disappeared. Now, more than ever, the people praised Jesus—but his enemies also hated him all the more.

Time after time, in many ways and in many places, Jesus stretched forth his hand and cured the lame, the blind, and the suffering. He became so popular, in spite of his wish, that people lined up for hours to gain admittance to the house or the street where he was preaching.

One day, he was visiting a small house in Galilee. Such a great crowd had gathered that no one could get in or out of the door. Outside some people had brought a sick man on his bed so that Jesus might cure him. Because they could not force their way in through the door, they decided to remove the roof and lower the invalid down, bed and all. Some of Jesus' enemies were watching. They were always prepared to make fun of Jesus or to cast doubts upon his wisdom and holiness. Now, when they saw the sick man being lowered on his bed, they laughed aloud.

But Jesus admired the resourcefulness of the invalid and his friends, and he blessed them and stretched forth his hands. The man who, for years, had been unable to rise from his bed, now walked and was cured. He was so well, in fact, that he lifted the bed on his back and marched out of the house, praising God.

Jesus' enemies were angry. What right did this carpenter's son have to take upon himself the powers of God and the ancient prophets? they asked. Deliberately, they started to spread the word that Jesus was actually a sinner, a man who purposely broke the laws of God. This was like saying that night was day and black was white. But many aristocrats thought that Jesus was becoming too powerful and too well loved by the poor and unhappy people of Judea.

JESUS WAS always looking for upright men who could help him spread the word of God. He had felt that Simon, the fisherman, was such a man. Now he saw Matthew, and he wished him to join the great cause.

But Matthew was not a fisherman or a farmer. He pursued a very unpopular profession, and it caused him to be disliked and hated, for Matthew was a tax collector. It was his duty, though a Jew himself, to round up money from the Jews so that it might be paid to Herod and to Rome. Matthew was not happy in his work, but he knew that someone had to do it. Being kind by nature, he was, at least, a pleasant tax collector, and never persecuted anyone.

It was Jesus' hope that he would attract a following of many different kinds of people; rich and poor, wise and simple, tax collectors as well as fishermen. One day, he approached the place where Matthew was counting taxes. Standing to the side, Jesus raised his arm and beckoned Matthew, saying:

"Follow me."

Matthew, a publican, as tax collectors were called, had heard of Jesus and believed in him. Without hesitation, he followed Jesus, and became a disciple. He invited other publicans to dine with Jesus.

Jesus' enemies were delighted with this latest piece of news. Imagine, they thought, now he has taken tax collectors into his company. Following Jesus to an inn, they confronted him and said:

"If you are a holy person sent by God, how can you sit here eating supper with tax collectors, beggars, and all sorts of common people?"

Jesus was never flustered by the question of his enemies. He smiled peacefully, and said:

"God has sent me to be a doctor to the sick. Why should I spend my time with those who are already well and sound? I must help the unhappy man, the hopeless man, and the sinner, whatever his calling or his station in life."

Thus Jesus spoke words and ideas that were new to the world, and, wherever he went, he gathered the sinners and the lowly, so that he might redeem them. But his detractors still complained.

The Calling of Matthew

"Why should God be concerned with sinners?" they asked.

And Jesus replied:

"God waits for all men to pay their debts to Him. The greater the debt, the greater the repentance, and the greater God's forgiveness."

To the fair-minded people of Judea, these words made sense. But the enemies of Jesus continued to argue and complain. When they heard that Jesus and his disciples had picked some grain to eat on the Sabbath day, they jumped on this infraction of the law, and cried out that Jesus had sinned. But the man from Nazareth simply reminded them that King David of old had done the same thing when he was hungry. David, in fact, had eaten the showbread meant for the rituals, yet the Lord did not punish him.

"That is all very well and good," said the enemies, "but you profane the Sabbath. You walk around preaching and do not go to the Temple."

Jesus answered quietly:

"A man need not be in the Temple to feel the presence of God, nor was man made just to worship on the Sabbath. The Sabbath was made for man."

Jesus' enemies even criticized him for curing the sick and suffering on the Sabbath. But Jesus explained:

"If you had a sheep and it fell into a pit on the Sabbath, you would not leave it there until the next day; by then it might be dead. Should we treat a sheep any better than we treat a man? No, God does not wish man to suffer needlessly, even on the Sabbath."

The enemies could not answer and turned away.

"This man Jesus must be destroyed," they whispered to themselves.

AT DIFFERENT TIMES in his life, Jesus visited the great city of Jerusalem in order to worship at the Temple. The favorite time for such a visit was at Passover, the great celebration of the Jewish Exodus from Egypt under Moses.

With several of his disciples, Jesus came into Jerusalem unnoticed

*Jesus
Visits
Jerusalem*

OPPOSITE: Plate 77. THE CALLING OF MATTHEW, by Caravaggio (Italian, 1565–1609), Church of San Luigi dei Francesi, Rome.

in the great throng of holiday visitors. At another time, in the not-too-distant future, he was to enter the city again, triumphantly—and he was to die there as well. This Jesus knew in his heart, but he said nothing to his disciples.

There was a man in Jerusalem to whom Jesus confided some of the most important concepts of his faith and of his mission on earth. This man was Nicodemus, a wealthy and influential Jew. One night, Nicodemus secretly sought out Jesus in a quiet room.

"I have heard of your miracles," said Nicodemus, "and I have listened to you speak. I want to know more about what you believe."

For many hours Jesus talked to Nicodemus. He told him that man was capable of everlasting life in the Kingdom of God, that, to enter this Kingdom, man had to have a pure heart and faith in God. Then Jesus reminded Nicodemus of the time when Moses fashioned a snake out of brass so that those beholding it might be saved from the poisonous bites of real serpents. Such a miracle would take place again through the Son of God, who, like the brazen snake, would be suspended on a cross and die for the salvation of mankind. Jesus then revealed an amazing thing to Nicodemus.

"God so loved the world," he said, "that He gave His only begotten son, so that whoever believes in Him will not die, but will live forever."

Jesus did not say directly that he was the Son of God to Nicodemus —but, clearly, he was speaking of himself and envisioning the time of his own death and resurrection.

The visit with Nicodemus, including the discussion held that night, is one of the most important and meaningful events in the whole story of Jesus and his teachings.

The Woman at the Well

AFTER THE PASSOVER FEAST, Jesus journeyed back to Galilee. He took the long way home, and thus passed through the land of Samaria, a place not friendly to the Jews. Jesus had a purpose in doing this, for he wanted to spread the word of God to people other than the Jews. So he went to the well in the center of the town of Sychar and sat there to rest. Soon a Samaritan woman came along to fetch some water.

"Would you give me a drink of water?" Jesus asked. The woman was surprised. Usually, Jews did not speak to Samaritans, let alone ask them for water.

"Why do you ask me?" she said.

"If you knew who I am," he answered, "you would ask me to give *you* the living waters that I possess."

The woman was confused. She wanted to know what waters he meant. Jesus said:

"Whoever drinks of ordinary water soon becomes thirsty again. But if you drink the waters I bring, you will never be thirsty again and you will have everlasting life."

The Samaritan woman became all excited. Naturally, she wanted some of this wonderful water, and asked Jesus to provide it. She did not understand that he was not speaking of real water, but of faith.

"First, you must purify your heart," said Jesus to the woman, "for I know that you are a sinner and have done some wicked things."

The woman blushed. It was true, she had been wicked. Realizing that she was talking to a religious prophet, the woman tried to excuse herself by saying:

"I am not a Jew, and I do not worship as you do."

Jesus assured her that the message and blessings of God were meant for all mankind, and that God had chosen the Jews as a means of bringing this salvation to the world.

"I know," the woman said. "I have heard that the Messiah called Christ will come from them—and that the whole world awaits him."

Jesus then spoke some startling words.

"I am he, the Messiah," he said.

The Samaritan woman was thus the first one to hear, directly from Jesus' own lips, these magnificent words. She immediately believed what she heard and rushed off to spread the news.

Jesus remained at the well. Soon some of his disciples came along with food, which they had purchased in the city.

But Jesus did not eat. His talk with the Samaritan woman had so filled his spirit that he felt no need of food. Later, he preached in Samaria at the well where he had revealed his divinity to the humble Samaritan woman.

ALL OVER GALILEE, in Syria, to the north and to the south, the word of Jesus' powers and holiness was spreading. Multitudes of people came to hear the Master and to be cured by his outstretched hand. Though Jesus knew that this was his role on earth, he nevertheless shunned the praises and adulation of the crowds. Often, he would stand in a small boat at the water's edge while the people listened from the shore. Then he would preach and heal, and, straightway, he would leave the scene to meditate by himself in the hills.

To assist in his great work, Jesus appointed twelve of his followers

The Sermon on the Mount

to be apostles, and thus to possess the powers of healing and the insight to preach the Word of God. These apostles were Simon the fisherman, who was later called Peter; Andrew, his brother; James and John the sons of Zebedee; Philip; Bartholomew; Thomas; Matthew the tax collector; James Alpheus; Thaddeus; Simon from Canaan; and a man named Judas Iscariot. These twelve preached to the people, as Jesus had instructed them.

Then one day, as he was meditating, Jesus saw thousands of people wending their way up the side of the mountain so that they might hear him preach. He called his disciples and told them to prepare the throng, for he would make a sermon there on the mountain, and, in this sermon, he would say all those things that mankind had to know for its salvation. The undying words he spoke that day are beyond compare in all history. He said:

> Blessed are the poor in spirit:
>   for theirs is the kingdom of heaven.
> Blessed are they that mourn:
>   for they shall be comforted.
> Blessed are the meek:
>   for they shall inherit the earth.
> Blessed are they which do hunger and
>   thirst after righteousness:
>   for they shall be filled.
> Blessed are the merciful:
>   for they shall obtain mercy.
> Blessed are the pure in heart:
>   for they shall see God.
> Blessed are the peacemakers:
>   for they shall be called the
>   children of God.
> Blessed are they which are persecuted
>   for righteousness' sake:
>   for theirs is the kingdom of heaven.
> Blessed are ye, when men shall revile you,
>   and persecute you,
>   and shall say all manner of evil against you
>   falsely, for my sake.
> Rejoice and be exceeding glad: for great is
>   your reward in heaven:
>   for so persecuted they the prophets
>   which were before you.

The blessings that Jesus pronounced are called the Beatitudes. They were the first part of his Sermon on the Mount. In the second part, Jesus went on to assure the Jews that his task was not to upset the Laws of Moses, but, rather, to fulfill them. For that reason he recited the famous Golden Rule: *Do unto others as you would have them do unto you.*

He also gave the humble and the poor great hope and courage, for he told them that they did not need wealth and high station to enter the kingdom of God, but, rather, righteousness and purity. Recalling the Ten Commandments, he warned that if we hate a man without cause and wish him dead, it is as if we murder him. He then urged the people to be merciful and forgiving, even with their enemies, and he said:

"Whosoever shall smite thee on thy right cheek, turn to him the other, also."

By this he meant: do not hastily strike back at someone who attacks you, but, rather, show him the peaceful intentions of your heart.

Furthermore, Jesus inspired the people to believe that God was always with them. They did not need the Temple, he said, or the synagogue, or the elaborate rituals of their religion to feel the presence of God and to become holy. Instead of repetitious prayers and chantings, Jesus taught a simple prayer, which all men might offer, for he said:

"Your Father in Heaven knows what is in your hearts."

The words he pronounced are called the Lord's Prayer, the most beautiful prayer in all the world:

> Our Father which art in heaven,
> Hallowed be thy name.
> Thy kingdom come.
> Thy will be done in earth,
>   as it is in heaven.
> Give us this day our daily bread.
> And forgive us our debts,
>   as we forgive our debtors.
> And lead us not into temptation,
>   but deliver us from evil:
> For Thine is the kingdom, and the power,
>   and the glory, for ever. Amen.

After this, Jesus spoke many more immortal words, and taught the meaning of faith and love, of justice, and salvation. Then he departed, and left the people astonished and inspired beyond all their dreams.

Jesus Saves Two Young Men

IN THE CITY of Capernaum there were about one hundred Roman soldiers stationed to keep the peace. At the head of this small army was a centurion, or a captain, as we would call him. He lived very well and had many servants, one of whom became quite ill. The centurion loved this servant like a son, and was distressed to see him suffering without hope of being cured.

Jesus was in Capernaum, and the centurion sent word beseeching him to save his dying servant. The disciples told Jesus that this Roman had been very kind to the Jews, and that he had even helped them build their synagogue. Jesus went to the centurion's house immediately. But as he approached, the centurion's messengers came running down the stairs with a note from their master. It said:

"Lord, I do not feel worthy enough to have you honor my house, nor do I think myself worthy to appear in person before you. But I have great faith that you can cure my servant without seeing him, even as I command many soldiers whom I do not know. I beg you to show mercy."

Jesus was deeply impressed with such faith. Moreover, he rejoiced to see that people other than the Jews were accepting his teachings and his power. He prayed for the dying man. That night, the centurion found that a miracle had taken place, and that his servant was well.

In the city of Nain, a poor widow was in grief. Her only son, her hope and support, had died of a fever. Jesus came to see the widow and found her kneeling beside the bed on which her son's body was laid. With great compassion, Jesus stretched forth his hand and called out:

"Young man, arise and live."

To everyone's amazement the boy who had been dead arose as one awakes in the morning, and embraced his mother. Soon the entire country heard about this miracle, and many, many more people began to believe that Jesus of Nazareth was indeed the Saviour of whom the prophets had spoken.

Yet many also doubted and hated Jesus. Some were sincere, others merely wicked. The followers of John the Baptist were honest in their doubts of Jesus, for they believed John to be the Messiah. After all, they said, John lived a life of pain and suffering in the desert; he never ate meat or drank wine; he now awaits death in Herod's prison. Is he not the real Messiah?

Jesus understood their doubts.

"You can't imagine that the Saviour should come to you neatly dressed, eating with tax collectors, going to weddings, and drinking wine. But God is wise, and knows what He is doing."

Then he continued:

308

"Come unto me, all you that labor and are heavy laden and I will give you rest."

JESUS WAS ESPECIALLY anxious to preach in Nazareth, where he had spent most of his life. There his mother Mary lived and his father, Joseph the carpenter, was buried. One day, Jesus asked permission to preach in the synagogue at Nazareth, and, according to custom, he was invited to do so.

Taking the Book of the Law in his hand, Jesus read about his own ministry among the poor and suffering, just as the prophets had described it many hundreds of years before. Though Jesus was very convincing in his speech, the elders of the synagogue in Nazareth rejected him.

"Isn't this the carpenter's son?" they asked in ridicule. "Is he trying to say that he is the Messiah of whom the prophets wrote?" And they laughed.

Jesus' disciples were unhappy to see their master rejected, especially in his own home town. But Jesus was philosophical.

"No prophet is accepted in his own country," he said. "Therefore, we must preach among other people. After all, you remember how Elisha, the prophet, converted Naaman, a man from Syria. God wishes us to spread His word among all the people of the world."

So they went on their way, preaching and teaching in the nearby towns. As usual, the enemies of Jesus followed close behind. They hoped to trap Jesus in public, so that the people would no longer believe in him. For this purpose, they brought a sinful woman into his presence. This woman had been taken in adultery—a crime that was punishable by stoning, according to the ancient laws.

"What would you do with this wicked woman?" shouted Jesus' enemies. Jesus was silent at first. He stooped down and wrote something in the sand at his feet.

The enemies smiled. They thought they had truly trapped Jesus. If he said that the sinful woman should go free, they could accuse him of disobeying the sacred laws. And if he condemned the woman and had her stoned to death, they could say that he was cruel and without mercy.

Jesus sought neither path. He rose and said simply:

"He that is without sin among you, let him cast the first stone at her."

Everyone was amazed. For in that crowd there was no one without sin—and no one worthy of condemning another human being. One by

The Rejection in Nazareth and the Sinful Woman

one, the conscience-stricken people left the scene until Jesus was alone with the sinful woman.

"We must not condemn each other," said Jesus to the woman. "We must forgive and pray to be forgiven. Go then, and sin no more."

The sinful woman was so grateful to Jesus that she became one of his followers. Some believe that this was Mary of Magdala, or Mary Magdalene. It is also said that, one night, while Jesus was dining in a rich man's house, Mary Magdalene entered with rare spices and oil so that she might anoint Jesus' feet. In those days, people always removed their shoes when they went inside, and bathed their feet and sprinkled them with fine spices and oils.

Magdalene anointed Jesus' feet with her tears and dried them with the hair of her head. Then she sprinkled them with spices and oil. The rich man at whose table Jesus was dining watched all this in surprise, and wondered how Jesus could allow a woman of such bad reputation to touch him, let alone anoint his feet.

Jesus spoke softly and reminded his host that God forgives all sinners who repent; the greater the sin, the greater is the repentance and the greater God's forgiveness.

"You are a rich man," said Jesus to his host. "But when I came into your house tonight, you did not anoint my feet and sprinkle them with spices and oil. You think your sins are few and you need not repent. But this woman knows her sins, and they are great. Thus will she be forgiven."

Then Jesus told a parable, to illustrate his point. Two men owed money to another man. One owed five hundred pieces of silver, the other only fifty. The man to whom the money was owed was generous and disclaimed both debts. Which of the debtors do you think was most appreciative? asked Jesus. And the rich host answered:

"The man who owed five hundred pieces of silver."

"Exactly," Jesus replied. "He who is forgiven the most will love the most. Just as this woman whom I forgave loves me and believes in me more than you do."

Jesus Answers His Enemies

NO MATTER HOW KINDLY Jesus spoke and how wisely he proved his teachings, his enemies taunted him and tried to cast doubts upon his mission. They began to spread the rumor that Jesus was in league with the devil himself, because he cured people and brought them back from death. They argued that, since the devil brought about disease and suffering, only the devil could call them off.

Jesus answered boldly:

"How can Satan cast out Satan?" he asked. "If a house is divided against itself, that house cannot stand. The fact is that God and only God can undo the devil's treachery, and you who are evil at heart cannot know good or speak wisely."

Then Jesus spoke of Jonah, who had been three days in the belly of a whale.

"So shall the Son of Man be three days in the heart of the earth," said Jesus. But no one grasped the meaning of these prophetic words.

In the crowd listening to Jesus were Mary, his mother, and his brothers and sisters. When someone pointed them out to him, Jesus exclaimed:

"All people are my brothers and sisters, for all of us have the same Father, who is God in heaven."

JESUS WAS A GREAT TEACHER because he made his lessons clear and easily understandable. To do this, he often told parables, or stories with a message. One day, while standing in a boat on the shores of Galilee, Jesus told this story to the crowd:

A farmer filled his apron with seeds, and set off to scatter them in the fresh earth. As he tossed the seeds this way and that way, some fell by the wayside, where the blackbirds ate them; some fell upon stony places; some fell among the brambles; and others fell into the earth, as they were supposed to. Jesus explained the story to his disciples.

"My words are like the seeds," he said. "Some will fall by the wayside and be ignored, so that the devil, like a blackbird, will come and eat them up. Some will fall upon people who are like rocks where no seed can take root, and therefore perishes. My words will also fall among brambles—among people who are too caught up with other things, such as money and pleasure, to concern themselves with the teachings of God. And my words will also fall upon those people, who, like fresh earth, are ready and willing to accept them and let them grow and bear fruit. This is the meaning of my parable."

Jesus often used the example of seeds being scattered in the fields as a way of clarifying his message. He knew that many of the people who listened to him were farmers and would understand the comparisons. Once, he compared heaven to a mustard seed, which is the least imposing of all seeds until it grows. Then it becomes a great tree, with many branches upon which many birds may live.

Parables of the Sower and the Kingdon of God

AFTER TELLING his parables, Jesus decided it was time to travel, and he beckoned his disciples to follow him across the sea of Galilee to the distant shore. They all boarded a ship, which then set sail.

Jesus was weary. He stretched out on the deck and soon fell fast asleep. As the ship made its way across the sea, a ferocious storm began brewing in the heavens. Within minutes, thunder and lightning were striking, and great waves were tossing the ship without mercy.

The disciples became fearful of their lives. Rushing to Jesus, they roused him from his sleep, crying:

"Save us, Master, save us!"

Without hesitation, Jesus lifted his arms and ordered the heavens to be at peace. In that same instant, the storm subsided and the great waves disappeared, so that the sea was peaceful and calm. Then Jesus turned to his friends and said:

"Why did you doubt that you would be saved? If I am with you, and you believe in me, then you will never perish."

The disciples, who knew Jesus and had seen his miracles before, were nonetheless amazed that he could command the very heavens themselves to obey.

When the ship docked on the far side of the sea, Jesus beheld a poor, sick man wandering in the graveyards of the countryside. This man, long afflicted with madness, had been abandoned by his family and friends. Now he was alone and he could do nothing but cause himself harm.

Jesus approached this piteous person and asked his name.

The man replied:

"My name is Legion."

By this, he meant that there were many sorry souls like him throughout the world possessed by many demons. Jesus lifted his hands and ordered the evil spirits out of the man and into the bodies of some swine that were feeding nearby. Then these swine ran, possessed, into the sea and disappeared.

Now the man whose name was Legion was cured, and he begged to join the disciples. But Jesus urged him to stay among his own people

The Great Storm at Sea

OPPOSITE: Plate 78. THE WOMAN TAKEN IN ADULTERY, by Rembrandt (Dutch, 1606–1669), The National Gallery, London.

313

and spread the word of God, for the people would believe him, seeing him cured and having known how hopeless he once had been.

Jairus' Daughter

JESUS AND THE DISCIPLES returned to Capernaum aboard their ship. This time the sea was calm. But upon the shore a great crowd awaited with excitement, for many had come to be healed.

Most eager in the crowd was Jairus, a high official of the synagogue. His twelve-year-old daughter lay dying, and he knew that only Jesus could save her. As the Master set foot on the shore, Jairus rushed forward and begged Jesus to hasten to his house and save his child. Jesus immediately responded and started to make his way through the crowd.

Waiting on a side road was an elderly woman who had suffered from a blood disease for many years. Countless doctors had been unable to help her; now she knew that Jesus was her only hope. But, as he passed, the crowd was so thick that she could not speak to him. Hurriedly she followed behind, having faith that to touch the hem of his robe would be enough to cure her illness. With great effort, the elderly woman managed to place her fingers just at the hem of the Master's robe.

Though hundreds of people pressed in from every side, Jesus knew that someone in need of him had touched his robe. He stopped.

"Who touched me?" he inquired.

"Everyone is touching you," his disciples replied, "for the crowd is very large."

"Yes," said Jesus, "but there is someone here who was ill and now she is healed, for I felt my curative powers entering her soul."

The sickly woman fearfully raised her hand and admitted that she had touched the Master. Jesus was pleased.

"So great is this woman's faith," he said, "that she need but touch my robe to be healed."

At this same moment a messenger came running toward Jairus with the terrible news that his daughter had died. The poor man broke down in tears. But Jesus spoke words of comfort.

"Only believe," he said, "and all will be well."

Then Jesus hastened to Jairus' house, where many people were mourning and weeping.

"She is dead," they said to Jesus. "Why try to save her now?"

"She is not dead," Jesus replied. "She is merely asleep."

Though the others were scornful, he went to the little girl's bed and commanded her to rise. Miraculously, the child opened her eyes and walked from her bed into the arms of her joyous parents.

"Give her something to eat," said Jesus, "and tell no one of this miracle. I do not perform these deeds in order to win praise, but to prove the power of God."

After this, Jesus journeyed through the streets, and blind men and deaf mutes followed him and cried out their faith in his powers, so that they were cured. From Capernaum to the shores of Galilee, in the cities beyond, the word spread fast; no one had ever seen such miracles as the miracles of Jesus.

TIME WAS SHORT and Jesus had a great deal of work to do. In order to spread the word of God, he instructed his twelve disciples in the purposes of his mission and he endowed them with the miraculous power of healing.

"Heal the sick, cleanse the lepers, raise the dead, cast out devils," he said, "and ask nothing in return."

He further warned them to be very careful.

"I send you forth as sheep in the midst of wolves," he said. "Therefore, be as wise as serpents and as harmless as doves."

The disciples were inspired, and set off for many distant cities in order to heal and preach in the manner of Jesus.

Weeks later, the disciples joined Jesus again. They saw how hard he had worked and urged him to rest. But, as he went up to a quiet place in order to sit beneath a shade tree, he found a great throng of people awaiting him.

"They are like sheep without a shepherd," said Jesus, and, forgetting his own need of rest, he went into the midst of the crowd and preached.

By evening, more people had joined the throng, and all were hungry. The disciples thought that it was time to send them home to eat.

"No," said Jesus. "They are poor and we must feed them."

"But we have only a few pennies," answered the disciples, "not enough for even a small loaf of bread."

Jesus looked around. Seated nearby was a boy with a picnic basket. In the basket were five loaves of bread and two small fish. Jesus took the food and performed a great miracle. With only five loaves of bread and two little fish, he was able to feed five thousand people, and, when they were done eating, there were twelve baskets of food left over.

The throng was astonished. They wanted to make Jesus king and put him on a throne. But Jesus wished no such earthly praise, and he quietly left the scene and disappeared into the hills.

The Disciples Are Instructed and Many Persons Are Fed

OPPOSITE: Plate 79. THE STORM ON THE SEA OF GALILEE,
by Rembrandt (Dutch, 1606–1669), Isabella Stewart Gardner Museum, Boston.

BELOW: Plate 80. CHRIST WALKS ON THE SEA OF GALILEE,
by Tintoretto (Italian, 1518–1594), The National Gallery, Washington, D.C.

Jesus
Walks
on the
Water

AFTER THE MIRACLE of the loaves and fishes, Jesus instructed his disciples to cross the Sea of Galilee, so that they might continue their preaching. He stood on the shore bidding them good-by as they set sail.

However, when night fell, the sea became very rough, and the disciples had a hard time rowing the boat. Suddenly, they saw a figure apparently walking on the water. At first, they were afraid, because it was dark and they could not recognize their Master. But, once Jesus made himself known, they rejoiced.

Peter had doubted that anyone could walk on the sea, and asked Jesus to endow him with the same power. Stepping out of the boat at Jesus' bidding, Peter found that he could also walk upon the waves. But, suddenly, a wind blew up and Peter became afraid, thus losing faith. Immediately, he began to sink. Jesus rescued him, saying:

"Man of little faith, why did you doubt?"

Peter was ashamed, but now, more than ever, he was convinced of his Master's divinity. Later, Jesus sat among his disciples and asked them:

"Who do you think I really am?"

Some said that he was the prophet Jeremiah, reborn, or Isaiah, or even Elijah. But Peter said:

"You are Christ, the Son of the Living God."

Jesus was deeply impressed with Peter's understanding and faith, and he said to him:

"You, Peter, are the rock upon which I will build my church, and you will also sit at the gates of heaven and hold the keys to my kingdom in your hands."

The other disciples now realized that their Master was indeed the Messiah, the Christ, for whom the world had prayed. But Jesus warned them not to speak of this news in public.

The
Mission
of Mercy
Continues

FOR MANY MONTHS, Jesus and his disciples traveled through Galilee and other parts of the Holy Land, curing the sick, preaching, and debating their ideas. Jesus made no distinction among the suffering. Jews and gentiles (or foreigners) were healed by him. Children and old people came to be comforted; the blind and deaf, the sick in body and mind, all were saved by faith in his word and teachings.

But, still, the scribes and the Pharisees and the rulers of the cities believed Jesus to be a dangerous and troublesome man. In spite of the proofs of his power, these enemies of Jesus continued to plan ways to ensnare and perhaps destroy him.

Yet he continued his work. One day, at the city of Bethsaida, Jesus restored a blind man's sight. Later, he healed an epileptic boy.

Jesus also continued to instruct his disciples in the ways of the Lord. It was important that they be able to answer their enemies, so that the people would respect their wisdom.

Once a tax collector stopped Peter, and said to him:

"You are a follower of Jesus, and he says many things about the proper way to live; but, tell me, does he pay his taxes?"

Peter immediately answered, "Yes."

Nevertheless, Peter wondered if Jesus, a divine being from God, should actually have to pay taxes, for a king did not pay taxes in Judea. He asked Jesus about this, and Jesus replied:

"I will pay the tax and keep the peace. We want no trouble over such a little matter."

"Very well," said Peter, "but there is no money to pay the tax."

"Go to the sea," said Jesus, "and cast your line."

Peter did so. The first fish he caught had a coin in its mouth. Peter took the coin, sought out the tax collector and said:

"Here is my master's tax."

Thus, the disciples learned the proper conduct of their lives. But they learned the hard way.

One day, they were arguing among themselves about which one of them was the most important and would, thus, receive the most reward in Jesus' eyes. Jesus overheard this foolish argument, and he said.

"If any man desires to be first in the kingdom of heaven then he must really be last; he must be humble, serve others, do good things, and expect no reward. But he who thinks of himself as great and righteous and expects glory, he shall be considered lowly in the eyes of God."

Jesus then prophesied his own death and resurrection, and said that many would come after him who would take up the burden of his work and suffer the same fate, but that they who did so and died for the cause would gain eternal life in heaven.

"What does a man profit if he gains the whole world," said Jesus, "but gives up his chance to live after death?"

SOMETHING JESUS HAD SAID troubled the disciples, and they spoke of it among themselves.

"What did he mean about his death and resurrection?" they asked.

Several times now, Jesus had made reference to a time, not far off, when he would go to Jerusalem, be condemned, and later be forced to

The Transfiguration

carry a weighty cross upon which he would die. Then, Jesus said, he would rise from the dead, after three days, to show all the world God's great mercy and power. The disciples could not understand the mystery and wonder of these prophecies.

Jesus did not explain further. One night, he asked three of his followers, Peter, John, and James, to walk with him to a high mountain in the north country. He wanted to pray there.

The three men walked with Jesus and became weary. When they reached the peak, they lay down, wrapped their cloaks about them, and slept. Jesus, meanwhile, knelt in prayer. Then a wonderful thing happened: the heavens opened, a great light poured forth, and two mighty figures appeared, from the clouds above the peak. They were Moses and Elijah, the great ancient prophets of God. They had come to speak with Jesus, the Messiah.

The bright light and the glory of this moment roused Peter and his friends from their sleep. When Peter saw the figures of Moses and Elijah and the transfiguration of Jesus into a being of radiance and great beauty, he fell on his knees and cried out:

"Let me build a temple here to commemorate this great moment." But, as he spoke, a voice was heard far above, saying:

"Behold, this is My beloved Son in whom I am well pleased. Believe in him, and that is enough."

When Peter raised his head, the vision had disappeared, leaving Jesus in a glowing light. Now, more than ever, Peter and his friends knew that their Master was the Son of God, in other words, God in the form of man. But Jesus advised them to keep this knowledge to themselves. Again, he foresaw his fate in Jerusalem, but he comforted his disciples, saying:

"Even my death is part of God's great plan."

THE TEACHING of God's word was now going forth with great speed. Jesus appointed seventy righteous men to visit seventy cities in order to preach. Others took up the task of healing: and many evil spirits were cast out of the land.

The Good Samaritan

OPPOSITE: Plate 81. (Frontispiece) CHRIST BLESSING THE CHILDREN, School of Rembrandt, (Dutch, 17th century), The National Gallery, London.

Still Jesus' enemies tried to ensnare him. One day a lawyer stood up
and called out to Jesus:

"How shall I achieve eternal life? What is the way?"

And Jesus answered:

"You shall love the Lord your God with all your heart, and you
shall love your neighbor as yourself."

The lawyer was cunning, and he said:

"Love my neighbor? How do I know who my neighbor is? Suppose
he is a stranger to me?"

To answer this insincere question, Jesus told a parable, as follows:

Once a certain man was journeying from Jerusalem to Jericho,
when he was suddenly attacked by robbers, who left him badly beaten
and stripped by the side of the road. As the poor man lay there, a high-
and-mighty priest rode by. Seeing the suffering man, he turned his face
and quickly galloped away. He wanted no part of any trouble. Similarly,
a Levite, one of the officials of the Temple, came by, looked at the injured man, and also hurried off without trying to help.

322

Then a humble man from Samaria, a Samaritan as he was called, journeyed by and, seeing the wounded man, rushed to his aid, and carefully dressed his injuries. Then the Samaritan lifted him onto his horse and took him to a nearby inn to recuperate. Moreover, when morning dawned, the Samaritan gave the unfortunate man some money, so that he might find his way home.

Now Jesus turned to the lawyer and asked:

"Which of the three men would you consider the neighbor of the injured man?"

And the lawyer answered:

"The Samaritan, because he helped him and showed him mercy."

"Indeed," said Jesus, "we are all neighbors if we show mercy to each other. Now you go and do the same."

A POOR BEGGAR lay in the streets, blind and helpless. Jesus was passing, and took pity on the man, who begged for comfort. Taking some clay from the ground, Jesus moistened it and applied it to the blind man's eyes. Then he told him to wash himself in the pool at Siloam, nearby.

The beggar obeyed, and, when he had finished bathing, he found his sight restored and his whole body well and straight. He returned to his home to declare the wondrous miracles of Jesus. But his neighbors were suspicious. They didn't believe that this healthy-looking man was the same beggar whom they had seen every day lying in the streets.

Jesus' enemies took advantage of the situation. They implied that the so-called blind man was a fraud. Some people sought out the beggar's parents and asked them, "Is this your son, and was he ever really blind?"

The old people realized they might get in trouble with the high priests and the rich men of the city so they simply replied:

"He is old enough to answer for himself."

The beggar was angry, and insisted that he had been blind since

*The
Man
Born
Blind*

birth and that Jesus had miraculously restored his sight. But he was greeted with threats and ridicule. Discouraged, he sought out Jesus for comfort, recalling that Jesus had once said, "None is so blind as he who will not see."

The Raising of Lazarus

IN THE TOWN of Bethany lived Lazarus and his two sisters, Martha and Mary. They believed in Jesus, and knew that he was the Messiah sent from God. Such knowledge made all three very happy.

But, now, sad times befell the family, for Lazarus was grievously ill, and his sisters feared that he would die. Hurriedly they sent word to Jesus, who was preaching nearby.

"Come and save our brother, your friend Lazarus," they pleaded.

But, oddly enough, Jesus did not seem anxious. Instead, he continued his mission, telling his disciples that Lazarus' illness was part of God's plan.

Then one day word came of Lazarus' death. Now Jesus was determined to go to Bethany. His disciples begged him to remain where he was. Once, in Bethany, some people had thrown stones at him, because they said he had broken the Sabbath. But Jesus was not afraid.

"Our friend Lazarus is asleep, and I must wake him," he said.

The disciples were confused. They thought Lazarus was dead, not asleep. Nevertheless, they followed their Master into Bethany.

It took Jesus four days to arrive at the home of Lazarus. It was a house of sorrow. Many people had gathered to comfort Martha and Mary, the grieving sisters. When Jesus appeared, Martha ran to him.

"Oh Lord," she said, "if only you had come sooner, you could have saved our brother. Now he lies in his grave these last four days."

Jesus spoke comforting words.

"Lazarus will rise again," he said.

"I know," Martha replied, "he will arise on Judgment Day, in the Resurrection, for he was a righteous man. But, for now, he is gone and buried."

Jesus then proclaimed a mighty message.

"I am the Resurrection and the Life," he said. "Whosoever believes in me, *though he be dead,* he shall live again. And whosoever lives and believes in me, he shall never die."

With these words ringing in her ears, Martha led Jesus to the tomb of Lazarus. Meanwhile Mary had heard of the Master's arrival. She rushed from the house in the midst of all the mourners, seemingly joyful, for she knew the power of the Lord.

At Lazarus' tomb, the sisters knelt and wept with Jesus, who had great compassion in his heart. All those around them were struck by Jesus' devotion, and wondered could he, who had cured the lame and the blind, also raise from the dead a man buried four days in the earth?

Jesus ordered the stone rolled away from the tomb of Lazarus. Then, lifting his eyes to heaven, he cried,

"Lazarus, come forth!"

God heard Jesus' prayer, and, in a miracle surpassing all others, He restored Lazarus to life, so that the man who had been dead emerged from his tomb, still wrapped in his shroud, and stood before the astonished crowd.

Word of this mighty miracle reached the priests and rulers of Jerusalem. The most influential of these men was Caiaphas, a high priest of the Temple. He was very crafty and knew how to balance his power between the Jews and the Romans who ruled the nation.

"If this man Jesus becomes too powerful," he said, "the Romans will get angry and cause us harm. We must rid ourselves of this so-called Messiah from Galilee."

At first, it was thought to exile Jesus. But he would not leave his country or abandon his work, for the people now joined him in greater numbers. Some openly approached him in the streets and asked to become disciples.

"Do you know that it is hard to be a disciple of mine?" Jesus would inquire. Some agreed, but joined him. Others found the task too hard, and fell by the wayside. Jesus understood, for he was always aware of man's weaknesses.

JESUS CONTINUED to preach his parables, using examples from everyday life. He told the story of *The Missing Coin.*

Once, he said, there was a woman who had ten silver coins. By accident, one of them rolled off the table to the floor. The woman was determined to find that coin, so she lit her candle and began searching in every corner of the room. When she found the missing piece, she was so overjoyed that she threw open the windows and called to her neighbors:

"Rejoice with me, for I have found the coin I lost."

In this same way, said Jesus, God rejoices when even one lost sinner repents.

Another story had the same message. It was the *Parable of the Prodigal Son.* Once there were two brothers who lived at home with their father. The younger was impatient and restless. He wanted to see the

Some
Famous
Parables

ABOVE: Plate 83. CHRIST HEALING THE BLIND MAN, by Duccio
(Italian, about 1255–1319), The National Gallery, London.

OPPOSITE: Plate 84. THE RAISING OF LAZARUS, by Geertgen Tot Sint Jans
(Dutch, about 1455–about 1490), The Louvre Museum, Paris.

world and enjoy the life of the big cities outside. Accordingly, he asked his father to give him his share of his inheritance, so that he might venture forth into the world.

The father did as his youngest son asked; and the boy went off to the city. There he gambled and lived a riotous life, until he was without money and friends. Then a famine came upon the land. Poor, disgraced, and hopeless, the young man made his way back home. It was his plan to become a servant in his father's house, so that he might pay off his debts and make himself worthy once again.

As he approached the house, his father saw him and ran to greet him joyously.

"But, father," said the prodigal son, "I am not worthy of your forgiveness, for I have sinned."

The father would hear no more. He ordered the finest robes brought from the house, and a fattened calf killed for a feast in celebration of his son's return. The older brother became angry.

"I have been faithful and steadfast," he said to his father, "but with no reward. My brother, however, wasted your money and disgraced himself. You never had a party for me, but you kill a fattened calf and prepare a feast for him."

The father replied with wisdom.

"I do not love you less than your brother," he said, "but it is fitting that we should make merry and be glad; for your brother was as good as dead, but now he is alive again. He was lost, and now he is found."

Some of Jesus' parables concerned the Pharisees, who had set themselves against all new ideas and prophecies. In one story called *The Beggar and the Pharisee,* a poor man named Lazarus, who was too ill to work, stationed himself at the door of a rich Pharisee's home. There he lay, hoping to catch a few crumbs from the rich man's table. But he was ignored, and chased by dogs in his misery. Finally Lazarus died and went to heaven, where the angels carried him to the comfort and peace of Abraham's bosom.

In time, the rich Pharisee also died. But he did not go to heaven. Instead he fell among flames and torture, so that he lay in perpetual agony. From this wretched place, the rich man could see Lazarus, the beggar, in Abraham's bosom, and he called to him and cried:

"Help me. I am thirsty and in pain. Just dip your finger in some water so that I may wet my lips."

But the gulf between Lazarus and the rich man was too great, and the beggar could not help him. The Pharisee, realizing the error of his ways, sought to prevent his brothers and his sons from knowing a similar fate. So he cried out to Abraham:

"Send Lazarus back to earth, to warn my kinsmen of the fate that awaits them if they remain hardhearted and cruel."

"They have the words of Moses and the prophets, let your kinsmen listen to them," said Abraham.

"They won't," said the Pharisee, "but if someone from the dead goes to them they will repent."

"If they hear not Moses and the prophets," said Abraham, "they will not be persuaded by one from the dead."

Jesus told a similar story of the *Pharisee and the Publican*. The Pharisee and a humble publican went to the Temple to pray. The Pharisee raised his eyes toward Heaven and said:

"I am a righteous man, not like the others. I pray; I give money to the Temple; and I fast twice a week."

The publican standing nearby lowered his eyes and bowed his head. His prayer was quite different.

"I am a lowly sinner," he said, "and I can only pray for my forgiveness."

Jesus assured his listeners that God was much more impressed with the publican than with the Pharisee, for, as Jesus said, he who exalts himself shall be brought low, and he who humbles himself shall be exalted in the eyes of God.

Jesus told another parable about wealth and humility:

A rich young Pharisee once came to Jesus and asked:

"How may I gain eternal life?"

Jesus reminded the young man of the law and the Commandments.

"Yes," said the Pharisee. "I have obeyed the law and I follow the Commandments, but I feel that there is something else I must do."

Jesus knew what the rich man lacked.

"Go," he said to him. "Sell all your possessions and give the money to the poor. Make yourself a disciple of mine, and you shall inherit a greater treasure in heaven."

But the rich man could not bring himself to part with his worldly goods, so he went away with his head hung low. Then Jesus turned to his friends and said:

"How hard it is for a wealthy man to part with his goods. Indeed, it is easier for a camel to pass through the eye of a needle than for a rich man to enter the Kingdom of God."

The people loved to hear Jesus' parables, for they were easily understood and dealt with everyday events. For example:

A man had four servants who were very trustworthy. Because he was going on a long journey, the man divided his money among the servants and told them to take good care of it. Three of the servants took the

Plate 85. THE RETURN OF THE PRODIGAL SON, by Bartolomé Esteban Murillo (Spanish, 1617–1682), The National Gallery, Washington, D.C.

money and invested it so that they could show a profit when their master returned. But the fourth servant was lazy, and merely buried the money in the ground. Of course, money does not grow in the ground. So, when the master returned, the clever servants were able to show a profit, but the lazy man could only hand back the same amount of money he had been given. The master was angry with this lazy man and dismissed him.

So it is, said Jesus, with the word of God. Some shall take it and use it profitably. Others will do nothing and gain nothing in the end.

Jesus considered God's teachings more important than everyday affairs. One day, he visited Martha and Mary, the sisters of Lazarus, who had been risen from the dead. They were preparing a feast to celebrate the great event. When Jesus entered the house, Mary would not leave his side, for she was anxious to hear his teachings. Her sister Martha, however, bustled around with her pots and pans. Finally, she went up to Jesus and said:

"Lord, it isn't fair that my sister Mary sits here and doesn't help with the housework. Tell her that she must help."

But Jesus smiled. "Martha, Martha," he said, "you can do housework every day, but how often is it that I come to your home with the word of God? Mary knows this, and she will be rewarded."

Jesus told many other parables. In some of them, he compared himself to the Good Shepherd who will go any distance to save one lamb who has gone astray. Furthermore, said Jesus, the Good Shepherd is willing to lay down his life to save his sheep. This, too, Jesus was prepared to do.

SINCE THE PASSOVER FEAST was soon to be celebrated, Jesus and his disciples made plans to visit Jerusalem, so that they might worship in the Temple. In his heart, Jesus knew that he would die in Jerusalem, as the prophets had predicted. But his destiny was meant to be fulfilled; and he approached the final journey with great serenity.

While passing through Samaria, on the way to Jerusalem, Jesus continued his preaching and healing. At one village, ten unfortunate lepers waited at the crossroads, hoping to be healed. When they saw Jesus they rushed forward and fell on their knees. The crowd drew back, for leprosy was considered to be contagious. But Jesus knew no fear. He lifted his hands over the lepers' heads, and they were healed. Only one of the cured men remained kneeling in thanks. Jesus was very pleased, for this man was a Samaritan, not a Jew. Now, even the Samaritans believed in Jesus and his miracles.

Jesus Prepares to Visit Jerusalem

While passing through the town of Jericho, Jesus once again proved that all men might gain salvation, even unpopular tax collectors.

Zaccheus was the richest man in Jericho—and the chief tax collector. He was a small, unattractive person, neither better nor worse than anybody else. He was also a determined man. When he heard that Jesus, the famous prophet, was coming to town, he wanted to catch a glimpse of him. Eagerly he left his money bags and rushed out into the crowd. But, being small, Zaccheus couldn't see a thing. So he climbed a sycamore tree and sat there right over the place where Jesus passed.

"Make haste, Zaccheus," called Jesus, seeing the man in the tree, "I will stay at your house while I am in Jericho."

Everyone was surprised to see Jesus enter the home of the tiny tax collector. But Zaccheus was overjoyed. To celebrate his salvation, he gave half his money to the poor and became a devoted follower of Jesus.

After Jericho, Jesus passed through Bethany, his last stop before entering Jerusalem. There, in Bethany, he visited Martha and Mary and their brother Lazarus, who had been raised from the dead. It was the Saturday before the feast of Passover. For the next few days, Jesus would pass from triumph to death, and, then, to glory. The story of his last week in Jerusalem is sometimes known as the *Passion of the Lord.*

The Fate of John the Baptist

WHILE JESUS WAS PREPARING to enter Jerusalem, John the Baptist lay in chains deep in the dungeon of King Herod's palace. From the depths of his cell, he continued to preach the coming of the Lord and Saviour. Occasionally, his followers managed to get a message to him, and they told him of Jesus and his wonderful work.

King Herod feared John the Baptist, and was content to keep him in prison without doing him further harm. But Herod's wife, Queen Herodias, was wicked and sinful. Because John had spoken against her, for she had been the wife of Herod's brother, she wished him dead.

One night, during a birthday feast for the king, Herodias introduced her beautiful daughter, Salome. King Herod was delighted, and wished the maiden to dance for him. He promised to award her anything her heart desired, even half his kingdom, if she would perform.

Salome agreed, and danced before the king and his guests. When she finished, Herod said:

"Now, tell me. What do you wish?"

Salome went to her mother, Herodias, for advice. Then she returned to Herod with a terrible request.

"Give me the head of John the Baptist on a silver platter," she demanded.

Herod was shocked. He tried to talk Salome out of her request, promising her jewels and great wealth. But Herodias' daughter insisted. Finally, the king reluctantly gave in, and the great prophet John was slain in the dungeon.

When the followers of Jesus heard this news, they were afraid for their Master, for the whole city of Jerusalem was seething with unrest. Everywhere, Roman soldiers were stationed, prepared to quell any riot that might begin because of the Baptist's death. In the Temple, the Pharisees and Sadducees, sworn enemies of Jesus, were plotting ways of doing him harm. Ever since Lazarus had been raised from the dead, they had feared Jesus' power and popularity. Thus, hatred and trouble were brewing in Jerusalem while Jesus prepared to make his entry.

But there were great expectations as well, for the humble Jews of the city looked forward to seeing the great Master from Nazareth. His reputation had spread in spite of his enemies' greatest efforts.

AT A PLACE called the Mount of Olives, Jesus gathered his disciples. He told them that his visit to Jerusalem would be a time of fulfillment of all the ancient prophecies. In accordance with these prophecies, Jesus sent two of his men into the village nearby, in order to fetch a spotless white colt that had never been ridden. The prophets had said that the Messiah would one day enter Jerusalem astride a perfect white colt.

In due time, the disciples found such an animal and brought it to the Mount of Olives. There, Jesus mounted the colt and began the journey into Jerusalem. As he passed through the villages outside the city's walls, his disciples cried out:

"Behold the King that cometh in the name of the Lord!"

The Pharisees hearing this were alarmed. They feared a violent revolution that would make Jesus king, for they didn't understand the spiritual meaning of the word. Angrily, they cried to Jesus:

"Make your disciples stop all this shouting."

But Jesus replied:

"If these people are silent, then the stones will cry out—for my message must be heard."

Finally the procession approached the city gates. When Jesus beheld Jerusalem, the great city of the Jews, he began to weep silently, for he knew the destruction and sorrow that would someday befall every house and stone within. But then his heart was made glad, for the multitudes came out in throngs to greet him, laying their cloaks on the road in his path. Many climbed trees for a better view, and others plucked palm leaves from the trees to wave at the Lord. Thus, the first Palm

The Celebration of the Palms

Sunday was celebrated in Jerusalem amid cries of "Hosanna"—which means "Salvation"—and amid great rejoicing.

At twilight, Jesus and his disciples returned on foot to Bethany. The first day had ended in triumph.

The Cleansing of the Temple

ON THE DAY following his triumphal entry, Jesus returned with his disciples to Jerusalem and went directly to the Temple. In ancient times, it was the custom to erect stalls alongside the Temple's walls for the purposes of selling food and objects for the sacrifice. Gradually, many merchants moved onto the Temple grounds themselves, and conducted their business in sight of the main altar.

Money lenders and changers also set up tables in the Temple, where they conducted themselves in a generally noisy and ungodly manner. Jesus understood these outrages, but this did not soothe his anger. With a whip in his hands, he rushed into the midst of the money lenders and overturned their tables and stalls, crying:

"The House of God shall be a house of prayer, not a den of thieves!"

Hastily, the merchants and money lenders retreated, but they were not soon to forget this incident. A few days later, many of them were on hand to condemn Jesus to death.

When the defilers were out of the Temple, the poor, the lame, and the blind came before Jesus, and they were miraculously healed. The priests who watched in amazement would not admit Jesus' greatness, fearing to lose their own high status in the city. In fact, they stepped forward and challenged Jesus, demanding to know who he was and by what authority he spoke. As they were speaking, a group of children entered the Temple grounds singing:

"Hosanna to the Son of David, the Messiah."

Jesus turned to the priests and said:

"You asked who I was? Out of the mouths of babes will you hear it."

OPPOSITE: Plate 86. CHRIST DRIVING THE MONEY CHANGERS FROM THE TEMPLE, by El Greco (Spanish School, 1541–1614), The National Gallery, London.

Parables
and
Events
in the
Temple

AFTER CHASING the money changers and healing the sick, Jesus continued to preach in the Temple. As a teacher, or rabbi, he was entitled to do so, even though the priests and rulers of the city challenged him and wished him away. They were very cautious about causing a riot, however. Many people had gathered in the Temple to hear Jesus, and, if the soldiers had arrested him or stoned him, hundreds would have risen to his defense. So the wicked men merely tried to make Jesus look foolish in the sight of his followers.

One of them held up a coin and asked a treacherous question.

"Since you tell us to pay homage only to God," he asked, "should we continue to pay taxes to Rome?"

Jesus knew this question was an attempt to entangle him. If he said, "Don't pay taxes to Rome," he would surely be arrested. If he seemed to be fearful of Roman authority, then he would appear cowardly and weak. With perfect control, Jesus asked the man to show him the coin. The man complied.

"Whose picture is this on the coin?" asked Jesus.

"That is Caesar," the questioner replied.

"Very well," said Jesus. "Give this to Caesar, since it is his, but give unto God the things that are God's."

Properly rebuked, the troublemakers left the Temple.

On the following day, Jesus came to preach again. This time, many Pharisees and priests assembled to challenge him and interrupt his work.

"Woe unto you, scribes and Pharisees!" he called to them. "You exalt yourselves on earth, but you will be as nothing in the Kingdom of God. Even this great city of Jerusalem will one day fall to ruin; and this Temple, by which you swear, it shall crumble again, because you have based your values on material things and not on God."

The mighty rulers of the city were angered.

"This man says he is the Savior, the Christ," they said. "But he is just a teacher from Nazareth—and no prophets ever came from Nazareth!"

Patiently, Jesus urged the sinners to repent. There was always room at God's table for the penitent, he said. Then he told the parable of *The Wedding Guest*.

A rich man once held a feast to celebrate his son's wedding. For selfish reasons, those invited failed to come. The rich man was upset, for he had prepared much food and gone to great trouble. After a while, he called his servants and told them to remind his guests of the feast. But the wicked people killed the servants rather than leave their businesses and their other tasks. Fortunately, the king of the city heard about this crime, and sent his army to arrest the murderers.

The rich man then decided to open his doors to anyone who wished to attend the celebration, and he ordered his servants to go out into the streets and invite all those at hand. Many poor and hungry people eagerly came to the feast, first dressing in their best garments as a sign of respect. One man, however, was too eager. He did not bother to change his clothing or to cleanse himself before the meal. He was forcibly made to leave. As Jesus said: "Many are called, but few are chosen."

Jesus explained his story thus: The Kingdom of God is like the feast; it is there waiting for everyone. Some people will be foolish, and refuse God's invitation to attend. Others, humble though they might be, will accept and enjoy the bounty of Heaven. Still others will be unprepared, like the man who was not properly dressed. They will be cast out of Heaven.

Another parable had a similar message. It was called *The Foolish and Wise Virgins*:

Ten young ladies were supposed to accompany a bridal party on its way to the Temple. Each girl had a small oil lamp, which was to be lit at the proper time so that the procession would appear festive and beautiful. The bridegroom was detained in arriving, so the maidens sat patiently by the side of the road awaiting him. The hour grew late, and they all fell asleep. About midnight a cry was heard:

"Get ready; the bridegroom is coming!"

The girls hastily prepared themselves. But five of them suddenly discovered that they had forgotten to put oil in their lamps. Nervously, they asked their wiser friends to lend them some oil. But the others needed every drop, and advised the foolish virgins to hasten and purchase the oil they needed. Then the wise maidens lit their lamps and went forth to greet the bridal party.

The foolish girls ran all over town, seeking oil. But the hour was late, and none was to be found. Finally, when they returned to the wedding feast, the doors of the house were locked, and they could not enter.

So it is with the Kingdom of God, said Jesus. God's call may come at any moment, even while you are asleep; therefore, always be ready, or you may not be able to enter the Kingdom of Heaven.

Jesus then prophesied many strange and wonderful things that would happen in the future. He spoke until evening approached; then he prepared to leave the Temple. At the door of the building, there was the customary poor box. Jesus paused and watched as the rich men of Jerusalem dropped in large sums of money to impress their neighbors.

When they were gone, a poor widow approached the box and deposited the sum of two mites, or one penny. Jesus turned to his friends and disciples, who had been with him in the Temple, and said:

"For all the wealth of the rich, God will appreciate this poor woman's gift many times over, for the rich will never miss what they gave. But this poor woman gave all she owned."

So saying, Jesus and his friends left the Temple of Jerusalem for the very last time.

The Plot against Jesus

IT WAS WEDNESDAY of the final week. Jesus and his disciples decided to preach in the city and in the villages nearby. As they walked from Bethany, the group passed a withered fig tree. Peter was surprised. He remembered having seen that same tree standing tall and straight only the day before.

Peter soon learned that Jesus had cursed the fig tree so that it withered. On Monday, Jesus had been hungry, and when he approached the tree in order to eat some figs, he found that it was bare. Jesus did not mean to be vengeful toward a harmless fig tree. But he wanted to teach his disciples a lesson.

"When the word of God comes to you and you are bare as that fig tree," said Jesus, "then you will also wither."

Peter was nonetheless amazed that the tree had withered so fast.

"Have faith," said Jesus. "Faith can move mountains and fulfill all righteous desires. There is nothing like faith in God. He will feed you when you are hungry, and give you drink when you are thirsty. All these things can be accomplished by faith."

In the evening, Jesus and his followers returned to Bethany. But one disciple was missing—unnoticed by the rest. He was Judas Iscariot, a quiet, brooding man, who had remained behind in Jerusalem to take part in a terrible plot against Jesus.

Judas Iscariot

IT WAS DARK in the city. Judas crept along the narrow streets until he found the house of Caiaphas, a high priest of the Temple and the enemy of Jesus. In Caiaphas' room, several men were planning to capture Jesus so that they might turn him over to the Roman authorities.

They had to be careful. If they arrested Jesus while he was preaching, a riot might result. Therefore, it was best to take him by surprise when he was alone. Caiaphas turned to Judas:

"When would be the best time to capture your Master?"

Judas was trembling and worried.

"First you must tell me what I will get if I betray him," he said.

"The price is thirty pieces of silver," answered Caiaphas. "Tell us when it would be best to capture your master!"

Judas was afraid, yet he accepted the deal. He told the conspirators that Jesus frequently prayed alone in the garden of Gethsemane and that he would be an easy victim at such a time.

"I shall be nearby," Judas continued. "In case you don't recognize the Nazarene, I will go up to him and kiss him on the cheek. That will be your signal."

Caiaphas was pleased, and told Judas to return to his friends. Judas left the room thinking that the priests merely wanted to arrest Jesus. He did not know that they planned to accuse him of treason against Caesar and thereby enable the Roman authorities to nail him to a cross until he was dead. The priests and Pharisees had no power to put a man to death; that power rested with Pontius Pilate, the Roman governor of Jerusalem. But the priests did have the power to bring charges against their enemies.

Jesus knew what was about to happen. Once again, he told his followers that he would be crucified in Jerusalem, and that, three days later, he would rise from the dead, for he was Christ, the Messiah, and it was his destiny to be sacrificed. Centuries before, Moses had commanded his people to sacrifice a paschal lamb and place its blood on their doorposts, so that the Angel of Death would pass over them and they would be spared. Now, Jesus would give his life on earth, so that all mankind, believing in him as the Messiah, might be spared the hopelessness of death and be redeemed of all the sins and transgressions of the world.

ON THURSDAY, the entire Jewish nation prepared to celebrate the Passover feast, which commemorated the ancient Exodus from Egypt. As religious Jews, Jesus and his disciples sought a place where they might hold the ritual supper. At first, the disciples were worried about finding such a place, but Jesus said:

"In the city, you will see a man carrying a pitcher of water. Follow him. In his house, upstairs, a room will be ready and a table set. We shall hold our supper there."

As Jesus had said, the disciples found a man carrying a pitcher of water; and he led them to a modest house, where the Passover table was set and ready. That evening, Jesus and his twelve disciples, including Judas Iscariot, came into Jerusalem for the meal.

Though it was a joyous holiday, a somber mood seemed to hang

The

Last

Supper

Plate 87. THE LAST SUPPER, by Leonardo da Vinci
(Italian, 1452–1519), Church of Santa Maria della Grazie, Milan.

over the festivities. The disciples, remembering Jesus' prophecy that he would die in Jerusalem, were sad and concerned. Nevertheless, they gathered around the table and began talking quietly among themselves. Soon a slight argument began.

"What is wrong?" asked Jesus.

One of the men replied:

"We should like to know which of us you favor most and which one will be most highly exalted in Heaven?"

Once before, the disciples had wondered about this and, at that time, Jesus had said:

"He who wishes to be first in heaven must be last on earth."

Now, as a demonstration, Jesus removed his outer cloak, filled a basin with water, and knelt down before Peter.

"Let me wash your feet," he said.

Peter was amazed. How could the Lord perform such a humble service?

"Please rise, my Lord," insisted Peter.

But Jesus explained:

"When I wash your feet, you become a part of me."

Peter reflected.

"If that is true," he said, "then wash not only my feet but also my hands and my head."

Jesus was pleased at Peter's devotion and proceeded to wash his feet and the feet of all the other disciples. Then Jesus resumed his place at the table and said,

"Now you are clean; all but one of you. For one of you will betray me."

These words fell like thunder on the ears of the disciples. Nervously, each one asked:

"Is it I, Lord?"

Jesus did not immediately reply. Instead, he dipped some bread in a bowl of herbs and vinegar and passed it to Judas Iscariot as a sign of his knowledge that Judas would betray him. The others did not seem to understand this, and they remained perplexed and uneasy. Then Jesus turned to the deceitful Iscariot and said to him:

"What you must do, go and do quickly!"

Judas immediately rose from the table and fearfully left the room. The others thought that he had been sent on an errand, since Judas often handled finances for the group. They did not question Jesus any further, nor did he tell them that Judas would betray him as part of God's great plan.

Instead, Jesus rose, lifted a piece of bread in his hand, and said:

"Take this bread, which I have blessed, and eat it, for it is my body."

Then he took a cup of wine, blessed it and said:

"This is my blood of the new testament, which is shed for many in the remission of sins."

The disciples knew that they were witnessing a sacred act, and they knelt, and each received a piece of bread and a sip of wine in communion with Jesus. Then he said to them:

"I will not drink wine again until I drink it with God, my Father, in Heaven."

And, as they rose, he further announced:

"A new commandment I give unto you: Love one another as I love you—and all men will know that you are my disciples."

Thus, the first Communion was performed in a modest room in Jerusalem.

AFTER THE MEAL, the disciples sang a hymn and went out into the streets. They headed for the Mount of Olives, where it was Jesus' habit to pray alone. As they walked, Jesus turned to Peter and said:

"When I am gone, I fear my disciples will flee."

"Not I," Peter exclaimed. "I would go to prison and even to death for my Lord."

But Jesus knew the weakness of men.

"Peter," he said, "before the cock crows twice, before the morning comes, you will deny me three times and say you never knew me."

Peter was amazed and protested. Indeed, all the disciples pledged anew their undying faith. Jesus said nothing more. He walked into the quiet garden of Gethsemane on the Mount of Olives. There he signaled Peter, James, and John to follow him and keep guard while he prayed. Jesus felt sorrowful and uneasy. Kneeling alone in the darkness, he experienced the fear and terror common to all mankind, and he called out to God:

"Father, if it is possible that I might be spared the suffering and the pain that I know will come, let me be spared. But if I must suffer as part of Your plan, let it be done. I am ready."

And, as he prayed thus, an angel appeared above him, holding forth a cup of comfort. But Jesus knew no comfort. His agony was so great that great drops of blood fell from his face. Then he seemed to swoon. When he regained his strength, the fear and terror passed away. He rose and returned, calm and unafraid, to Peter, John, and James.

*The
Agony
in the
Garden*

343

ABOVE: Plate 88. THE AGONY IN THE GARDEN, by El Greco
(Spanish School, 1541–1614), The National Gallery, London.

OPPOSITE: Plate 89. THE TAKING OF CHRIST (JUDAS' KISS), by Giotto
(Italian, about 1276–about 1337), Arena Chapel, Padua.

344

Unfortunately, the three disciples had fallen asleep while they waited for their Master.

"Could you not watch even one short hour?" Jesus asked them as they awakened.

The men were embarrassed, and tried to make excuses.

"I know," said Jesus. "The spirit was ready, but the flesh is weak."

Then he asked them to watch again while he returned to his prayers. At the same moment, led by Judas Iscariot and the high priests of the Temple, a group of Roman soldiers entered the garden.

Quietly, their swords drawn, they stationed themselves behind trees, waiting for the signal from Judas.

The Arrest

JESUS ROSE from his prayers, ready to enact God's plan. As he turned to walk from the garden, Judas came up alongside him.

"Hail, Master," he said in a friendly voice. Then holding his torch close to Jesus, he leaned over and kissed him on the cheek. Jesus understood. Quietly, he said to Judas:

"So, you have chosen to betray me with a kiss."

No sooner had he spoken, when a dozen Roman soldiers led by a priest surrounded him, their swords in the air. Angrily, the disciples jumped to their feet and attacked the soldiers. But Jesus cried out:

"Put up your weapons, for all those who live by the sword shall die by the sword!"

One of the disciples acted hastily and slashed the ear of the priest's servant with his sword. Jesus held him back and gently touched the servant's ear, so that it was cured. The disciples, seeing this, retreated into the shadows as other soldiers and priests came to capture Jesus. Cruelly, the soldiers bound him with ropes and poked him with their spears.

"Am I a common thief," asked Jesus, "that you treat me like this? Only yesterday I preached in the Temple, and you heard me and did not attack me."

But the assailants would not listen. Hurriedly they dragged Jesus from the garden of Gethsemane amid their flickering torches and upraised spears. The fateful prophecy was about to be fulfilled.

Jesus Before the Priests

WAITING IN JERUSALEM were Caiaphas, the high priest, and his father-in-law, Annas, who was also an official of the Temple. Before these men, Jesus was brought as a prisoner to answer charges.

First, Caiaphas asked Jesus about his disciples and his doctrine. Jesus answered that he had never preached secretly or maliciously.

"I spoke openly to the world and in the Temple as a good Jew," he said. "You know this, your people have seen me."

Caiaphas was not pleased with this answer. He signaled one of the soldiers to strike Jesus across the face.

"Why do you strike me?" asked Jesus quietly. "If I have spoken evil, God will strike me, not you."

Outside in the courtyard of Caiaphas' house, Peter waited nervously in the shadows. He had followed the band of soldiers that had captured Jesus, and he was anxious and afraid. While he waited some men built a fire since it was cold in the morning air. As Peter moved close to warm his hands a young woman saw him and said:

"This fellow was with the prophet Jesus who is now a prisoner."

Peter was alarmed.

"That's not so," he said. "I don't even know that man."

Another person looked up.

"Oh, yes," he said, "you were one of his followers."

"No," Peter insisted. "I never heard of Jesus before tonight."

The first girl laughed.

"Don't fool us. You are his disciple. Come on, tell us what he's like."

Peter became angry. Again he denied ever knowing Jesus or being part of his band. Then, suddenly in the distance, the cock crowed in the dawn. A cold chill ran over Peter's skin as he remembered Jesus' prophecy, *Before the cock crows, you will deny me three times.*

Horrified at his weakness and disloyalty, Peter burst into tears and rushed from the scene.

Inside Caiaphas' house, the long questioning of Jesus continued. Many witnesses were brought in to testify against the man from Nazareth. Some of them were paid to lie; others purposely misinterpreted what Jesus had said, so that it might be used against him. Throughout, Jesus made no reply.

Finally Caiaphas rose and pointing his finger at Jesus, he demanded:

"Are you Christ, the Messiah, the Son of God?"

Jesus replied very simply.

"You have spoken the truth," he said.

This was too much for the high priest. Shouting "blasphemy," he turned to his council of priests,

"You have heard this blasphemy against God," he cried. "It is a sin to call oneself the Messiah; and such a sin must be punished by death. What is your decision?"

The council dared not go against Caiaphas' wishes. Without further discussion, they condemned Jesus and ordered him taken to the Roman governor, for they had no authority to put him to death. The soldiers grabbed Jesus by the arms and took him out into the street. Once alone with him, they began to punch him and spit in his face, laughing all the while and saying:

"If you're the Messiah, tell us which of us hit you and spat in your face."

OPPOSITE: Plate 90. CHRIST BEFORE PILATE, by Tintoretto (Italian, 1518–1594), Scuola di San Rocco, Venice.

BELOW: Plate 91. THE CROWNING WITH THORNS, by Hieronymous Bosch (Flemish, about 1450–1516), The National Gallery, London.

Jesus did not reply. He bowed his head in prayer as they led him away.

Watching from the shadows was Judas Iscariot, who had come to Caiaphas' house to get his thirty pieces of silver. Now he saw Jesus being led away, bound and disgraced. He knew the Romans would put his Master to death and he said to himself:

"My God, what have I done?"

Trembling, he took the money and returned to Caiaphas.

"I have sinned and betrayed a righteous man," he cried. "Take back this blood money; I'll have no part of it."

Then Judas ran from the scene to his house where he took his own life by hanging.

The priests did not want his money, for they knew it was accursed. So they took it and purchased a plot of land owned by a potter. Here the poor and unknown of the city were buried free of charge. Today such places are known as Potter's Fields—lonely memorials to the treacherous Judas Iscariot.

The Trial Before Pontius Pilate

IT WAS EARLY Friday morning. Bound and guarded, Jesus was led to the palace of Pontius Pilate, the Roman governor of Jerusalem. Many of Jesus' enemies lurked outside the palace, waiting for news of what was happening.

Pilate sat on his throne surrounded by his soldiers. Before him were the representatives of the high priests.

"What charges do you bring against this man?" asked the governor.

The priests stated their case, saying that Jesus had spoken against Caesar and that he had corrupted the people with false teachings. Pilate looked over the bill of complaints that the priests had submitted. Then he summoned Jesus before him.

"Are you the King of the Jews?" he asked.

Jesus answered very quietly.

"Yes," he said, "but my kingdom is not of this world, but of the world hereafter."

Pilate was hesitant. Assuming that the complaints were religious, not political, he turned to the priests and said:

"I find no fault in this man."

The priests were emphatic. They continued to demand action from Pilate, for the law gave them no power to put Jesus to death.

"This man has corrupted the entire nation," they said, "all the way from Galilee to Jerusalem."

When Pilate heard mention of Galilee, he decided to unburden the case on King Herod, who was responsible for order in Galilee, and he ordered Jesus taken to Herod's palace in Jerusalem.

For a long time, King Herod had been submissive to the Roman authorities. When Jesus came before him, he hardly knew what to do.

"Can you perform some miracles for me?" asked the foolish king.

Jesus was silent. Outraged by this indifference, Herod, in mockery, ordered Jesus dressed up in gaudy robes, as would befit a comic "king." But he did not want to take responsibility for Jesus' death. So he ordered:

"Send him back to Pilate, and let the Romans handle him."

And so Jesus returned to the Roman governor. He was questioned again and again. For hours, Pilate listened to the arguments of the priests, and he became bored and short-tempered.

"I will have this man whipped," he said. "Then we will release him with a warning. That should satisfy you."

But the priests would not be satisfied. Pilate had a new idea. It was the custom during Passover for one prisoner to be freed upon the people s request. Pilate thought that the crowds would ask for Jesus, since he was not a murderer or a robber like the other prisoners. But Jesus' enemies had gathered in that crowd—all the merchants and Pharisees— and, when Pilate asked them which prisoner they wanted released, they called, "Barabbas! Barabbas!" although Barabbas was a common thief. While Pilate was trying to resolve his dilemma, his wife came to him. She had dreamed about Jesus and believed him innocent of all the charges made by the priests. She urged her husband to release him.

Pilate went before the crowd and asked:

"Do you want me to crucify this man just because he called himself King of the Jews? This is hardly a crime."

But the people continued to shout for the release of Barabbas. Pilate was annoyed. He had other things to do, so he took a basin of water and poured it over his hands.

"I wash my hands of this matter," he cried to the crowd, "because I find no fault in this man."

Nevertheless to please the mob, he freed Barabbas the robber, and had Jesus flogged. Then he ordered his soldiers to dress Jesus in an old purple robe, such as a king might have worn, and crown him with a wreath of thorns. The soldiers enjoyed this cruel sport, and they hit Jesus and spat in his face as they dressed him.

Finally Pilate brought Jesus out into the courtyard before the mob.

"Here is the man," he said. "For the last time, what shall I do with Jesus who is called Christ?"

Jesus' enemies shouted:

"Crucify him! Crucify him!"

Pilate turned to Jesus, and urged him to say something, or do something that could appease the crowd. But Jesus knew that it was his destiny to die, and he said to Pilate,

"It is not in your hands, for you have no power except the power given to you by God."

Pilate then called the priests from the crowd. Once more, he argued with them, trying to avoid responsibility for Jesus' death. But the crafty priests said:

"He has called himself a king. There is only one king and that is Caesar. Any man allowing him to live is no friend of Caesar's, as Caesar will learn."

Hearing this very meaningful threat, Pilate no longer argued. He turned to the mob and announced:

"Behold your king!"

The people shouted:

"We have no king but Caesar."

"Very well," said Pilate—and he sentenced Jesus to be crucified.

BEYOND THE WALLS of Jerusalem was a spot called Golgotha. There condemned prisoners were crucified upon great wooden crosses, and their bodies tossed into a pit. To this place Jesus of Nazareth came, dragging a heavy wooden cross upon his back while Roman soldiers led the way.

By now, it was midday, and many of the poor and common people of Jerusalem were out on the streets and in the markets. They could see the sorrowful procession of prisoners, weighed down under heavy beams of wood, heading toward Golgotha. Many recognized Jesus, the kindly teacher from Galilee, and they left their work to follow, weeping to see Jesus burdened by the heavy cross, an ugly crown of thorns on his head and the wounds of his whipping still fresh upon his skin. But Jesus turned to them, in his agony, and said:

The Crucifixion of Jesus

OPPOSITE: Plate 92. CHRIST CARRYING THE CROSS, by Simone Martini (Italian, about 1283–1344), The Louvre Museum, Paris.

353

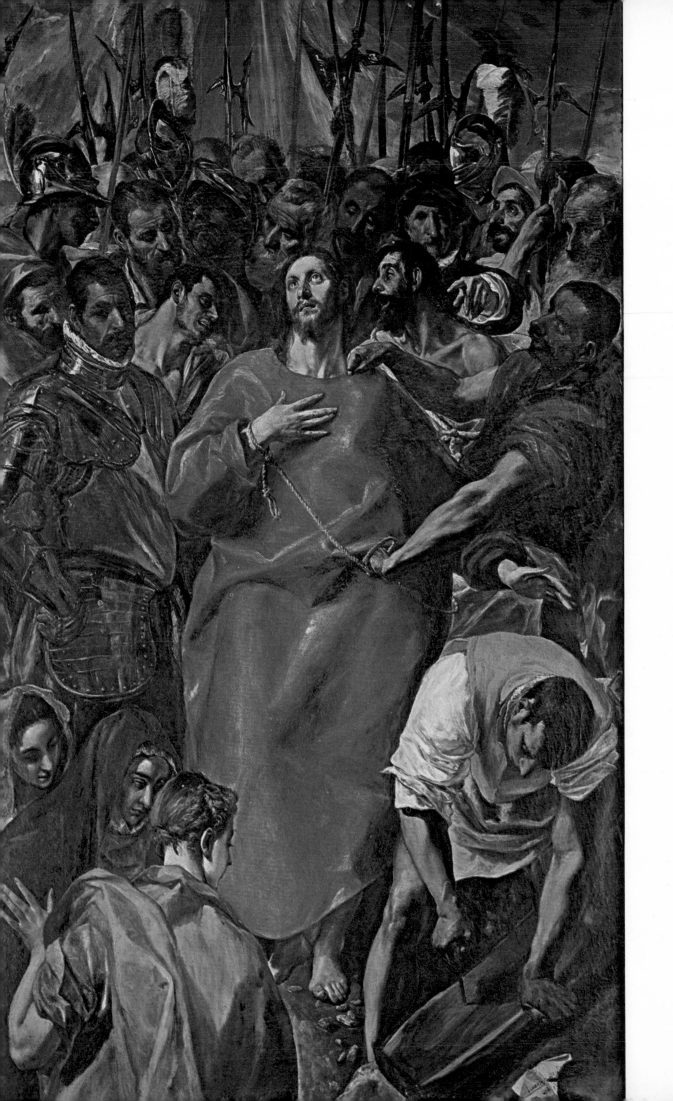

OPPOSITE: Plate 93. THE DISROBING OF CHRIST, by El Greco
(Spanish School, 1541–1614), Toledo Cathedral, Spain.

BELOW: Plate 94. CALVARY (THE CRUCIFIXION), by Paolo Veronese
(Italian, about 1528–1588), The Louvre Museum, Paris.

"Do not weep for me, but for yourselves and your children. For, behold, evil days are coming to Jerusalem."

Then he faltered under the weight of the cross, and he fell, and lay in the gutter. The soldiers ordered a man named Simon of Cyrene to lift the cross, so that Jesus might continue his final journey. So it was that Jesus, falling and in agony, reached the pinnacle of Golgotha.

Now it was time for the cruel execution. The soldiers disrobed Jesus and flung his garments to the ground. There, others grabbed up his seamless robe and began rolling dice to see which one should claim it. All this they did as Jesus was nailed by his hands and feet to the beams of the cross. He neither struggled nor cried out. But he lifted his eyes toward Heaven, and exclaimed:

"Forgive them, Father, for they know not what they do."

Then the soldiers fastened to the topmost beam of the cross a sign that read *Jesus of Nazareth, King of the Jews*. It was meant in mockery.

Once this was done, they raised Jesus on his cross to an upright position, so that he hung most painfully above the ground by the nails in his hands and in his feet.

Below, many scornful people watched this execution, calling to Jesus,

"If you are the Son of God, then save yourself and come down from the cross."

But Jesus knew his destiny. He had even refused to drink a potion that might have numbed his pain, knowing that he had to suffer for the sins of the world. And so he looked out across the city of Jerusalem in prayer, while the crowd taunted him from below.

Then he turned his eyes to the left and to the right, where two other prisoners were nailed to crosses. Both were thieves and feared death, and one of them cried to him:

"If you are the Christ, save us from this torture."

But the other said:

"If you are the Christ, remember me when you enter into Heaven." And Jesus promised to remember him.

Now, also, in the crowd at the foot of the cross, stood Mary, Jesus' mother, Mary, the mother of James, and a third Mary, who was Mary Magdalene. Some of the disciples had come there as well, fearfully and in sorrow. When Jesus saw his mother and his friends, his heart was very heavy, and he whispered to the disciple John:

"Take care of my mother when I am dead."

Then a strange darkness began to fall over the city, though it was early in the afternoon; and Jesus lifted his head toward Heaven, and cried in pain:

"My God, my God, why hast Thou forsaken me?"

Feeling pity, someone raised a wet sponge to Jesus' lips so that he might have some small relief. But it was too late for comfort.

"Into Thy hands I commend my spirit," cried Jesus, the man from Nazareth, and he departed his earthly life and died.

At this dark moment, the sky became pitch black. Buildings trembled, and the graveyards gave up their dead. Even the veil that hung before the Holy of Holies in the Temple suddenly tore in two, as though rent by invisible hands, and the air seemed filled with moans and crying, so that many who had scorned and mocked Jesus as he died fell on their knees and cried out:

"Truly, this was the Son of God!"

The Burial

A KINDLY JEW named Joseph of Arimathea had often heard Jesus preach and been impressed with what he had heard. This man wished to claim Jesus' body, so that he might give it decent burial.

The hour was late and the Sabbath was approaching. By Jewish law, it was forbidden to bury anyone on the Sabbath, so Joseph hurried to Pilate, the governor, to request permission to remove Jesus from the cross. At first, Pilate wished to leave Jesus there, in humiliation. But Joseph would not be dissuaded, and, finally, the Roman governor granted his wish.

Joseph then hurried to Golgotha. As he watched, a Roman centurion pierced Jesus' side with a spear to make sure he was dead. Then they removed his body from the cross.

Carefully, Joseph wrapped Jesus in fine linen. With the aid of the sorrowing disciples, he carried the body to his home, where there was a garden. In this garden was a cave, prepared especially for burials. Here Joseph wished to bury Jesus, but, first, he called the three Marys to his side, and, together, they anointed Jesus' body with fine oils and spices. Then, with reverence and sorrow, they buried him.

In Jerusalem, the Pharisees and the priests came before Pilate and said:

"This man Jesus boasted that he would rise from the dead on the third day after his death. We must make sure that his disciples do not steal his body away and then pretend that he is risen from the grave."

"What do you want me to do?" asked Pilate.

"Place a guard at the tomb," they answered, "and roll a heavy stone before the opening, so that it is sealed. Then his disciples will be helpless, and will not be able to fool the people."

OPPOSITE: Plate 95. THE DESCENT FROM THE CROSS,
by Rembrandt (Dutch, 1606–1669), Pinakothek (Picture Gallery), Munich.

BELOW: Plate 96. CHRIST AND THE MAGDALENE
(NOLI ME TANGERE—DO NOT TOUCH ME),
by Titian (Italian, about 1487–1576), The National Gallery, London.

Pilate agreed, and sent three soldiers to watch at the grave, where an enormous boulder was rolled in front of the opening. Then the Sabbath came and the city was quiet. Jesus' ordeal had ended.

The Resurrection

ON SUNDAY MORNING, Mary the mother of Jesus, Mary the mother of James, and Mary Magdalene came to the garden where Jesus was buried, wishing to pay him final homage. As they approached the tomb, they saw an astounding sight. The Roman soldiers had vanished; the great boulder that had been set against the opening of the grave was now rolled away down the path; and a glorious angel, all dressed in white, sat at the entrance to the tomb.

"Fear not," said the angel to the women. "Jesus of Nazareth, whom you seek, has risen from the grave as he promised, and will shortly go to Galilee and appear before his followers."

Then the angel pointed inside the tomb where the women had seen Jesus laid to rest. Now, there was his empty shroud, and nothing more. The women were stunned. What could they believe? Had someone come and stolen Jesus' body? Mary Magdalene began to weep, and started down the path toward the city. Suddenly, she saw a shadowy figure of a man in the road.

"Why are you weeping?" asked the man.

Magdalene lowered her head to hide her tears, and she replied:

"I believe that someone has stolen the body of my Lord."

"Look at me," said the man. "Don't you know my face?"

Magdalene looked up to see Jesus standing before her, his face radiant and serene. The amazed woman reached out to touch him, for she could not believe her eyes. But Jesus withdrew, and said:

"Do not touch me now, for I have not yet ascended to Heaven."

Then he vanished.

Joyously, Magdalene ran back to the garden where Peter and John had come to behold the empty tomb. She told them what she had seen. But they were baffled and confused by her story.

In the city, word spread that Jesus of Nazareth had disappeared from his tomb and was actually risen from the dead. Many disbelieving persons said that his body had been stolen and hidden by his followers. But others believed in the resurrection, and took great encouragement from the news. Thus dawned the first Easter Sunday amid doubt and hope, for as Jesus had said earlier that week:

"Destroy this temple of my body,
and in three days I will raise it up."

Two men from the city of Emmaus heard the news about Jesus' resurrection. They staunchly believed that he had risen from the dead and was the Savior promised by the prophets of old. As they walked upon the road toward their home, they spoke of the events in Jerusalem, bemoaning the tragic death of the kindly teacher from Galilee.

As they were talking, another man, a stranger, joined them and entered into the conversation.

"What has happened?" the stranger asked.

Cleophas, one of the first two men, told the story of how Jesus had been cruelly tortured and crucified.

"But," he added, "Jesus also rose from the dead this very day, as he promised, for he was a great and wonderful prophet."

The stranger, seeing that Cleophas and his friend were greatly upset over Jesus' death, spoke to them with words of profound meaning.

"You must understand," he said, "that it was Jesus' destiny to suffer, according to what the prophets of old have taught us. That is why he will enter into glory."

The men from Emmaus were strongly impressed by the stranger and invited him to their home to share their evening meal.

"Abide with us," they said, "for evening fast approaches."

All three then went to the house of Cleophas. There a loaf of bread was placed before the stranger, so that he might have the honor of blessing it. This he did, and, when he raised his hands, suddenly the men saw that it was Jesus Christ, the Messiah, who had walked with them along the road and now sat at their table. As they looked on in amazement, Jesus vanished from sight.

Joyously, and in haste, Cleophas and his friends rushed back to Jerusalem to spread the word that Jesus had truly reappeared.

The disciples heard the good news from Emmaus. They were overjoyed and yet afraid, — Jerusalem had become a dangerous place for Jesus' followers. For this reason, they hid themselves in a small room in a friendly house. Here they spoke of the wonders of the resurrection.

As they talked, Jesus himself suddenly appeared in their midst and said to them:

"Peace be with you."

The disciples were overwhelmed. Was this a spirit or was it really their beloved Master risen from the dead? Jesus sensed their doubts.

"Look at my hands and see the marks of the nails that pierced them," he said. "Look at my chest, where the spear was thrust. Have you not read the Scriptures that predicted these events?"

Jesus at Emmaus

Jesus Appears to His Disciples

Plate 97. CHRIST AT EMMAUS, by Diego Velázquez
(Spanish, 1599–1660), The Metropolitan Museum of Art, New York.

Plate 98. THE ASCENSION,
by Andrea Mantegna
(Italian, 1431–1506),
The Uffizi Gallery, Florence.

The disciples were ashamed of their doubts, and they fell down before Jesus in prayer. He blessed them and instructed them in their tasks. Then he asked for some food, and they served him broiled fish and honey.

When he had finished eating, Jesus comforted his disciples once again.

"It was necessary for me to suffer," he said, "so that I might relieve the world of its sins."

Doubting Thomas

AFTER JESUS LEFT HIS DISCIPLES, Thomas came into the room. He had been out on an errand, and had missed seeing his Master. The other men excitedly told him that Jesus had actually appeared and eaten with them in that very room. Thomas would not accept their story.

"Until I can touch him with my own hands," he said, "I will not believe it."

Eight days later, the disciples were gathered in the room again, when Jesus suddenly appeared as before. Thomas was surprised, but still doubtful.

"Come forward," said Jesus. "See my hands and the place where the nail has pierced, and see on my side where I was wounded by the spear. Touch these, so that you will believe."

Thomas went over to Jesus and touched the wound on his side and the hole in each hand where a nail had pierced him on the cross. Then Thomas fell on his knees, exclaiming:

"My Lord and my God, I do believe."

Jesus pointed up a lesson from this incident:

"Thomas is blessed; he believes in me because he has seen me and touched my wounds. But more blessed are they that believe in me, even though they have not seen me."

The Ascension

AFTER MANY DAYS, the disciples returned to their homes in Galilee, and took up their old calling as fishermen. They needed time to collect their thoughts and fully appreciate the great tasks that lay ahead.

One day, they all set out in different boats to fish on the Sea of Tiberias. For hours they threw out their nets and lines, but caught nothing. Then Peter saw a man standing on the shore, and at once he recognized Jesus. Overjoyed, he leaped into the water and swam to the beach. The other disciples followed him in their boats.

It was a joyous meeting. With Jesus in their midst, the men found many fish in their nets, for he had performed a miracle as in days past. After they had eaten the fish, they gathered at Jesus' feet to hear his message.

"Go into the world," he said, "and feed my sheep—for all people are like sheep in need of a shepherd. Each one of you has his duty to spread my message and to glorify God in the name of the Father, and of the Son, and of the Holy Spirit." Then he repeated his great commandment:

"Love one another, as I love you."

For forty days, Jesus remained on earth after his resurrection. During this time he met with his disciples and continued to instruct them. One day, he asked them to meet on the Mount of Olives near Jerusalem. There he stood before them for the very last time on earth. Then, lifting his hands in a blessing, he ascended to Heaven and to God amid singing angels and great glory.

Thus ended the earthly life of Jesus, the Savior, who, as the Lamb of God, had been sacrificed in the remission of sins for all mankind.

THE ACTS OF THE APOSTLES, AND THE EPISTLES

Stories of the Early Christians; Their Miracles and Hardships; of Paul, His Journeys and Letters and His Teachings.

The Heavenly Fires

TEN DAYS after Jesus ascended to Heaven, the city of Jerusalem became crowded with visitors who had come to celebrate the harvest feast of Pentecost. It was to be a supremely important day for the disciples of Jesus. They had returned to Jerusalem waiting for a sign from heaven that would mark the beginning of their mission. Once they received this sign they could go out into the world and baptize people, as John the Baptist had done, in the name of the Risen Christ. Those they baptized were later known as Christians.

At the time of Pentecost, there were only eleven disciples, because Judas Iscariot was dead. Peter had become their unofficial leader, and it was now his thought that another man be chosen to bring the number once again to twelve. An upright Jew named Matthias was selected. He and the eleven others now became known as the Apostles, or those who were to establish the new Christian faith.

Knowing that their mission was at hand, on Pentecost the apostles went to the Temple in Jerusalem. As they were in prayer, they heard the sound of a rushing wind coming from heaven. When they raised their eyes, they saw mysterious tongues of fire flickering over their heads, and they were filled with a marvelous sensation of communion with God, for the Holy Spirit had descended upon them. In addition, they experienced great intelligence and found they had received the gift of languages, whereby they could speak and understand all the foreign tongues in Jerusalem. The apostles could thus communicate with all people directly and without interpreters. They immediately began preaching the word of Christ. At first, the crowd thought that the apostles were drunk, because their voices sounded like babbling. But Peter stepped forward and announced:

"This is as the prophet Joel predicted; that all men should one day be filled with the Spirit of God; that your sons and daughters shall prophesy; and your young men shall see visions; and your old men shall dream dreams."

Plate 99. THE PENTECOST, by El Greco
(Spanish School, 1541–1614),
The Prado Museum, Madrid.

Then he recounted the miracle of the resurrection, and verified the report that he and the other apostles had seen Jesus risen from the dead, and announced that Jesus was God, the true Messiah. Thousands of persons in the crowd were deeply moved by this sermon, and they asked what they could do in acceptance of Christ. Peter urged them to be baptized for the remission of their sins. That day thousands became Christians in the Temple, and the Christian Church was born amid fellowship and brotherly understanding.

New Miracles of the Apostles

THE HEALING POWER of Jesus had passed to his apostles, who were now filled with the Holy Spirit. One day, Peter and John came to the Temple for prayer, and walked through an arch called the Beautiful Gate. Here was stationed a crippled beggar, who was known throughout the city as the "beggar of the Beautiful Gate." When he saw the apostles, he stretched out his hand for some coins. But Peter and John had no money. Instead, Peter exclaimed:

"Look at me, and I will give you something better than money, in the name of Jesus Christ."

Then he took hold of the crippled beggar and drew him to his feet. Suddenly the man, who had been crippled since birth, found new strength in his legs, and, before long, he was leaping and jumping about and praising God at the top of his voice. Many people who knew this beggar saw the miracle, and were convinced of the powers of God. They now came to Peter to be baptized as Christians.

But the Pharisees and the Sadducees, the priests, and the other enemies of Jesus, were still set against the new religion. The high priest Caiaphas ordered Peter and John arrested. He feared the growth of Christianity, and commanded that all references to the resurrection immediately cease. But Peter was firm in his cause and would not submit. Besides, Caiaphas had heard about the beggar of the Beautiful Gate, and he knew that a miracle had taken place. Rather than excite the people by punishing Peter and John, he released them with a warning.

The two apostles returned to the Temple, where they joined their friends. As they prayed, the earth trembled beneath them, and they knew that God approved of their devotion.

The Brotherhood

AS MORE AND MORE people were converted to Christianity, it became necessary to establish some kind of brotherhood or community. A

Plate 100. THE STONING OF ST. STEPHEN, by Fra Angelico
(Italian, about 1400–1455),
Chapel of Nicholas V, The Vatican, Rome.

369

plan was devised whereby money would be pooled together for the common use of all Christians. Thus, a poor man could pursue his new faith without fear of going hungry. Many agreed to this plan, and sold their possessions in order to supply the fund.

A man named Ananias and his wife Sapphira were Christians who did not like this idea. They sold their possessions, but kept a good portion of the money they had received. Peter knew what they had done and questioned them, but they swore that they had deposited all their wealth in the common treasury. Because of their deceit, they both died suddenly. The others, as a result, realized the importance of honesty, and never tried to deceive the apostles.

The Sadducees and priests watched the growth of the new brotherhood with increasing alarm. They had warned Peter to cease his preaching, and yet they saw more people joining his ranks every day. Caiaphas finally ordered Peter and the apostles arrested and thrown in prison.

That night, as the apostles knelt in their cells, an angel of God appeared, and, unseen by the guards, opened all the prison gates. The apostles returned to the Temple and continued their work. When the priests came to the Temple in the morning and saw Peter preaching, they were amazed.

"Didn't we put him in prison?" they asked.

Peter stepped forth, and again announced the truth and power of Christ. But Caiaphas would hear no more. He ordered the apostles brought before the high council on charges of blasphemy. If the council found them guilty, all the apostles would be stoned to death.

Fortunately, a man named Gamaliel, a respected member of the council, rose and spoke to Caiaphas:

"We have seen many so-called messiahs appear in Jerusalem, claiming all sorts of miracles and gathering many followers to their cause. All of these groups eventually break up and disappear. I recommend that we leave these men alone. If they are false prophets, they, too, will disappear. If they are truly doing the work of God, they will survive, and we cannot fight them."

The council accepted Gamaliel's wise advice. They ordered each apostle whipped and sent away with a warning. But Peter was firm.

"We shall not heed or obey the council," he said to his friends, "for we must obey God rather than men."

The Deacons

As THE CHRISTIAN COMMUNITY continued to grow, dissensions arose among its members. Some persons complained that they weren't getting a fair share of the food. Others felt generally neglected. Accordingly, Peter and the apostles realized that they needed help in governing the community. They set out to find seven righteous men who would minister to the poor and hungry while the apostles preached. The men chosen were called deacons. They soon organized the community and restored harmony and order.

One of these deacons was Philip, who chose to minister to the converts of Samaria. On his way along the road from Jerusalem, Philip saw a splendid chariot drawing near. Seated in the chariot was a fine-looking Negro who had come from the country of Ethiopia, far to the south of Palestine. He wanted to know more about the Hebrew religion, and, for that reason, he was heading toward Jerusalem. To prepare himself, he had selected the book of Isaiah to read along the way. Philip approached and asked the man if he understood the words he was reading. The Ethiopian admitted that he was puzzled about certain references to the coming Messiah made by Isaiah. Philip spent many hours telling the Ethiopian about Jesus Christ, who had fulfilled Isaiah's prophecies by his death and resurrection. The dark man was so impressed that he urged Philip to baptize him in the nearest stream, and he returned to his own land as the first Christian of Ethiopia.

ONE OF THE MOST NOBLE and courageous of the deacons was Stephen, a young man totally devoted to the teachings of Jesus Christ. Because he was an eloquent speaker, Stephen frequently lectured and debated with non-Christians about the new faith. Eventually, the Sadducees and priests heard of his work and ordered him arrested for blasphemy.

Stephen was obliged to go through the same sort of trial that Jesus had endured. He had to answer the cruel questions of the priests and stand by while false witnesses lied about his teachings. When Stephen finally had a chance to speak, he was filled with the Holy Spirit and began a sermon of such intensity and truth that the men of the council were frightened, and they covered their ears so they could not hear him.

Then, in a heavenly vision, Stephen saw Jesus standing by the side of God. The young deacon was completely unafraid and reaffirmed the glory of Christ to the angry priests. They pounced upon him, and had him dragged into the courtyard.

There, a group of burly men tied him hand and foot and began to hurl rocks at him. Stephen knelt down in pain, and called upon God to

The
Martyrdom
of Stephen

forgive his enemies and to receive his spirit into heaven. Then he collapsed under the hail of stones.

Standing nearby, watching over the garments of those men who were hurling the stones, was a Jew named Saul from the city of Tarsus. He hated the Christians and scorned the stories of Jesus Christ. Every day, he was paid to persecute Christians and send them to prison. This he did without fail, and he was greatly feared. Yet this man, later known as Paul, was to become the greatest Christian of his time.

The Conversion of Saul

SAUL HAD FINISHED his relentless work in Jerusalem; as a result, many Christians were in prison. He now wished to round up others in neighboring lands, and so he started off for the city of Damascus, in Syria.

On the road to Damascus, Saul became enveloped in a blinding light of such intensity that he could not see, and fell from his horse. Lying on the ground, he heard a faraway voice calling:

"Saul, Saul, why do you persecute me? I am Jesus; and by harming my people you harm me, as well."

Dazzled by the light and astounded by the voice of Jesus, Saul could hardly believe what was happening. Trembling with emotion, he asked:

"What shall I do, my Lord?"

Jesus instructed him to continue his journey to Damascus, but to do nothing until he was visited by a follower of Christ named Ananias. Saul rose from the ground, still blinded from the light, and staggered toward Damascus with a fresh spirit of kindness and charity in his soul. He had become a different man.

On the street called Straight stood the house of a man named Judas. Here Saul waited, still unable to see and still dazed by his marvelous encounter on the Damascus road. Three days later, Ananias appeared at the house, just as Jesus had predicted in Saul's vision. Ananias went straight to Saul and blessed him. In that instant, Saul regained his sight. Falling to his knees, he begged Ananias to baptize him, so that he might follow Jesus Christ.

Saul now changed his name to Paul. With a new name and a new

OPPOSITE: Plate 101. THE CONVERSION OF SAUL, by Caravaggio (Italian, 1565–1610), Church of Santa Maria del Popolo, Rome.

religion, he went to the synagogue of Damascus to preach the message of Jesus. The Christians of the city, however, did not know of his conversion, and feared him as a powerful enemy; the Jews believed that he was a friend. When he was heard praising Christianity, all were amazed. At first, people thought that he might have lost his mind; but, as he continued to preach and practice Christianity, he became more and more hated by his former friends. One night, they conspired to kill him. But Ananias and other Christians helped Paul escape from Damascus by lowering him in a basket over the city walls.

Paul then returned to Jerusalem. Here, again, he amazed his former friends by preaching in the name of Jesus. The Christians were especially suspicious, wondering how a man who had once hated Jesus so violently could now preach his message. One Christian named Barnabas trusted Paul, and convinced the apostles that he was indeed an honest man who had changed his ways for the sake of Christ. Thereafter, Paul was entrusted with many duties of the new church, and he traveled great distances to preach and convert.

The Conversion of Cornelius

IN THE CITY of Caesarea lived Cornelius, a Roman officer in charge of a company of soldiers. Though he did not practice the Hebrew religion, Cornelius was charitable to the poor and respected his neighbors. One day, a heavenly vision appeared to him and told him to seek out the apostle Peter who was staying in Joppa, for God was pleased with Cornelius and wished him to become a Christian.

At the same time, Peter beheld a baffling vision of birds and beasts; from this he learned that God no longer considered the old dietary laws necessary. In fact, it seemed to Peter, that many of the old laws were being liberalized.

When Cornelius' messengers found Peter, they brought him to the Roman's home. Cornelius immediately fell on his knees before the apostle, and wished to worship him. But Peter raised him up, and said:

"Do not worship me; I am only a man. But let me tell you of Jesus Christ, so that you may worship him."

Outside Cornelius' house, many Christians watched as Peter and the Roman conversed. It had never been the practice to admit non-Jews into the Christian community, for most of the apostles believed that Jesus had come as a Messiah only for the Jews. But the words of God and Peter's vision of the birds and beasts seemed to point in another direction. Peter now believed that it was God's will that all men and all nations become followers of Jesus Christ, for, as Peter said:

"I know God is no respecter of persons, but in every nation he who fears Him and does what is right is acceptable to Him. He sent His word to the Children of Israel, preaching peace through Jesus Christ . . . so that all may be relieved of the burden of their sins."

Then Peter baptized Cornelius the Roman, who was the first gentile to become converted. From then on, Christianity was to spread throughout the earth.

PETER CONTINUED to preach in small towns, bringing the word of Jesus Christ to Jew and gentile alike. News of his work reached King Herod Agrippa. Since Jesus' death, Herod had cruelly persecuted the Christians and was responsible for the death of the apostle James. Now he wanted to slay Peter, so he sent an order for his arrest. In due time, Peter was arrested and thrown in jail. To make sure that he could not escape, he was chained to two soldiers, while other men stood guard outside the door of his cell.

At midnight the soldiers fell asleep, and at the same moment an angel descended into the cell and quietly broke the chains that held Peter a prisoner. Then the angel beckoned Peter to follow him out of the dungeon. At first Peter thought that he was dreaming, but he soon found himself safely outside the prison walls and on the road to town. He hurried along and came to the apostles' house, where he anxiously knocked on the door. A servant girl answered, and was amazed to see Peter, who, she thought, had been killed by Herod. Joyously, she went to tell the apostles, but they were doubtful.

"You must have seen his ghost," they said.

Peter couldn't wait. He strode into the room and stood before his astonished friends.

"I want you to see this proof of God's deliverance," he said. Then he hastened away to hide from Herod's soldiers.

In the morning, Peter's escape was discovered. Herod blamed the soldiers, and put them all to death. He was angry, indeed. Soon after, he attended a banquet, dressed in his finest array. Suddenly, while he was making a speech, he slumped in his throne and died. After this, the apostles were not persecuted so bitterly.

BACK IN JERUSALEM, the apostles decided to send Barnabas to the city of Antioch in Syria. A large Christian community had developed

Peter Is Rescued

The Missionary Work of Paul

Plate 102. THE LIBERATION OF ST. PETER, by Raphael
(Italian, 1483–1520), The Vatican, Rome.

there, and the people had waited many years to hear from their leaders.

Barnabas arrived in Antioch, and was delighted to see the great number of believers assembled to greet him. For days, he preached, and talked to his friends, but, after a while, he found the work too much for him. He then sent a message to Jerusalem requesting that Paul of Tarsus be allowed to assist him. The apostles were a bit suspicious of Paul, for they still wondered about his sudden conversion. Barnabas, however, believed in him, and journeyed to Tarsus to see him and ask for his help. Paul was enthusiastic. God had spoken to him and urged him to preach among the gentiles. Now he would have his chance. Together with Barnabas, Paul journeyed to Antioch and, for a whole year, the two men preached the gospel and encouraged the believers.

A prophet in Antioch predicted that a famine was coming. Accordingly, Paul and Barnabas arranged to collect food and water well in advance of a drought or bad harvest. Then, when lean days came upon the land, they were able to feed the hungry. When the people of Antioch were fed and out of danger, Paul and Barnabas took the extra supplies to Jerusalem. The missionaries stayed a short time in Jerusalem, and then prepared to return to Antioch. A young man named Mark, a nephew of Barnabas, asked to join them, so that he might preach the gospel. Paul and Barnabas eagerly accepted the young man's aid.

After another stay in Antioch, the missionaries felt the urge to go beyond and preach to the people of distant cities. They journeyed to the island of Cyprus, which was part of the great Roman Empire and was ruled by a Roman governor. When the governor heard about Paul and his work, he ordered the missionaries brought before him. Doubtful at first, the governor questioned Paul about the new religion. Paul spoke eloquently and convincingly, and softened the governor's heart. But a scheming magician in the court, an enemy of Christians, began to argue against the teachings of Jesus. Paul was enraged:

"You enemy of righteousness!" he exclaimed. "The Lord will strike you blind until you repent."

In that instant the magician lost his sight. The Roman governor was so amazed that he became converted on the spot, and established a Christian church in his city.

PAUL AND BARNABAS left Cyprus and traveled through Asia Minor, the area that we know today as Turkey. At first, the Jews of that land listened to them courteously, and many accepted the teachings of Christ. But, soon, the religious leaders of the city became jealous and ridiculed

*Trouble
in Various
Lands*

the Christians. As a result, the Jews stayed away from the missionaries. In their place, many gentiles gathered at the feet of Paul and Barnabas to hear the story of Jesus.

Soon, the whole city was talking about the strange missionaries and their wonderful message. But the Jewish leaders decided to punish Paul and Barnabas for preaching blasphemy, for they did not believe the story of Jesus' resurrection. They ordered the two Christians to leave their land.

Paul and Barnabas next journeyed to Iconium, nearby. Here, again, they preached and won over many converts. Here, again, the local religious leaders were angry and took action against them. This time, their lives were threatened; and they had to flee to the town of Lystra.

A strange thing happened in Lystra. In this city, the people worshiped idols, for they had never heard of the one true God. Nevertheless, they gathered to see Paul and Barnabas speak of Jesus and his miracles. A poor cripple was in the crowd. When he heard of the wonderful healing powers of Christ, he begged Paul to cure him.

"Stand up on your feet," said Paul.

To everyone's amazement, the cripple rose and began to walk.

"These men are surely gods," said the people of Lystra. "They have come from heaven, as our forefathers promised."

Eagerly, the entire village turned out with gifts and sacrifices for Paul and Barnabas.

"You are Mercury and Jupiter," cried the people of Lystra, referring to the ancient gods of Rome; and they bowed down before the two Christians.

Paul and Barnabas were horrified. They were not gods and did not want to be worshiped. Calling for silence, they insisted that the one true God of all the world was alone responsible for life and death, for sunshine and rain, and for all the many wonders of life. Then the Christians spoke of Jesus Christ, who had brought God's message so forcefully to earth. Many of the idol worshipers were converted. Others still wondered about Paul and Barnabas.

A short time later, troublemakers from Iconium came to Lystra and spread rumors about the evil doings of the Christians. Many of the idol worshipers who had been puzzled by Paul and Barnabas now became angry and vicious. They found Paul preaching in a secluded spot, and immediately began to hurl stones at him. He fell under the crushing blows and appeared to be dead.

That night, however, he miraculously revived and dragged his aching body to the seaport, where he set sail for the city of Derbe. Again, he and Barnabas preached the word of Jesus Christ. From Derbe they went to other cities of the Middle East, and finally returned to Antioch, in Syria, where they were greeted by their fellow Christians.

THE FIRST DISCIPLES of Jesus Christ had all been Jews brought up in the Laws of Moses. When they began to preach the word of their Master, they converted other Jews to the new faith. They remembered that Jesus, as a devout Jew, had said, "I come to fulfill the Laws of Moses, not to change them."

Now, many gentiles, or non-Jews, were being converted to Christianity and certain early leaders of the new faith thought that it was wrong to accept them. They sent messengers to Antioch, where Paul and Barnabas were staying. These two missionaries, because they had converted many gentiles, were told to return to Jerusalem for a conference on whether or not gentiles would be admitted to the new religion.

Great tension existed in Jerusalem among the Christians over this matter, for many were opposed to allowing non-Jews into their community. After much debate, the aged apostle Peter rose and said:

"God urged me to preach to the gentiles, and I converted Cornelius, a Roman. I found the gentiles eager for the word of Jesus Christ and greatly receptive to his message. Therefore, let us not set up a barrier between man and God at the risk of man's salvation."

The apostle James the Less spoke along the same lines, saying:

"As long as the gentiles are pure in heart and fully accept the one true God, why should we deny them the teachings of our Lord Jesus Christ?"

These arguments were convincing. The leaders in Jerusalem decided to allow non-Jews into the Church, and sent a message to the city of Antioch confirming their decision. Paul and Barnabas, with two other men, Judas and Silas, returned to Antioch with the news. Thenceforth, all men who were pure in heart and believed in the one true God could become faithful Christians.

PAUL WAS EAGER to set out again on his missionary work. He approached Barnabas, and said:

"Let us revisit all the places where we have been in order to see what our fellow Christians are doing."

Barnabas agreed, and summoned his nephew Mark to join them. Paul was not pleased with Mark. Earlier, on their mission to Asia Minor,

An Internal Fight

Paul's Second Mission

Mark had left their company and suddenly returned to Antioch. Paul decided that Mark was too inexperienced for the second mission, and told Barnabas, who became very upset. Rather than leave his nephew behind, Barnabas took Mark on his trip to Cyprus, while Paul went back to Asia Minor. Because of this matter, the two great missionaries did not part on the most friendly terms.

Paul chose Silas to accompany him to Syria and to the familiar cities of Lystra and Derbe. In Lystra, he learned about the work of a young Christian named Timothy, who had a gentile father and a Jewish mother. When Paul met young Timothy, he was so impressed with his intelligence and devotion that he asked him to join the missionary expedition.

For months, the three Christians preached and established the foundations of their new religion. They finally reached the seaport of Troas, which was located near present-day Istanbul. When Paul finished his work at Troas, he first thought of returning eastward, back toward Antioch. But, one night, as he slept, he had a vision in which a man from a more distant country called Macedonia urged him to "come over and preach to us."

Paul was convinced that this was a message from God urging him to expand his missionary work into the western part of the world, which we know as Europe today.

The next morning, Paul advised Silas and Timothy that they would embark for Macedonia, and the city of Philippi. In those days, this vast area belonged to Rome, and the people there worshiped many gods. Nevertheless, there were a few Jews in the land, as well as many gentiles hungry for a new faith and a new salvation.

Paul sought out the Jewish community in Philippi and found that the people met for their prayers on the Sabbath by the river bank. He joined them, and, afterward, spoke of Jesus and his teachings. In the group was a wealthy lady named Lydia. She was deeply moved by Paul's words and asked to be baptized there at the river, along with her servants. Then she invited the missionaries to stay at her home while they were in Philippi. By this time, a young doctor named Luke had joined Paul and his friends. Luke was a gentile who believed in Jesus Christ. He kept faithful records of all the things that Paul said and, eventually, he wrote one of the most important Gospels.

The Fortune Teller

IN PHILIPPI there was a man whose servant girl was gifted in telling fortunes. The girl herself was not aware of her powers, for she had been possessed by an evil spirit. Every day, she fell into a trance, speaking the words of the evil spirit, while her master collected money for the fortunes that she told.

Paul and Silas used to pass the house where the fortune teller lived. Every time she saw them, she cried out:

"Behold the men of God, who have come to bring us salvation!"

Paul knew that the girl was possessed, and wished to cure her. Approaching the place where she was, he cried:

"In the name of Jesus Christ I command the evil spirits to leave you!"

In that same hour, the girl was restored to her right mind and she was at peace; however, she could no longer tell fortunes. Her greedy master was enraged. When he was told that Paul and Silas had cured the girl, he called the Roman soldiers and had them arrested.

By this time Paul and Silas were well known in Philippi, and they had many enemies. The Romans, knowing this, ordered them to be severely beaten and thrown into prison. This was done. Paul and Silas were placed in stocks, fastened by their hands and feet, and left alone in a dark, dirty cell.

At midnight, the two missionaries heard a fearsome rumbling in the earth, and, suddenly, all the doors of the prison swung open and all the stocks and chains fell apart. The prisoners, including Paul and Silas, were overjoyed, but a young Philippian jailer was fearful for his life. How could he explain this miracle and not be charged with treason? He was so alarmed that he decided to kill himself rather than face disgrace. Paul leaped to his side and held his sword.

"Do not kill yourself!" he cried. "We will not run away!"

True to his words, not one of the prisoners left his cell, even though the doors were opened. The jailer realized that he was in the presence of holy men, and fell at their feet, crying:

"How may I be saved?"

Paul then spoke of Jesus Christ, and won over the jailer to Christianity. In the morning, the jailer spoke to his friends and to the Roman officials. He described the wonderful teachings of Paul and Silas and how they had been kind to him.

The two missionaries were fed and told that they were free. But, oddly enough, Paul would not go. He demanded an audience with one of the Roman judges.

"I have a serious complaint," said Paul. "I am a Roman citizen, like you, and yet I was dragged through the streets, beaten, and put into jail without a trial."

The judge was afraid. He knew that Paul was right and that the officials of Philippi had acted hastily. He apologized, and begged Paul to leave peacefully, if not for his sake, then for the sake of the young jailer who had been converted the night before. Paul knew that he had made his point and, with Silas, he left Philippi.

The missionaries continued to preach throughout Macedonia. From Thessalonica to Berea, their message was heard in many cities. Often they were attacked. Riots flared up against them. Many believed; others scoffed. Danger and success went hand in hand for the missionaries; but they were undaunted. At last, Paul decided to enter the ancient land of Greece, and he summoned Timothy and Silas to join him.

Paul in Athens

THE MOST BEAUTIFUL CITY in Greece was Athens. Not only was Athens an important center of business, science, and religion, it was also adorned with the noblest buildings and sculpture to be seen anywhere in the world. Paul could not help but be impressed by the city and especially by the Acropolis, a mighty hill, crowded with many temples and statues, that overlooked the ancient city.

Though Paul found Athens nobly beautiful, he was distressed by the idol worship there. No one spoke of the one true God or of Jesus Christ. Instead, they paid homage to statues representing warriors, hunters, and supernatural beings. There was even one monument built to the "Unknown God." This intrigued Paul. At least, he said to himself, the Athenians were aware of the possibility that a greater God did exist.

In order to preach to the widest audience he could find, Paul went to the Hill of Ares in the center of the city. Here, learned men and philosophers met every day to exchange ideas. Everyone was interested in what Paul had to say; and at first he was given a courteous hearing.

"I have seen your altar to the 'Unknown God,' " he said. "I declare to you that this is the one true God who made all the heavens and earth and who sent us His only son, Jesus Christ. I also tell you that Jesus Christ suffered and died for our sins, and that he was resurrected from the dead so that he might sit in judgment of all men upon the appointed day of reckoning."

The mention of Jesus' resurrection was apparently too much for the Athenians, and they began to laugh. Worldly-wise as they were, however, they left Paul in peace and told him to come again, next year, and speak of his "Unknown God." Then they went about their business as usual. One man named Dionysius did believe what Paul said. He and a few others became Christians that day in Athens.

FROM ATHENS PAUL journeyed to Corinth, another Greek city. Here he stayed with some Jewish friends and helped them at their business of sewing canvas for tents. Paul had been trained as a boy in this trade. On Sabbath, he went with the Jews to the synagogue and spoke of Jesus and the new faith. Timothy and Silas joined him in Corinth. All three vigorously preached the new testament, but the Jews were unreceptive. This angered Paul.

"From now on I will speak only to the gentiles!" he exclaimed.

A few Jews did convert to Christianity, and held secret services in their homes. After a year, this practice spread, and began to alarm the enemies of Christ. When the new faith seemed to be getting out of hand, the religious leaders of Corinth arrested Paul and his colleagues and brought them before Gallio, the civil ruler of the city. Gallio listened to the complaints of Paul's enemies and was annoyed.

"Don't bring me your religious problems," he said. "I am here to deal with civil matters and not with God."

He then dismissed the case and retired, without putting an end to the fighting and disputes. Paul continued to preach in Corinth, but, with Passover approaching, he decided to return to Jerusalem for the great religious festival. After a brief rest in the Holy City, Paul was off on his mission again, this time returning to Antioch.

Paul in Corinth

IN THE CITY OF EPHESUS, across the water from Athens, most people worshiped the goddess Diana. There was, however, a synagogue for the Jews, who believed in the one true God and who read the Holy Scriptures of Moses. One of these Jews, named Apollos, had learned about John the Baptist and his concept of a new religion. Apollos had accepted these ideas and baptized many of his friends. However, neither he nor his followers had ever heard of Jesus Christ or knew the events of his life and death.

One day, some Christians came to Ephesus and were told about Apollos and his group. They sought him out and asked:

"Have you never heard of Jesus Christ and the Holy Spirit?"

Apollos confessed his ignorance, but was eager to learn. He soon realized that what he had established was only a part of the religion of Christ; and he hastened to inform his followers of the great news. After this, the Christian faith began to take form in Ephesus.

When Paul arrived in the city, there were many persons ready to accept the new religion. He taught and preached for months. He also performed many miracles of healing, so that his fame spread far and

The Uproar in Ephesus

wide. Every day, countless numbers of the sick and infirm came to be cured. When the people of Ephesus saw the power of God, many repented their old ways. They burned their books of black magic and accepted the teachings of Christ.

But not all the Ephesians were sympathetic to Jesus. The greater number of them still worshiped the goddess Diana and, every day, they bowed down before tiny silver statues made in her image.

Demetrius was the leading silversmith of Ephesus who fashioned the idols of Diana. He became worried that the increasing number of converts to Christianity would ruin his business, so he called together many other silversmiths of the city and said:

"We earn our money by making idols of the goddess Diana. Now this man Paul comes along and says that such idols are false and that the one true God needs no idols. If this keeps up, we shall all be paupers."

Demetrius' argument was very convincing, and his colleagues joined him in an attempt to discredit Paul. They marched up and down the streets of the city crying:

"Great is Diana, the goddess of Ephesus!"

Some of Paul's followers heard this cry and came out to investigate. When the silversmiths saw them, they attacked them, and there was a great riot in the streets. Paul tried to help his friends, but was prevented by other Christians who knew that the angry mob would tear him to pieces. By nightfall, the riot still continued and many were hurt. Finally, a high city official came upon the scene and demanded silence.

"People of Ephesus," he cried, "by such a commotion you bring discredit upon the great goddess Diana. The men whom you have attacked are not robbers or criminals. If the silversmiths have a complaint against them, let them go to a court of law. Remember! We have the good reputation of our city to consider."

The Ephesians were convinced by this appeal to reason, and released the Christians. Nevertheless, a few Ephesians lay in wait for Paul, who was supposed to board a ship that night for Syria. Fortunately, Paul learned of the plot. He escaped and set sail for Macedonia instead.

For many months, Paul traveled the familiar route of his mission; from Macedonia back to Asia Minor and the cities of Derbe and Troas. As always, he preached and made new converts to Christianity. More important, he enriched the faith of those already following the ways of Christ, often solving difficult problems faced by the young churches.

At last, Paul decided to return to Jerusalem, the center of all religion. He knew that danger awaited him there, and, each time he met with old friends along his route, he made a special effort to bid them good-by and to leave them with a memorable message.

One day, when he was boarding a ship for the long journey back to Palestine, a multitude of the faithful followed him to the shore. They warned him of the dangers ahead and prayed for a last message. Paul raised his hands and said:

"The best thought that I can leave you is very simple. As our Lord has said, it is more blessed to give than to receive. Remember this, and be kind to the weak and suffering."

Then Paul set sail along the route to Palestine, touching the ancient ports at Cyprus, in Syria and, finally, Caesarea—the last stop before Jerusalem.

WHEN THE JEWS of Jerusalem heard that Paul had returned, they became enraged.

"This is the man who has gone around the world trying to destroy the Jewish faith," they cried. "He has even allowed non-Jews into the synagogues, and he must be punished."

Paul's friends heard these accusations, and urged him to prove his good intentions by going to the great Temple and worshiping in the manner of a faithful Jew. Paul agreed. He went to the Temple, and performed the rites of purification according to the Laws of Moses.

On the streets, near the Temple, were some of Paul's most relentless enemies. When they saw him, they began to rouse the crowd:

"There he is! There is the man who is trying to bring down the Temple and destroy the faith!"

Paul had entered the Temple alone, but he was accompanied to the door by two friends from Greece. The angry Jews thought that he had defiled the Temple by allowing these strangers inside, so they rushed upon Paul and dragged him into the streets.

A great riot followed instigated by angry and dissident men. Fortunately, a band of Roman soldiers heard the commotion. They rescued Paul and allowed him to climb to the highest stair of the Temple. There, speaking in Hebrew, Paul told the crowd the story of his life, from the time when he persecuted Christians to his great revelation of Christ on the road to Damascus. Paul also described his missionary work and kept repeating the fact that he had always been a good Jew and that the work that he was doing in the name of Jesus was in accordance with Jewish prophecy. The crowd listened patiently. But when Paul spoke of converting the gentiles, they became enraged again alarming the Roman authorities, who bound Paul and led him away to be flogged. When he was brought before the judge, Paul asserted his independence as a

Trouble
in
Jerusalem

Roman citizen and demanded a fair trial. The judge was cautious. He ordered that Paul be turned over to the Jewish priests.

During the trial, Paul noted that the two great factions of Jewish rule, the Pharisees and the Sadducees, were assembled. In order to cause dissension among them, he cried out:

"Listen to me, I am a Pharisee and I believe in the resurrection of the dead."

The Sadducees did not believe in resurrection. They immediately began to call for Paul's execution, while the Pharisees, taking him for one of their own, loudly advocated his freedom. The Romans, seeing the futility of this trial, brought Paul back to the prison.

The Midnight Escape to Caesarea

THOUGH PAUL was locked up in a cell, his enemies were determined to kill him. Forty of them took a pledge that they would not eat a bite of food until Paul lay dead at their feet. Then they began to plot a way to kidnap the Christian as he was led from the prison to the courtroom.

Paul's young nephew overheard the plotting and sent a warning to his uncle. Once again, Paul used the fact of his Roman citizenship as a means of salvation. Calling upon the prison commandant, he described the plot against his life.

"In order to save me," said Paul, "I recommend that several hundred soldiers take me to Caesarea and the Roman governor, Felix. This way I will be out of your authority and saved from my enemies."

The commandant agreed and wrote to Felix, asserting Paul's innocence and bidding him protect Paul as a Roman citizen.

That night several bands of soldiers entered the prison courtyard. They wrapped Paul in a cloak, placed him on a horse in their midst, then galloped away toward Caesarea. Paul's enemies were hardly aware of what was happening.

The next day the apostle was put in the prison of Caesarea to await a trial. He knew that he was now on the road to Rome, and that it would be his mission to preach in the great capital of the world, where many waited for the Gospel.

The Trial Before Felix

A FEW DAYS after his arrival, Paul was conducted to the throne room of Felix, the Roman governor in Caesarea, for still another trial. This time, Paul's enemies sent Tertullus, a skillful lawyer, to prosecute on their behalf in Caesarea.

Tertullus rose before Felix and bowed with a flourish.

"O mighty Felix," he said, "you are a great and noble ruler who has brought us all prosperity and peace. Every one of us owes you a debt of thankfulness."

Felix knew that this flattery was only meant to prejudice his judgment, so he urged Tertullus to get to the point. The lawyer from Jerusalem immediately changed his tone and began to lash out against Paul, describing him as a ringleader of the Nazarenes, a rabble-rouser and blasphemer! He then called for the severest possible punishment.

Felix now instructed Paul to defend himself. Once again the dauntless apostle of Christ rose and spoke of his work, his mission, and his honorable purpose. The Roman governor was perplexed. He realized that Paul was innocent, but he also wanted to appease the Jews, so he ordered Paul returned to prison pending further evidence.

For two years, Felix kept Paul in prison, allowing him many privileges. At times, he even brought Paul into his private chambers, so that he might hear more about Christ and the new testament. On one such occasion, Felix became overwhelmed by his troubled conscience and his many sins. Trembling, he sent Paul back to his cell. He secretly hoped that someone would offer him a bribe for the prisoner's escape. But no one did.

AFTER A TIME, a new governor named Festus replaced Felix in Caesarea. Festus was very serious about his job, and journeyed to Jerusalem in order to learn more about the Jewish people over whom he ruled. In Jerusalem, Paul's enemies appeared before Festus and urged him to release Paul in their custody. They intended to kill him.

Festus was very cautious. He advised the Jews that he would return to Caesarea and investigate the case. In ten days, he said, they could come there for another trial.

Ten days later, Paul stood before his accusers. Once more, he firmly asserted his innocence and described his noble work. Festus was perplexed, as Felix had been. He dismissed the council and turned to Paul.

"Let me send you back to Jerusalem," he said. "I am sure you will receive a fair trial."

Paul knew differently.

"I shall not go to Jerusalem," he exclaimed, "but rather to Rome. I appeal to Caesar himself—as is my right under Roman law. If he finds me guilty, then I will accept my punishment."

Paul
Appeals
to Caesar

Festus, not wishing to pass judgment on Paul himself, was relieved.

"You have appealed to Caesar," he said. "To Caesar you shall go."

A few days later Festus entertained a royal visitor, King Agrippa of nearby Jordan. While the two men were dining, Festus related the story of Paul, the prisoner, who had caused so much debate and dissension. King Agrippa was anxious to see Paul for himself.

The next day, Paul was led into the throne room of Festus, where he found a large crowd assembled. There was the Roman governor with King Agrippa and the king's sister Bernice. Agrippa ordered Paul to tell his story.

Once again, the apostle began the story of his life, from the time of his revelation on the road to Damascus to the days of his missionary work among Jews and gentiles alike. Paul also spoke eloquently of Jesus Christ—his life, his death and his resurrection and he preached the path to salvation through belief in the resurrected Lord. King Agrippa was deeply moved and said:

"You almost persuade me to become a Christian."

Paul was honored.

"I wish you would become a follower of Christ," he replied. "I wish all men could hear my message."

But Festus was not as easily moved.

"Too much learning has made you crazy," he said to Paul, and he ordered him taken back to the cell.

Agrippa then turned to Festus and shook his head.

"It is too bad," he said. "This man seems innocent enough, and he could go free. *But* he has appealed to Caesar, and to Caesar he must go."

The Great Shipwreck

PAUL WAS SENT to Rome in chains, under the care of Julius, a Roman centurion. With several other prisoners and passengers, Paul set sail on a cargo ship bound for Italy. Luke, the physician, accompanied Paul and kept a diary of the fearsome journey that followed. This is what he wrote:

"We set sail from Caesarea amid many well-wishers who had come to bid farewell to Paul. At the port of Sidon, we were allowed to go ashore briefly to visit some Christians there, for Paul had become friendly with Julius, our captain. At the seaport of Myra we made our last stop. There, we boarded a larger ship, loaded with grain and other cargo. Then we headed out into the vast Mediterranean Sea.

"At first all seemed well, but soon dark clouds arose in the heavens and the seas became choppy and fierce. Paul went on deck and told the captain that much injury and damage would follow if we continued. So the ship was steered to a small harbor, called Fair Havens, on the island of Crete. Shortly after, the captain was anxious to continue the journey, in spite of Paul's warnings, and as the storm had somewhat abated, he set sail once more—venturing far out onto the sea. This time, a great gale arose, and the sky was black, day and night, for weeks. We could not go forward and we could not turn back, so we foundered in the waves, helplessly. The captain was alarmed. Rather than see us all drown, he ordered much of the cargo tossed overboard, to lighten the ship. This helped little, and the storm continued to rage, causing the passengers to be afraid. Only Paul was courageous. He appeared and told us of a dream in which God promised that no one would be lost in the storm, since it was destined that Paul reach Rome.

"For two weeks, we rocked back and forth on the waves, and then someone sighted land far off in the mist. A few of the sailors were too anxious to get off the ship. Secretly, they headed toward the lifeboats in order to get away. But Paul saw this, and warned the captain that God wanted all the crew and passengers to remain aboard. So the captain cut the lines of the lifeboats, and they floated away without anyone in them. The people then demanded food, for they had been fasting in order to conserve our meagre supply. Paul said we might eat and thank God for our safety. When we had eaten enough, we tossed the remaining supplies overboard to lighten the ship.

"By now, the ship had floated close to land, and we could see a rocky harbor nearby. The mainsail was raised, the rudder loosened and many anchors dropped so that we could climb off the ship and swim ashore. But then, the prow hit a rock and the entire vessel began to split apart. Even so, not one passenger drowned or was lost. We all swam safely to the island of Melita, where the inhabitants welcomed us and built fires for our comfort. Thus, we survived a terrible sea voyage, and Paul was at last on his way to Rome."

ON THE ISLAND of Melita, or Malta, Paul, Luke and the others rested for three months. The islanders at first thought Paul was a common prisoner, for they saw his chains and heard many wicked rumors about him. Then, one day, while Paul was carrying wood to a fire, a poisonous snake bit his hand. The people surely thought he would die because he was a wicked man. Instead, nothing happened at all, and Paul went about his work. Now the islanders knew that Paul was favored by God, and they respected him.

Paul's
Last
Journey

On that same island lived Publius, a chieftain, who invited Paul to his home, where Publius' old father lay ill and dying of a fever. But Paul prayed for him and eventually he was healed. Once again, many came to believe in Paul, and, by the time he was ready to set sail again, the people of Melita had proclaimed him their friend forever, and gave him many presents as a token of their respect.

From Melita, Paul went by ship to Rome, stopping along the way at the ports of Syracuse and Puteoli. The Roman captain, Julius, was kind to his prisoner, and allowed him to visit the Christians at these places.

Finally, the ship reached the port of Rome. At last, Paul had arrived at the world's chief city where the emperor Caesar lived, surrounded by a vast population, and by luxuries unlike any in the world. In such surroundings, Paul was at first anxious and unsure. But, as he walked the roads toward the center of the city, many Christians who had heard of his coming rushed out to greet him and to cheer his heart. Paul was no longer afraid, even when he was handed over to the Roman authorities. They treated him well, gave him his own quarters, and set only one guard over him.

A few days later, Paul went before the Jewish authorities in Rome and learned, to his great surprise, that they had never received any message from their colleagues in Jerusalem about Paul or his supposed crimes. As far as they were concerned, the case was closed. Greatly relieved, Paul went about his work preaching to Jews and gentiles alike.

Paul settled in Rome in his own house, and widened his circle of friends and followers. He had one servant, a young man named Onesimus, who devoted his life to serving the great apostle. At first Paul didn't know that Onesimus was a slave who had run away from his master, Philemon. In those days a slave was the personal property of his master and he could not do as he pleased. When Paul learned this news, he wrote a letter to Philemon, begging for Onesimus' freedom—a letter so eloquent that it probably softened Philemon's heart, for he wrote:

"Perhaps Onesimus fled you for your own good, since it is better that we all look upon our fellow men as brothers, not as servants."

Paul's Great Letters

PAUL WROTE many other letters, mainly to his friends in the churches he had visited. These letters were intended to clarify many difficult points of faith and to strengthen belief and love in Jesus Christ.

The letter that he wrote to the church at Ephesus was called the *Epistle to the Ephesians.* Those he wrote to the people at Thessalonica were called the *Epistles to the Thessalonians.* Especially beautiful was one letter that he wrote to the Christians in Corinth. In this letter, the *First Epistle to the Corinthians,* the great apostle declared the glory and the beauty of spiritual love and charity. He said:

"Though I speak with the tongues of men and of angels, and have not love, I am become as sounding brass or a tinkling cymbal. And though I have the gift of prophecy, and understand all mysteries, and all knowledge; and though I have all faith, so that I could move mountains, and have not love, I am nothing . . . for love suffereth long, and is kind; love envieth not . . . but beareth all things, believeth all things, hopeth all things, endureth all things . . . and never faileth."

Paul was very old. He could look back on his life and say with honesty that he had "fought the good fight and kept the faith." Thousands and thousands of weary souls had been converted to Christianity by Paul, and he truly established the religion now known in every part of the world.

We do not know exactly what happened to Paul after his letters were written. But, in A.D. 64, the insane emperor of Rome, Nero, set fire to the city. When the conflagration had died down, he blamed the Christians for starting it and many were put to death. It is believed that Paul was executed at this time. It is also said that the aged apostle Peter died that same day, hanging on the cross, as Jesus had died—but upside down, by his own request, so that, in death, he would be lowlier than his Lord.

Thus, two of the greatest saints in all history, St. Peter and St. Paul, finished their days in Rome.

THE REVELATION OF ST. JOHN THE DIVINE

ABOUT THIRTY YEARS AFTER Peter and Paul had died, an old man sat in lonely contemplation on the island of Patmos in the Aegean Sea. He had been sent there as a prisoner by the Romans, who had intensified their persecution of the Christians. This old man was John of Ephesus. There is a difference of opinion as to whether he was the John who was a disciple of Jesus, or another man who had preached the Gospel in Asia Minor.

Whoever he was, this holy man saw awesome and majestic visions during his island isolation. The Revelation, or the Apocalypse, as it is sometimes called, is John's retelling of the things he had seen in his visions. He wrote:

"I was in the spirit on the Lord's day, and heard behind me a great voice, as of a trumpet, saying 'I am Alpha and Omega, the first and the last. What you see, write in a book, and send it to the seven churches which are in Asia.'

"And I turned to see the voice that spoke to me. And I saw seven golden candlesticks; and in the midst of the seven candlesticks one like the Son of Man, clothed with a garment down to his feet and girt around the chest with a golden girdle.

"And his countenance was as the sun shining in its strength. And when I saw him, I fell at his feet as if dead. And he laid his right hand upon me saying, 'Fear not; I am the first and the last. I am he that liveth and was dead; and behold I am alive for evermore, Amen; and have the keys of hell and of death. Write the things which thou hast seen, and the things which are, and the things which shall be.'"

John tells us of his being overwhelmed by seeing God enthroned; of seeing the destruction wrought upon the sinful cities of the earth— the Babylons; of viewing the final battle between the angels and the powers of evil, with Satan being chained for a thousand years. A memorable part of the book records the vision of the Four Horsemen of the Apocalypse setting out to devastate the earth. Pestilence rides a white horse, war rides a red horse, famine rides a black horse, and death rides a pale horse.

John writes of a majestic vision in which he saw the Lord on a great, white throne, surrounded by the Heavenly Host on the day of the Last Judgment.

"And I saw the dead, small and great, stand before God; and the

The
Wonders of
Future
Days

books were opened: and another book was opened, which is the book of life. And the dead were judged by what was written in the books, according to their deeds."

In a final vision, John saw the wonders of future days. He wrote:

"And I saw a new heaven and a new earth: for the first heaven and the first earth were passed away; and there was no more sea.

"And I, John, saw the holy city, new Jerusalem, coming down from God out of heaven, prepared as a bride adorned for her husband. And I heard a great voice out of heaven saying, 'Behold, the tabernacle of God is with men, and he will dwell with them, and they shall be his people, and God himself shall be with them, and be their God. And God shall wipe away all tears from their eyes; and there shall be no more death, neither sorrow, nor crying, neither shall there be any more pain: for the former things are passed away.' And he said to me, 'It is done, I am Alpha and Omega, the beginning and the end. I will give unto him who is thirsty of the fountain of the water of life freely.'

"And one of the seven angels talked to me, saying, 'Come, I will show you the bride, the Lamb's wife!'

"And he carried me away in the spirit to a great and high mountain, and showed me that great city, the holy Jerusalem, descending out of heaven from God.

"And I saw no temple there, for the Lord God Almighty and the Lamb are its temple. And the city had no need of sun, neither of the moon, to shine in it, for the glory of God did lighten it and the Lamb is the Light thereof.

"And he showed me a pure river of water of life, clear as crystal, proceeding out of the throne of God and of the Lamb. Along the street, by the river, grew the tree of life, which bore twelve kinds of fruit, and yielded its fruit every month; and the leaves of the tree were for the healing of the nations.

"And the Lord God of the holy prophets sent his angel to show to his servants the things which must shortly be done. And he said to me, 'Behold, I come quickly. Blessed is he who follows the prophecy of this book.'

"Amen. Even so, come, Lord Jesus."

Plate 104. ST. JOHN THE DIVINE ON PATMOS,
by Hieronymous Bosch (Flemish, about 1450–1516), State Museums, Berlin.

INDEX OF ILLUSTRATIONS

PRONOUNCING GUIDE

This list includes a modern phonetic spelling of difficult names found in the stories.

A–bed′ne–go *uh–*BED*–nuh–go*
Ab′i–gail AB*–ih–gale*
A–bim′e–lech *uh–*BIM*–uh–lek*
A–bin′a–dab *uh–*BIN*–uh–dab*
Ad–o–ni′jah *add–uh–*NYE*–juh*
A–has–u–e′rus *uh–haz–oo–*EE*–rus*
A–ha–zi′ah *ay–huh–*ZYE*–uh*
A–him′e–lech *uh–*HIM*–uh–lek*
An–a–ni′as *an–uh–*NYE*–us*
An–ti′o–chus *an–*TIE*–oh–kus*
An′ti–pas AN*–tih–pass*
Ar–i–ma–the′a *air–uh–muh–*THEE*–uh*
Ar–ta–xerx′es *are–tuh–*ZERK*–zeez*
Ath–a–li′ah *ath–uh–*LIE*–uh*
Ba′al BAY*–ul*
Ba′laam BAY*–lum*
Ba–rab′bas *buh–*RABB*–us*
Bel–shaz′zar *bell–*SHAZ*–er*
Ben–ha′dad *ben–*HAY*–dad*
Be–thes′da *beh–*THEZ*–duh*
Bo′az BOH*–az*
Caes–a–re′a *cess–uh–*REE*–uh*
Ca′ia–phas KAY*–uh–fuss*
Ca′naan KAY*–nun*
Ca–per′na–um *kuh–*PURR*–nay–um*
Chal–de′an *kal–*DEE*–un*
Da–ri′us *dah–*REE*–us*
Do′eg DOH*–eg*
E′dom EE*–dum*
E–li–e′zer *ee–lih–*AY*–zer*
E–li′sha *ee–*LYE*–shuh*
Em–ma′us *eh–*MAY*–us*
Eph′e–sus EFF*–uh–sus*
E′phra–im EE*–frah–yim*
Ge–ha′zi *ghee–*HAY*–zye*
Ger′shom GER*–shom*
Geth–sem′a–ne *geth–*SEM*–uh–nee*
Gol′go–tha GAHL*–goh–thuh*
Haz′a–el HAZ*–uh–el*
Hol–o–fer′nes *hol–oh–*FUR*–neez*

Hu′shai HOO*–shy*
Ja–i′rus *jay–*EYE*–rus*
Ja′pheth JAY*–futh*
Je–ho′ram *jee–*HO*–rum*
Je–hosh′a–phat *jee–*HOSH*–uh–fat*
Jeph′thah JEFF*–thuh*
Jo′ash JOH*–ash*
Laz′a–rus LAZ*–uh–rus*
Lyd′da LEED*–uh*
Lys′tra LISS*–truh*
Mac′ca–bees MACK*–uh–beez*
Mag–da–le′ne *mag–duh–*LEE*–nuh*
Mat–ta–thi′as *mat–uh–*THIGH*–us*
Mel–chi′ze–dek *mel–*KIZ*–eh–dek*
Me–phib′o–sheth *meh–*FIB*–uh–sheth*
Me′shach ME*–shack*
Mo–ri′ah *muh–*RYE*–uh*
Neb–u–chad–nez′zar *neb–uh–cud–*NEZ*–er*
Ne–he–mi′ah *nee–heh–*MY*–uh*
Phar′i–see FAIR*–uh–see*
Phil′ip–pi FIL*–ip–pie*
Phi–lis′tine *fih–*LISS*–tin*
Pi′late PIE*–lut*
Pot′i–phar POT*–ih–fer*
Re–ho–bo′am *ree–hoh–*BOH*–um*
Sa–lo′me *sa–*LOW*–may*
Sa–ma′ri–a *suh–*MAY*–ree–uh*
Sap–phi′ra *suh–*FIE*–ruh*
Sa′rai SAYR*–eye*
Sen–nach′e–rib *sen–*NACK*–uh–rib*
Sha′drach SHA*–drack*
She′chem SHEE*–kum*
Sis′e–ra SIS*–uh–ruh*
Tra′os TRAY*–us*
Vash′ti VASH*–tee*
Zac–che′us *zack–*KEY*–us*
Zar′e–phath ZARE*–eh–fath*
Zeb′e–dee ZEB*–uh–dee*
Ze–rub′ba–bel *zeh–*ROOB*–bah–bell*
Zip–po′rah *zip–*POH*–ruh*